THE
FORMLESS
EMPIRE

THE
FORMLESS
EMPIRE

• • •

A SHORT
HISTORY
OF
DIPLOMACY
AND
WARFARE
IN
CENTRAL
ASIA

CHRISTOPHER MOTT

WESTHOLME
Yardley

Westholme Publishing, LLC
904 Edgewood Road
Yardley, Pennsylvania 19067
Visit our Web site at www.westholmepublishing.com

First Printing June 2015
10 9 8 7 6 5 4 3 2 1
ISBN: 978-1-59416-221-3
Also available as an eBook.

Printed in the United States of America.

CONTENTS

SIX

Rebirth Through Smothering 147

List of Maps

INTRODUCTION

If I determine the enemy's disposition of forces while I have no perceptible form, I can concentrate my forces while the enemy is fragmented. The pinnacle of military deployment approaches the formless: if it is formless, then even the deepest spy cannot discern it nor the wise make plans against it.

—Sun Tzu, *The Art of War*

EURASIA IS A CONTINENT SO VAST IT EVOKES NO IMMEDIATE IMAGE IN the same way that Africa, Australia, or even North and South America do. Often, due more to political and historical factors than geographic ones, it is even subdivided into Europe, Asia, and sometimes even the subcontinent of India. Even with these western and southernmost protuberances shorn off, Asia alone still is an epic and multifaceted landmass with a famous coastline and an often obscure interior, at least as far as the popular imagination in the developed world is concerned.

And it is precisely these less-famous places on the map that this book is concerned with. It is a region often referenced in Chinese, Russian, and Middle Eastern histories as a thronging pit of barbarians who periodically explode outward in a mindless rampage, and it has fared little better in comparative Western European narratives until somewhat recently. When it comes to politics and state building, it is an area that has always tended to get short shrift, more of an exotic background for foreign spies and intrigue than a dynamic, indigenous series of actors in their own right. Historical attention has been paid to how various nomadic and peripheral people adapted to being conquered by larger, more-"established" powers, but there has been comparatively little on the subject of how more-established cultures had to adapt to being conquered by these nomads.

Yet it was these supposedly peripheral powers to the main narrative of littoral states that were often the dynamic imperialists and great powers of a premodern era. While this is increasingly understood historically, it is often neglected from the perspective of political theory—specifically, that Inner Eurasia was a region of strategic and foreign policy innovation that was as influential in the development of regional international order as the more officially established civilizations like China, Russia, and Iran. By examining a wide variety of case studies from ancient times through the present, each chosen as an example of a critical moment of adaptation and change in the regional situation, a course can be charted of a region just as innovative and adaptable in its methods as any other. When they are taken together, the case can be made that there is an observable geopolitical strategy often at play in Central Asia—one built around indirect rule, government by proxies, large-scale grand strategy based on mobility and speed, and interdependent economic relationships. In light of recent and still (as of the time of this writing) ambiguous events occurring in parts of the Russian periphery such as Georgia and Ukraine, it may be more than just historical curiosity that compels the examination of forms of grand strategy that emerged within the heart of the world's largest landmass. In fact, it may be an entire regional context for the continuing evolution of strategy.

It is worth noting that despite such tropes as the "Tatar yoke" of Mongol rule in Russia, or hackneyed observations about "Eastern despotism" or "Oriental tyranny," it was often these looser kinds of political groups that were open and relaxed compared to their littoral contemporaries, in Europe or elsewhere. These were places where more often than not, the ethnic or cultural minority was the dominant military power. In order to prevent constant revolts among the majority, and also because in many cases the herders of the steppe simply did not care, the general rule seemed to have been that to pay one's taxes and not rebel was enough for the ruling classes of nomadic empires. Persecution of religious minorities or ethnic groups was a rare event in many of the cases we will be examining here, unlike in other parts of the world commonly held to be higher levels of civilization.

These are empires that did not seek total control or ideological or cultural conversion of their subject peoples but rather behaved as arbiters between different communities and guarantors of trade. They effectively positioned themselves as an elite cadre akin to a modern rapid-reaction force that seeks to retain the military benefits of a mobile lifestyle while at the same time feeding off the benefits of trade in goods and resources that they could produce themselves. I call this phenomenon "The Formless Empire." While these trends are surely not unique to the geographic scope of this book, their prevalence in the region makes it by far the most rewarding place to look when examining the history of regional geopolitics. Additionally, the presence of many more-established great powers in the region (many of which, such as Russia and China, are still with us) shows a particularly stark connection between eras of the past with the present. By examining certain key examples, the pattern of a regionally indigenous form of strategic practice becomes apparent, as does its lingering influence through the eras—right on up to the present.

Before getting into the meat of our case studies outlining the existence of such a thing as the Formless Empire, we must define the terms of this book as well as its scope.

The terms *Central Asia*, *Inner Eurasia*, and *Central Eurasia* can all apply to various examples, and often multiple terms will be used to show both minor distinctions and to break up linguistic repetitiveness. *Central Asia* is often employed to describe the oasis region corresponding to modern-day Uzbekistan, Kyrgyzstan, Kazakhstan, Tajikistan, and Turkmenistan, which is known historically as Transoxiana, and its surrounding steppes. *Inner Eurasia* and the nearly identical *Central Eurasia* are used to describe a somewhat vaster area that includes Transoxiana but extends farther past the steppe to encompass much of the terrain of nonlittoral Eurasia. This can include the Black Sea steppe in the west and the mixed steppe/forest land of Manchuria in the east.[1]

This massive region, often lightly populated and known for its overland rather than oceanic trade, is the geographic setting to which we turn our attention. Geography and ecology are the first building blocks from which the societies in a region grow, and so it is important to appraise these factors first.

The most important elements of this geography are its vast space and its diversity—both contained within a certain level of continuity connected by the flat, dry grasslands known as the steppe. For most of history, the steppe was a poor place for agriculture to expand into, aside from the occasional fertile river valley, but still the grass could support numerous domesticated animals. This flat and edible (for pack animals) highway enabled herding-based nomadism to take hold. This turned the apparently hostile and sparse landscape into an artery that connected the various mountainous, forested, and cultivated plains areas together through the mobile groups of herding people who migrated and traded across the steppe. As the steppe flows east from Ukraine to western Manchuria and much more narrowly south from the forest edge of southern Siberia to the mountains of the Caucasus and Afghanistan as well as the deserts of Xinjiang and Turkmenistan, a common ecological denominator makes this large and diverse area part of a unified geopolitical network.

This and the regions adjacent to it are often integrated into this network through the political and economic policies of history, and they share certain common attributes that make them a cohesive if somewhat nebulous whole in military and political history. Being on the interior of the world's largest continent, having a seasonal—if often more cold than warm—dry climate, and sitting between what is traditionally considered to be the major world civilizations create a unique context worth examining.[2]

If one were to attempt to use all of the possible examples in such a giant region, this book could spiral into volumes upon volumes of cases. Instead, we need only utilize the specific examples of cases that mark key evolutionary points in the cycle. These exist first as the ascendency of the Formless Empire, and later as its relative decline in importance, to finally end in the present with something that may be a partial resurgence. The fact remains that the most relevant major powers that still exist in this region's evolution are without a doubt Russia and China, and so the geography of Inner Eurasian peoples who directly influenced the fate of those states remains the primary recruiting ground of our examples. This involves using many more examples from the eastern half of the Eurasian supercontinent than from the western, but a few choice ones outside this range are included because they illustrate something particularly relevant, such as adaptation to or from the steppe into another geographic realm. But it should be noted that the omission of a case study like the Kazan Khanate or the Kuban Cossacks is not a disavowal of their relevance to the concept of a Formless Empire but rather simply setting limitations on how many examples are needed to illustrate a strategic concept.

These specific geographic and cultural circumstances naturally facilitate the decentralized multicultural empire as the lynchpin of governance. The modern term *multicultural* in this case describes a society of relative openness to foreign influence with an ethnically and often religiously diverse population. Though empires have historically been far more common than nation-states, significantly predated them, and are endemic to almost every part of the world, the modern study of empire often evokes negative emotional reactions. For the purposes of this book, the concept of empire will be treated neutrally as a geopolitical expression, just as the nation-state is largely viewed today. We will delve further into the importance of empire in the following chapter, but for now it is worth noting that, value judgments aside, empire is tied with tribes and city-states as the most historically typical political entities. As Jane Burbank and Frederick Cooper state succinctly in their overview of the subject:

"By comparison [with empire] the nation-state appears as a blip on the historical horizon, a state form that emerged recently under imperial skies and whose hold on the world's political imagination may well prove partial or transitory."[3]

Inside Inner Eurasia, this predilection for empire was perhaps even greater than elsewhere. Wide varieties of peoples, economic structures, and geographic diversity came together to imply that only a highly mobile, decentralized, and often informal type of power structure could suffice for optimal geopolitical governance. Often it was the tribal element of the nomadic peoples that held the decisive strategic niche of mobility and space control to be the ruling elite and the ones who preyed on the settled and littoral peoples around them. Other, more-settled people who emulated the military methods of the nomads often responded by changing their military structure or frontier policies as they, too, adapted into this system—though in time, technological and economic changes would swing the initiative in this realm to the more-settled and littoral powers. Even after supplanting the nomadic peoples as the dominant military powers, settled states would have to adapt themselves to the realities of governing in such a diffuse and decentralized region. These continuing cycles of inward and outward migration from the region spread these techniques of empire out of the region and also bequeathed them to foreigners who entered it.

ONE

OVERVIEW OF
CENTRAL ASIAN HISTORY

THE YEAR 2000 BCE IS THE ROUGH STARTING POINT OF THE GEO-political trend of nomadic imperialism, when the chariot was introduced to the region. The use of endemic regional horses to great effect in facilitating trade and travel on the flat steppe plains was the opening development in the evolution of the steppe empire. This was the first change that enabled the nomadic element of the population to become the decisive lynchpin in the system. But these societies did not hit their full integral stride until about a thousand years later, with the adoption of horseback riding and the high-endurance little steppe ponies that would become their staple. The first wave of nomads, such as the Huns and Xiongnu, was the vanguard of this increased potency among the nomadic tribes and showed the societies peripheral to them the deadly combination of horse-borne mobility and lifestyle in con-junction with accurate arrow fire from the horn-and-sinew recurve bows that could be fired from full gallop.

Another addition to the power of the nomads came a thousand years later, with the invention of the stirrup. Now the hammer of the light bow-wielding cavalry could have the complementary anvil of heavy cavalry armed with lowered lances, which the stirrup enabled. This greatly increased the combat effectiveness of such units and further added to the power of the nomadic armies. Armies that traveled entirely on horseback and lived in transportable tents, called *gers* (Mongolian) and *yurts* (Turkic), had many advantages for achieving total strategic dominance out of proportion to their numbers—as long as they had sufficient grazing land for the livestock. And so the steppe was a natural corridor for them. It would remain so until the nineteenth century, when the technological innovation of railroads enabled the settled peripheral societies to surpass this mobility.[1]

This nomadic system, whether it was employed by indigenous inhabitants of Inner Eurasia or by peripheral powers that had the time and perseverance to adapt, had certain political aspects in its structure that affected subsequent geopolitical change to varying extents. In his overview of Central Asian history, where he resets the position of Central Asia from its usual relegation to the periphery back to the core of Eurasian history, Christopher I. Beckwith uses the term *comitatus* (originally coined by Tacitus to describe Germanic kinship bonds as well as the practice of rewarding soldiers with land in the Roman Republic) to describe this method of governance. The nomadic ruling elite sustained its power through personal charisma and gift giving, ensuring a loyal retinue to the single ruler, who could then distribute it back to his followers as he saw fit. To do this, the leaders of various tribes and empires had to foster trade and tribute systems. Given the military flexibility and power of nomadic armies, this could be done over large areas. However, the constant migration of other tribes often meant such arrangements were temporary and subject to usurpation by others. It was through such processes that a cyclic system of informal empire and economic integration spread throughout the region. This is a comprehensive system not simply related to military affairs but to all of geopolitics.[2]

The ultimate example of this system was the first true Eurasia-spanning hegemonic power: the Mongol Empire. We will go into much more detail about that state and its critical importance to this book in chapter 2, but for now it is relevant simply to use it as an example of the many aspects of the Formless Empire coming together on a truly massive scale. As Burbank and Cooper so adequately summarize it:

> Although the Mongol empires fragmented quickly, the unification of Eurasia left its imprint on later politics. The Mongols' protection of religious institutions, their governing practices based on recognized difference, with no fixed center or core population; the cultivation of personalized loyalty as the sovereign's means of control; the fluid politics of contingent alliance, pragmatic subordination, and treaty making—this repertoire remained in play long after [Chinggis Khan's] empire disintegrated.[3]

The general trend of governance in the region was a type of consensus building and getting results through a relatively egalitarian distribution of powers. This was a flexible rule, with no state church or settled doctrine, and it became the norm throughout the steppes. It was particularly strong when the nomadic influence was at its highest.[4]

Halford Mackinder's Eurasian Heartland Theory, as expressed in several articles, including the seminal "Geographical Pivot of History," is the most famous grand geopolitical study of the region that this book covers (at least it is in Europe and America). Despite being concerned primarily with the issues at stake in his own time—British and Russian rivalry in Central Asia during the late nineteenth and early twentieth centuries—Mackinder offers great insight into how the low population density and vast inland spaces combined to make mobility the key element of study in the region. He provides the motivation and reasoning for such a form of domination and the purpose of achieving it in the specific context of Inner Eurasia.

Though it is the purpose of this book to study the indigenous evolution of geopolitics in what Mackinder christened "The Heartland" and thereby set up a type of counternarrative to the typical Eurocentric need to understand all parts of the world with exported European theories, it is worth noting that Mackinder showed an understanding of many of the dynamics of the region's history, particularly in regards to Russia and its geographic heritage. Most importantly, after charting the fall of this great inland steppe-highway in prominence compared to the maritime system of Western Europe, he postulates that industrialization (particularly railroads) has the potential to return the region to importance in the future.[5]

In a chapter in *Geostrategy: Mackinder and the Defense of the West*, Colin S. Gray makes the very topical point of Mackinder's continuing relevance for comparison to how contemporary scholars treat issues such as geopolitics:

> Just as history inherently is strategic, so also must it be geopolitical. The former quality speaks to the persistence of the threat or use of force, while the latter, the focus here, affirms that "real international relations occur in geographic space," and spatial relationships matter greatly. . . . [M]odern scholarship on International Relations has been well populated with theories which betray an all but complete indifference to geography in its political and strategic dimensions.[6]

Because the largest-scale conflicts in warfare and diplomacy during the twentieth century (the time, arguably, of lowest geopolitical relevance for Central Asia) have been attempts to either impose or thwart Eurasian hegemony, the method of regional power politics is clearly a significant subject.[7] Looking at the historical and indigenous evolution of this concept as well as its potential paths for the future is of vital importance, and human- geography interaction remains a key element in this book.

Taken together, the net effect of geopolitical strategy in Inner Eurasia overlaps with the thinking of the most famous of Chinese military theorists, Sun Tzu. Sun Tzu is not an absolutely verifiable figure of history. His identity is as formless as the geostrategic philosophy he advocated. He may be an apocryphal figure meant to represent the amalgamation of strategic thinking coming from multiple individuals during the Warring States Period (475–221 BCE) in Chinese history and put together in order to summarize the lessons of that 250-year period of warfare built on harsh and painful experience.[8]

For convenience's sake, we will treat Sun Tzu as a real person. After all, there is at least some biographical information for this nebulous figure. He was reputed to be a strategist in the service of the state of

Wu, and his military abilities were renowned enough that the king of Wu challenged him to instill martial discipline into the courtly ladies of his palace—a task Sun Tzu was able to accomplish to the satisfaction of the king. This enabled him to become the chief general of the kingdom and over the course of several campaigns raise the status and power of Wu over its immediate rivals. Somewhere in this busy life, Sun Tzu wrote his famous work of strategic thinking, *The Art of War*.[9]

Despite the declared martial focus implicit in that name, the book's primary concern is the same as statecraft itself: the ultimate survival of the state. Indeed, it sees warfare, diplomacy, and overall state welfare as holistically integrated—an attitude shared by the Mongols, who (knowingly or not) used many of the tactics in Sun Tzu's work. The strategic principles encapsulated in *The Art of War* are based on the ideas of deception, speed, mobility, flexibility, and indirectness. Mark McNeilly classifies them into six points based on the major subheadings of the text:

1. Win without fighting
2. Avoid strength, attack weakness
3. Deception and foreknowledge
4. Speed and movement
5. Shaping the enemy
6. Character-based leadership[10]

Winning without fighting involves the notion that having to resort to warfare is always a loss—even for the eventually victorious party—so the first strategy should be to force a foe to acquiesce without having to engage it in battle. "The general rule for use of the military is that it is better to keep a nation intact than to destroy it." There is an obvious parallel here to the common tactic of Eurasian empires to leave defeated foes alive as vassals rather than annex them outright. If force must be resorted to, aim for the enemy's weak points, which one can be made aware of through espionage and good intelligence services. To cripple the enemy by striking at its weak points, speed of action is the ultimate virtue, which in turn will mold the enemy into a vulnerable position by causing it to lose the initiative and only have enough time to react. Sun Tzu makes explicit that while military operations can be clumsy and swift, they are never skillful and slow as "victory, not persistence, is most important in battle." Finally, tying all of these principles together and greatly facilitating their execution are the leadership qualities of the field commander and his officers. In a striking parallel to Beckwith's observation on the bonds of personal loyalty fostered in Inner Eurasian politics, Sun Tzu remarks that the way for a commander to win the loyalty of his men is to instill fair discipline and share their dangers.[11]

Rather than only reveling in simply a decisive blow, which is still within the context of an attrition-based warfare paradigm, Sun Tzu's treatise is really a treatise *against* the very principle of attrition-based warfare whenever possible. Deception, speed, adaptability, and maneuverability are all ways to avoid direct confrontation and still achieve results. But if confrontation becomes inevitable (because of either error or circumstance), good strategy becomes about overcoming the opposition in such a way as to keep one's own forces as intact as possible.[12] As Sun Tzu says:

> A skilled attack is one against which opponents do not know how to defend; a skilled defense is one where opponents do not know how to attack. Therefore, those skilled in defense are not so because of fortress walls. This is why high walls and deep moats do not guarantee security, while strong armor and effective weapons do not guarantee strength. If opponents want to hold firm, attack where they are unprepared; if opponents want to establish a battlefront, appear where they do not expect you.[13]

Sun Tzu's model of strategy is a fitting example to keep in mind when looking at the behavior of empires in Central Asia.

Another thinker pertinent to the concept of the Formless Empire but who only overlapped with the region in question on the periphery—in this case the opposite side of the Eurasian landmass from Sun Tzu—was Ibn Khaldun.

A fourteenth century historian, traveler, and political theorist from Morocco who spent much time in the Middle East, Khaldun was partly inspired by the history of the Arab conquests as well as the successions of Turkic migration that washed over the various regions he called home. He even lived through one such migration, being in Syria during the Timurid invasion and getting to meet the conquering emir Timur in person during the siege of Damascus and to engage in discussion with him. Interestingly, despite Timur's fearsome reputation in official history, Khaldun saw him as a masterful prince and heaped praise on him (the Timurids will be discussed in detail in chapter 3). Khaldun is therefore a direct witness to some of the very events used as case studies in the following examples, and this shows in his largely secular and state-based analysis of the world he observed. Like Central Asian states, he adopted a cyclical view of the rise and fall of government for social control rather than the religious reasons—which were the common explanations in the Arab world at the time.[14]

In *The Muqaddimah*, Ibn Khaldun postulates a theory of history encompassing where civilizations arise and the impacts of science on policy and geography on such things as agriculture. But his main focus is the interaction of nomadic and sedentary people, and his general preference for the virtues of the nomadic people—at least as leaders for the state.

"Sedentary people are much concerned with all kinds of pleasures," he said. "They are accustomed to luxury and success in worldly occupations and to indulgence in worldly desires. Therefore, their souls are colored with all kinds of blame-worthy and evil qualities."

Nomadic peoples, according to Khaldun, have greater solidarity, or *assibiya*, which enables them to more effectively utilize leadership, armies, and build larger and better nations. Naturally, however, as they conquer more and more civilized and sedentary people, they lose this inherent nomadic virtue and adopt more of the customs of the conquered.[15] Without commenting on the subjective values of this process, we will still see something quite similar to this being repeated in cycles through the pageant of Inner Eurasian history.

Khaldun was concerned with creating a safe yet dynamic space for science and trade to progress while embedded within the nonprogressive and often cyclic system of international politics. He says explicitly why he felt that nomadic people would be more effective at setting up these temporary periods that would allow domestic society to advance:

> These savage peoples, furthermore, have no homelands that
> they might use as a fertile pasture, and no fixed place to which
> they might repair. All regions and places are the same to them.
> Therefore, they do not restrict themselves to possession of their
> own neighboring regions. They do not stop at the borders of
> their horizon. They swarm across distant zones and achieve
> superiority over faraway nations.

This type of panregional connectivity makes larger and more-pow-
erful states, and for a few generations at least (Khaldun estimated an
average of four such generations)—and in the initial periods when the
nomadic ruling elite can harness the wealth of the settled nations but
before it is corrupted by said wealth—the greatest combination of civic
and scientific virtue can be made.[16]

Of course, Khaldun had no way of knowing that one day the technological progress of the settled world would reset the balance of
power against the once-militarily dominant nomadic peoples—a phenomenon we will explore further in later chapters. But even with this
inversion of geopolitical power in the realms of the following case
studies, Khaldun's overall idea of the ruling clique having a broader
and more-flexible understanding that came from its often-peripheral
origins would hold true.

Another large text worth mentioning, mainly for its unexpected
lack of value, is Sir Basil Henry Liddel-Hart's *Strategy*, published in
1954. Because he wrote an entire treatise on indirect strategy and had
for decades before championed the value of modern strategists' study-
ing the campaigns of the Mongol Empire, one might be tempted to
assume Liddel-Hart's *Strategy* would be included in this book. The
problem is, he seems to have read and become enamored with Sun
Tzu but not actually learned many of the fundamental lessons that are
taught in the *Art of War*. Liddel-Hart correctly deduces that mobility
and unpredictability are the prize virtues of strategy in this method of
warfare, but he makes them rigidly predictable by advocating always
operating indirectly to a fault, which becomes formulaic.[17] What Sun
Tzu actually advocated was to always outsmart and outmaneuver your
enemy by being formless. This means primarily having the flexibility
to be unpredictable, which could even include very direct action.

Certainly, the case studies we will examine will have examples of steppe-space interaction of many geostrategic varieties. Examples in *Strategy* of a direct battle method working are ignored or unconvincingly explained away, most egregiously with the Franco-Prussian War and the Russo-Japanese War.[18]

Though writing neither primarily about history or international relations (while frequently citing both), the contemporary philosopher John Gray is worth at least mentioning for making a solid case for disparaging progressive ideologies in politics as a significant force for change within geopolitics. Just as the Soviet Union failed to install anything but the most temporary and superficial unifying order working for a modernistic sense of progress in the region, so, too, I would contend that other attempts to apply a globalist and universal framework to understanding Inner Eurasia would fail. Other progressive political projects—usually from Western Europe or North America—are unlikely to be any more successful or elucidating if applied to the region.

A large percentage of case studies in this book are from polytheistic, shamanistic, or just generally non-Abrahamic cultures. At no point is this work interested in dealing with comparative religion, but it is worth noting that most world views lack messianic aspects and a progressive ideal to import into politics. Christianity and Islam are uniquely idealistic, and most modernistic political projects are directly descended from them either by reaction or adaptation.[19] Even though much of the region studied here eventually converted to Islam, the values of a more heterogeneous order never really left the region, and this further feeds into understanding Inner Eurasia in a politically cyclic fashion. An Abrahamic culture might be far less likely to either produce a Sun Tzu or be the originator of the first Formless Empire.

Theories of state building and empire in Central Asia find a voice in the historical overview *Empires of the Silk Road*, by Christopher I. Beckwith, one that traces continuity from ancient history to the post-Cold War world. Given its scope, this is one of the key sources for the large-scale view of this book, but even it is a work of history, and it is this work's main objective to move some of his purely historical concepts of Inner Eurasia as a valid and equal civilization to its littoral competitors into a realm of overlap with politics and strategy.

Beckwith makes a compelling argument about the nomadic state being a vital lynchpin in the Eurasian system in such fields as diplomacy and pursuing economic objectives. This historical theory should be placed in a contemporary international relations context. Especially relevant is the nature of interpersonal networks in establishing power politics based on the acquisition and taxation of goods and commerce, rather than direct territorial exploitation. Beckwith is particularly strong in noting that the tradition of the indigenous empires of Inner Eurasia function in this unique way that sets them apart as a case study from the more conventional understanding of empire.[20]

In order to bring an international relations/geopolitics view to this grand perspective, it is necessary to introduce the theory of neoclassical realism. This is because it is a theory whose primary focus is on the way states behave toward each other and how they balance, both internally and within alliance networks, as well as how they are motivated by domestic political factors such as regime survival and prestige. Neoclassical realism takes into account numerous domestic considerations in the study of foreign policy, has a looser and more historically grounded and global definition of exactly what the state is, and thus does not discount the role of economics in power politics as both the cause and the symptom of power imbalances.[21] In fact, it is a holistic theory that takes into account the primacy of regime survival of the ruling class as more important than the state itself. Considering the wide range of ethnic turnover at the highest rungs of politics, which many of these case studies have, as well as indirect methods they use to ensure their order, it seems that neoclassical realism is in fact the best contemporary political theory to match with the historical examples of the Central Eurasian experience.[22]

These are relevant factors to keep in mind when discussing the ingredients of empire, such as power imbalance, hegemony, and alliance networks. In this way contemporary theory supports the historical experience. As can be seen in the case of the Golden Horde in Russia, or contemporary Russia in the Central Asian Republics, both of these theories can be combined with a hegemonic state using a system of internal alliance balance of power to keep its allies subordinate and maintain its position of dominance and access over and into the vassal states. The dichotomy between hegemony and balance-of-power theory itself often has a very modern and Western-centric view. For instance, hegemony, rather than balance of power, is the normal state of international affairs in many regions of the world and eras of history. Europe, the Middle East, and North Africa under the Roman Empire at its height was a decidedly hegemonic system, as have been any of the great unified dynasty periods of Chinese history or even the entire world from the fall of the Soviet Union until recently vis-à-vis the United States, as explained persuasively in *The Balance of Power in World History*.[23] But such concerns apply to the Formless Empire as well.

Needless to say, there are far more examples than are covered in this book; in fact, a multivolume series would have to be written just to make sure every single applicable example was touched on. What I have elected to do instead is to examine first several of the best examples of the original Formless Empire at work and then move on to case studies that show the adaptations in response to changes.

Eventually, the nomadic and seminomadic peoples who are the stars of the show get shunted off to the sidelines in their own lands, but their replacement by more-established powers shows the lingering influence of the concept not only across the eras of time but also from culture to culture. This book charts the evolution, rather than the destruction or obliteration, of the Formless Empire. This book shows how the Formless Empire, just like the geopolitical strategy it advocates, is constantly adapting to new technological and societal changes in order to stay relevant to the land of which it is endemic—and yet throughout it all it retains many of its key characteristics. Like evolution, the Formless Empire is neither progressive nor regressive but simply responds to changing circumstances. It is a blind system of adaptation for survival that suits a particular ecological and by extension geopolitical niche. One might argue that any region of the world does exactly the same thing, but the Eurasian steppe and its neighborhood is a region of particularly high levels of migration, mobility, and flux and thus makes the best starting point for examining the principles of geopolitical formlessness in theory as it relates to geopolitics and strategy. Overall, we will see the relevance, both historically and theoretically, of the uniquely strong geopolitical model that arose via indigenous roots in the very heart of the world's largest continent.

This indigenous concept of grand strategy encompasses political, military, and diplomatic aspects utilizing the key concepts of strategic mobility and flexible or indirect governance. These political power systems originated in their largest incarnations among the nomadic people of the steppe and other people commonly considered peripheral in history but who in a Central Asian context were the original centerpieces of regional politics until technological changes led to their eclipse by the big sedentary powers such as Russia and China. However, even these well-established states took elements of the Formless Empire into their policies (if largely relegated to frontiers, the military, and a few informal relationships alone) and therefore the influence of the region's past lingers in different forms in the present.

TWO

HISTORIC EXAMPLES OF THE PREMODERN FORMLESS EMPIRE

Such was the harvest of results produced by a cloud of ruthless and idealess horsemen sweeping over the un-impeded plain—a blow, as it were, from the great Asiatic hammer striking freely through vacant space.
    —Halford Mackinder, *The Geographical Pivot of History*

THERE HAVE BEEN MANY NOMADIC POWERS THROUGHOUT THE history of Inner Eurasia. Bounded to the north by taiga forests, the south by desert and mountains, and cut with rivers, lakes, and various other topographies, this region is still defined by the centrality of one all-encompassing feature, the steppe.[1] It is this grassland, dry and yet plentiful for horses and pack animals, that fuels what was arguably the longest lived and most successful set of military cultures of the premodern era. Armies existing entirely of cavalry and made up of nomads who had grown up in the saddle possessed the ultimate mobility.

The core unit of this success was the mounted archer, who could fire accurately from full gallop. Coupled with the shock forces of a heavy cavalry reserve—to stage a breakthrough at the decisive moment—such a potent and flexible combination often could not be resisted by the armies of settled agrarian neighbors and dominated the Eurasian military field until the rise of gunpowder and eventually railroads overtook them.[2] Such forces could also melt back into the endless steppe using their mobility and lack of permanent settlements (which would need to be defended) and avoid or trap a less-flexible enemy. It was quite normal for steppe armies to defeat enemies of significantly greater number by utilizing speed, adaptability, and superior organization.[3]

In order to fully understand the workings of the Formless Empire within the space of Inner Eurasia it is necessary to acknowledge how common this combined practice of strategic and political mobility has been in the history of the region. There are many examples of the Formless Empire in Eurasian states that originated from nomadic and seminomadic peoples. Therefore, we will focus on a few examples that illustrate the principle of indirect rule and geopolitical formlessness particularly well, especially in interacting with more-conventional neighbors (*see map 1*).

Various nomadic steppe people from both north and west of the Chinese civilization had long interacted with the settled kingdoms in China proper. Often when the Chinese were divided, the nomadic peoples could make inroads into the settled areas. At other times, such as the partially Turkic Tang Dynasty, when China was strong and united, it could strike deep into the nomadic steppe and keep the various peoples there divided. A rare historical example of a bipolar system developing among this perpetual conflict occurred in the earlier Han Dynasty (206 BCE–220 CE), which faced off against the Xiongnu, a nomadic people who occupied the Mongolian steppe and the area known today as Turkistan. Here a unified nomadic state and a unified Chinese dynasty existed at the same time, and the differences between the two could not have started off as any more distinct.[4]

The Xiongnu Empire was founded by Modu Chanyu. It was based on the mobility of the horse and of livestock through pastureland, but the Xiongnu had no agricultural capacity or economic power. Han China, on the other hand, had plenty of both as well as desirable trade goods. In order to be able to reward his vassals and warriors, as well as present diplomatic gifts to other non-Chinese people, Modu Chanyu had to acquire these goods as a vital foreign policy objective. Although the Xiongnu had captured cities and goods manufactories by taking over the Tarim Basin cities in the deserts of the western frontier, without some form of integration into the Chinese economy they were doomed to stagnation if they could not trade.[5]

Given that the only significant advantage the nation possessed over the Han Dynasty was its military capabilities, and that the Chinese were notoriously suspicious of trading with nomadic barbarians for various reasons, the natural course of action for the new Xiongnu state was to begin acquiring what it needed through raiding.[6] These raids eventually convinced the Chinese that it was easier and cheaper to allow trade with their northern neighbors, resulting in a treaty in 198 BCE stipulating that the Xiongnu were to be treated as diplomatic equals and rendered tribute in the form of grain and luxury goods in exchange for nonaggression.

This arrangement soon came to be seen by both sides as mutually beneficial—at least for a little while. The raid could be destructive to the economic patterns active on both sides of the border, therefore representing a potential burden for the nomads as well. After all, the treaty was in force for sixty years, and during the ensuing stability the Xiongnu, a nation supposedly built on war, kept wealth flowing into their territories continually and without a renewal of major war. The construction of one of the first almost entirely pastoralist states effectively became based on the control of trade networks and the exacting of tributes. Although this model of imperial governance may have arisen out of the unique nature of a state ruled by nomadic pastoralists, the plan of the army patrolling key areas and allowing large numbers of the people in its network a certain degree of autonomy was the beginning of a highly successful and often repeated type of grand strategy in the lands of Inner Eurasia. After all, rather than bear the costs and effort of direct rule, why not engage in a mutually beneficial—if unequal—relationship? To quote David Christian on the nature of the Xiongnu system, "Macro-parasites, like micro-parasites, have to protect their hosts."[7]

This dangerous game was, of course, being played by both sides. The Chinese had been building up a cavalry-based armed force of their own, often supplemented with various steppe peoples. The treaty system may have had benefits for them, but it was humiliating and clearly benefited the Xiongnu more. Eventually, the officials of the Han Dynasty came to the conclusion that it was time to overthrow this order for one more favorable to their interests and security. They did so by adopting many of the tactics and strategies of the Xiongnu.[8] It was time to make their own Formless Empire, only this time with the players reversed.

The Han spent their time fostering internal division in the empire that had opened up their trade routes. Freedom of travel can work both ways, and Chinese money and goods were effective at undermining the unity of the Xiongnu as well as opening up new contacts with peoples farther afield who also bordered the Xiongnu state. A lightning campaign launched by the general Ban Chao (the supposed originator, in China at least, of the maxim "Use barbarians to fight barbarians") accomplished this feat by heavy reliance on nomadic auxiliaries and a reported interest in the strategies of Sun Tzu. His actions surely imply this is true, as wreaking havoc indirectly through deception before even launching the main assault is a mainstay of the master's thinking, and that is precisely what Ban Chao did.[9] Soon the Xiongnu state was split in two, with one-half a tributary of the Han Dynasty and the other weakened but still a foe. Now the battles took place far from Chinese territory in one or the other of the Xiongnu states.[10] Both sides had played for total hegemony of the formless variety over the borderlands, and it seemed the Chinese had won, but this was only the first round.

The nomadic peoples were kept largely on the defensive for a while after this turn of events. As late as 120 CE, Pan Yung, a Chinese court official, was advocating a continued vigilance toward the western regions in a list of political objectives toward the western frontier that smacks of what evolved into the tropes of Eurasian Formless Empires:

1. The occupation of the Western Regions denies them to the Hsiung-nu [Xiongnu].
2. The cost of occupation is partially defrayed by the payment of tribute and advantageous trade.
3. Neglect of the region will put the Oasis States and the trade routes in the hands of the Hsiung-nu who will profit thereby.
4. A strong Hsiung-nu state inevitably turns to ravage the borders of the empire.[11]

Now that the shoe was on the other foot it was time for the Xiongnu and other Turkic peoples of the region to lament their fortunes as the Chinese redirected their trade networks and political order to suit their own ends. Gradually the cost of constant deployment of Chinese armies (who often could not live on their own without a massive infusion of supplies on the steppe) to border forts began to wear down the government, and as the Han Dynasty began to scale down its operations, it was pulled back closer and closer to the homeland. The Han eventually fell, and a long period of disorder ruled in China. It was the same on the steppe until the coming of the Turkic Empire. The (possibly) partially Turkic Tang Dynasty, which had its own nomadic heritage, did, however, largely pick up the policies of the Han and continue them toward the Turks. Chinese armies of the seventh and eighth centuries played the game of vassalage and indirect rule tit for tat with the Turkic peoples. China had gone from being an imitator of the Formless Empire to being an active player under Tang Taizong, combining the elements of both worlds built on the historical experience of the Xiongnu and Han Dynasties.[12]

As an early Turk inscription said:

> The Chinese people were wily and deceitful. . . . [T]he Turkish people let their state . . . go to ruin. . . . Their sons worthy to become slaves, and their daughters worthy of becoming ladies became servants of the Chinese people. The Turkish lords abandoned their Turkish titles. The lords who were in China held the Chinese titles and obeyed the Chinese emperor and gave their services to him for fifty years.[13]

The ruling classes of the Tang Dynasty (618–907 CE) kept their relative integration with the nomadic-style military culture that had originally helped them attract the necessary Turkic allies with which to seize the empire from the unstable Sui Dynasty that had preceded them. Among these allies of the Tang—whose imperial domain in Central Asia ended up being almost as extensive in space controlled (if not in population) as their Chinese holdings—it was common to refer to the emperor by the Turkish title of Khagan.[14]

If the Han Dynasty had pioneered adopting the military tactics of the steppe people to ensure Chinese security, it was the Tang who did the most of any native dynasty to adopt some of their political and cultural methods, in order to not only be able to conquer territory that overlapped with lucrative trade routes but also to administer it in a way unobtrusive and perhaps even familiar to the locals. Over the course of a century, such methods proved a success, and the Tang not only thrived in the distant frontier but also crept steadily west, often being led by foreign mercenary generals at the head of nomadic Turkic and Khitan (a proto-Mongolian tribe) cavalry contingents. This process continued to expand influence until its advance was finally checked by another dynamic and growing empire, that of the Arabs. At the Battle of Talas in 751 beyond the Chinese western frontier in modern-day Kyrgyzstan, the Arabs inflicted a heavy, though not crippling, defeat on Tang forces by encouraging the defection of their western tribal Uighur allies in the battle. Around this same time, the rise of imperial ambitions in the newly centralized state of Tibet and some military successes on the part of the Uighurs began to erode these gains.[15]

With the coming of Uighur and Tibetan power, a multistate rivalry came back to the region. Still, a native Chinese dynasty had never before, and arguably never would again, have such widespread success on the western frontier for such a sustained period of time until the rise of the People's Republic in the mid-twentieth century.

The nomadic state may have pioneered the Formless Empire, but the Han and Tang Dynasties showed that it could be applied by settled states as well. A Eurasian-wide phenomenon of power politics had begun, but it had yet to reach its apogee. That would come later, also evolving in the borderlands between China and the Eurasian nomad, though in a different location and with different results.

The Tang Dynasty was crumbling in the tenth century. It had previously been rocked by decreasing power of the central government and massive rebellions, in particular the An Lushan rebellion, in which the Transoxianan general, who was targeted by court intrigue, attempted to seize the throne. Now the declining government, which was on its last legs, invited a people outside the empire to come in and shore up its northern frontier in 936. These people were the Khitans.[16]

The Khitans had originated in the north in what today is known in much of the world as Manchuria, or the Northeast Province of China. For much of their history before they rose to prominence, the Khitans had been weaker than many of their neighbors and thus had learned to be canny and adapt to whatever balance of power held sway. Many of them had served as a major contingent of the army of An Lushan in his ultimately failed rebellion against the Tang.[17] But with the founding of their own state in the vacuum left by the Tang decline, followed by their conquest of the Po-Hai kingdom in Manchuria and the invitation by the Tang to enter the game of Chinese power politics, the Khitans' fortunes changed drastically.

Previously in Chinese history, the steppe nomads had largely waged war for access to trade and tribute. The governance of settled people was at best a sideshow to the actual purposes of regime support and acquisition that the nomadic rulers pursued. This began to change with the Khitans, who set a precedent of those based in the Liao River valley by adopting a different kind of political model for nomadic/settled interaction. The Liao River valley was a small, unique geographic area in eastern Eurasia that combined pastoralists, small agricultural villages, and cities. This was not the last time this region would create a unique hybrid dynasty (the Jurchens and Manchus would follow) but it was here, at the start of Khitan rule, that a unique kind of Formless Empire started to develop—one nomadic yet with a large settled element that was an important part of the state.[18]

In 907, a leader known as Abaoji united the Khitans and their immediate neighbors into a proper regional force. As the Tang collapsed utterly, the Khitans used their clout to justify annexing large tracks of northern China into their rule. Despite the immense opportunities this presented in terms of having direct influence over an agriculturally active and craft-producing populace, there were also dangers for the Khitans. The fragmented Chinese states south of them, though divided, could all potentially marshal more wealth than the new Khitan state through the tax base of their populations alone, and there were still other nomadic groups not in the Khitan alliance network that could simultaneously threaten the northern borders. Acquiring large numbers of Chinese farmers, merchants, and officials could become an internal danger in such an uncertain time.

Therefore, Abaoji improvised. He ruled his nomads and his settled subjects in ways that pleased them both and was a nomadic clan chieftain as a khan and a bureaucratic, Chinese-style emperor at the same time. Therefore, the Khitan Khanate became also the Liao Dynasty, named for the unique river valley that had spawned this innovative compromise between ways of life. This was the birthplace of hybrid dynasties through the 1930s (which we will discuss later).

The Liao Dynasty sought accommodation by maintaining a nomadic government that still conducted business in major cities designated as regional capitals that the ruling entourage continuously traveled between. Each city had its locally recruited permanent staff of bureaucrats. The northern and western sections of the empire were ruled in the manner of steppe people with personal relationships with the ruler and interwoven relationships between families, lords, and vassals.[19] Pastureland was the primary resource for these people, who remained the ruling elite even as they kept to their traditions. This way they could avoid the fate of many other conquest dynasties that had acculturated too much to the settled Chinese way, lost their military talents and flexibility, and succumbed to other invaders. To be a proper ruling class, these people had to maintain their nomadic way of life, as they saw it.[20]

The story in the south was quite different. The areas populated by Chinese were given a certain amount of regional autonomy, including the right to keep the traditional Chinese Confucian examination system to select their administrators. The overall number of governors started out as almost always Khitan, but over time there was syncretism between the two peoples, which allowed many Chinese to rise to very high positions in the southern districts. Given this level of decentralized autonomy, the Chinese sections of the empire pretty much conformed to the will of the state and remained loyal subjects, continuing on much as they had during the earlier Tang Dynasty.[21]

Aside from territories held in Manchuria, northern China, and Mongolia, the Liao sought to avoid a full grab at total control and rather extended their influence outward. This was accomplished by either using indirect methods or enforcing a peace treaty after launching a military campaign on their enemies that allowed them to retain their autonomy under certain conditions. Abaoji—then known to his Chinese subjects as Emperor Taizu of Liao—died in 933. By that time, Khitan armies had driven deep into parts of China, westerly lands north of Tibet, and the Korean Peninsula. Yet in each case, they withdrew once they had set up an open-trade relationship and at least some nominal form of tribute network that flowed from the defeated party to the five capitals. The raw materials and luxury goods, such as silk products and surplus agriculture, stimulated the Liao state's economy, and the integration with the nomadic Khitans controlling the trade routes (and becoming literate in order to manage this economic web better) made the ruling classes of the new empire a vital link in the territories north of native-ruled China. Without direct control, a relatively small number of Khitans could maintain a Formless Empire.[22]

The multitude of Chinese states in the south began to coalesce into something larger, and by 960, the Sung Dynasty had formed. In their quest to reunify all the lands holding a primarily Chinese population, the Sung struck north with their military to recapture the parts of northern China under Liao rule. Abaoji was dead, and the Sung forces hoped that without his leadership and only a preteen on the throne they could restore Tang-style unity to the lands by having no major rivals in East Asia.

The massive Sung armies were able to eradicate the small states that had been able to survive as tributaries of the Liao, but they hadn't considered the fact that Abaoji's widow, the dowager empress Chengtien, was as formidable as her husband had been. Khitan women had a far higher status in society then their Chinese counterparts, holding property, guaranteed rights in marriage, and, in the case of the empress, having knowledge of military strategy. Leading the Khitan armies into the field, she struck and defeated the massive numbers of Sung forces in multiple engagements, driving them back into southern China and then laying siege to their capital at the Battle of Kao-Liang River. The Liao counterattack did much damage to Sung territory, but the Khitans lacked the numbers to continue the advance against such a populated state far into enemy lines, and so the conflict to resolve hegemony of northern China descended into stalemate (*see map 2*).[23]

A peace treaty between the two powers was concluded, and a stable border was drawn as a result. A multipolar power structure once again emerged in the Chinese world system. The border did not remain entirely stable, because of various outbreaks over disagreements, but there were no full-scale wars once it was properly demarcated. Additionally, the Khitans began to prepare the Liao state, which was heavily outnumbered by the Sung, for a defensive posture toward its southern neighbor. Along the immediate area of the border, rice cultivation was banned (though not other forms of agriculture) in order to facilitate the movement of cavalry, which would be significantly hampered by the extensive irrigation needed to supply rice paddies.

Meanwhile, the less-settled frontiers of the Liao state began a process of further integration of their allies. Many of the minor tribal vassals who had been attached to the Liao state started to take lucrative government positions rather than remain as tribute-paying vassals. This process was noticed with some alarm by the bordering vassal state of Korea, which the Sung tried to make an alliance with on the pretext of common defense of "civilized values." But the mobility and striking power of the Liao armies, coupled with their economic integration within the policies of Korea, acted as enough deterrent to prevent this plan from becoming a reality.

Finally, after a long dance between Cold War-type jockeying and occasional flare-ups, an unexpected victory won by the Liao military convinced the much larger Sung Dynasty to give up any attempts to overthrow the balance of power, either by trying to diplomatically outflank the Liao or by pushing the irredentist claims on the border. The treaty of Shan-Yuan, signed in 1004, finally settled the matter for the long term. According to the treaty:

> 1. The Sung would pay the Liao annually two hundred thousand lengths of silk and one hundred thousand ounces of silver

as a "contribution to military expenses" (effective indemnity for the war—phrased to diplomatically avoid the word *tribute*).

2. An even more rigidly demarcated border would be established.

3. There could be no cross-border disturbances or interference with the agricultural output of the other state.

4. Neither side could give refuge to the fugitives of the other.

5. No new border fortifications could be built.

6. Both sides had to cultivate good relations and respect each other's territorial integrity.[24]

For a century after this treaty was drawn up, the borders remained stable and peace reigned between the two kingdoms, by and large. The two emperors went so far as to declare themselves of the northern and southern courts, meaning they were like royal siblings of different branches of the same family, the Liao and Sung respectively. The only way that the Liao state—with its significant lack of comparative strengths to the Sung in terms of economic might, population, agricultural output, and the like—could be considered an equal to the Sung was because of its wealth derived from mobility in its civic and military elements, and its formlessness in both organization and diplomacy, which enabled it to deploy an army anywhere across its vast territories with unmatched rapidity as well as keep order through granted autonomy to distant peoples. It was through these principles—whether they were naturally occurring evolutions of policy or a specifically planned grand strategy—that the formless nature of Eurasian empire pioneered by the Xiongnu (and possibly others from eras not recorded) reached its first germination into a codified state policy on multiple levels under Khitan administration.

The Liao Dynasty, for all intents and purposes, was as formless as an empire can get and still be recognizable as a state. Its diplomacy was about maintaining profitable resource extraction routes, and it enforced these objectives by keeping its nomadic warrior base sharp and deployed, ready to strike wherever it might be needed. That it survived in the face of such a large and daunting foe as the Sung Dynasty (as well as numerous other nomadic peoples swirling around its periphery) for more than a century is testament to its effectiveness.

Some scholars estimate, based on surviving records from the Liao, that 750,000 Khitans were able to maintain a privileged position over 2.4 million Chinese subjects and 650,000 other ethnicities. A state of 3.8 million people, led by an ethnic minority of politically and economically marginal origin, became a broker of international trade while simultaneously holding its own in a largely bipolar system against a far larger state. Estimates of the Sung population range over one hundred million, though there are no specific numbers for this period of its history.[25]

With a stable southern border, the peacetime elements of Khitan policy and their flexible systems' effectiveness at enacting what in more modern parlance might be termed "brain drain" from the Sung or the westward-lying Tangut Kingdom of the Xi Xia became apparent. Soon the Liao attracted immigrants, laid-off Sung bureaucrats and scholars, and those down on their luck or seeking new opportunities. Because of the peace of Shan-Yuan, the Sung and the Liao were no longer technically enemies, so many opportunists took advantage of the situation and became people who could work for both dynasties, circumstances depending. Going to the Liao and then returning later to the Xi Xia or the Sung was an option many people took, becoming a type of government temp worker. As Zhang Li, a scholar who pursued this path of migratory opportunity, wrote in the *Liao Shi*, "I am not accustomed to the local customs of the north, to the food and drink, or to the living accommodation, so I often feel depressed. And it was simply because of this that I ran away."[26] Such workarounds were not only possible but helped the Liao attract as much talent as possible.

Even with such a stable system, the Sung Dynasty was not content. As the Liao rocked from a tribal rebellion in its northeast, the Sung seized the opportunity to ally with the Jurchen people of northern Manchuria. The Liao Empire eventually unraveled under the pressure of warfare as the Jurchens jumped from victory to victory over the Khitans. By 1125, the Jurchens had fully taken over the heartland of the Liao state. They also turned on their erstwhile Sung allies and drove them farther south than the Khitans ever had. Thus the Jin Dynasty was born. It was a construct much more conventional (to

Chinese eyes at least) in that soon the ruling nomadic class began to settle down and become more-Sinified rulers, accommodated to Chinese culture and lifestyle. The bipolar system was soon recreated in China—at least until the coming of the Mongols a hundred years later. Much of the Khitan nobility stayed behind and ended up serving the new Jurchen masters, but many others, including much of the military aristocracy, who were still nomadic, packed up their gear and headed west. The story of the Khitan techniques of imperialism and great power politics was not yet over.[27]

Yelu Daishi, a royal descended from the noble Liao lineage and a successful general, led many Khitans west in the wake of the losses to the Jurchen people. Having escaped to freedom from Jin captivity, he rebelled against the incompetent figurehead Liao remnant government and took almost one hundred thousand Khitans out just in time as the government finally collapsed. They passed into the territory of the Uighurs, who submitted to their overlordship and looked to establish a new base somewhere in Central Asia proper.[28] Despite the positive reception of the Uighurs, it looked like the Khitan people had fallen from glory into obscurity, left to be trampled in the wake of other, newer power brokers. But having survived in large part owing to their mobility, the Khitans also brought their grand strategies and techniques of rule west with them. The Liao Dynasty may have been gone, but its influence was about to be reborn in a new region.

After realizing the Jin were too strong to effectively counterattack them from the west, the Khitan refugee army moved farther toward Central Asia. There the Karakhanid state invited the Khitans to annex parts of its former territory that it had lost to rebellious tribal army forces. This plan backfired for the Karakhanids, however, as the arrival of Khitans inspired the subject Qarlug people to ask for Khitan protection against the Karakhanids and their Seljuk Turk allies. Seeking to exploit this opportunity to build a new Khitan empire, Yelu Daishi gathered his forces for an epic battle against his combined foes, defeating them decisively at the Battle of Qatwan outside of Samarkand in 1143. The shock of this defeat unraveled the coalition against the Khitans and enabled them to take over large swathes of territory in Transoxiana.[29]

Once again the Khitan found themselves as a ruling minority controlling vastly different subjects who were largely tradesmen and settled farmers. They had not, however, forgotten the lessons learned during the Liao Dynasty. Their new state, the Kara-Khitai Empire, was a successor in more ways than just the ethnicity of the ruling class. Although retaining a pseudo-Chinese court culture (for the prestige it brought these otherwise totally alien Khitan shamanist-Buddhist syncretic conquerors of Muslim lands), the Kara-Khitai hired locally to man their bureaucracy and made sure to keep their nomadic traditions intact, as before.[30] Additionally, they made themselves appear more as arbiters than direct rulers by becoming the mediators of interests among cities, farmers, and nomadic populations.[31] In foreign policy they maintained very stable borders with their neighbors, and most military actions were small scale and focused on establishing tributary networks or preventing the rise of another regional power by balancing their forces against them. Most of the neighbors of the Kara-Khitai ended up as domestically autonomous and largely recognized as independent states, so long as they kept the supplies and money flowing through trade routes.[32]

This state continued for another hundred years in Islamic Central Asia, using the formless tactics Abaoji had developed to integrate into the periphery of Chinese civilization.[33] Eventually, though, this state was absorbed by another rising power, the Mongols. It is a testament to the adaptability of the Khitans that many of them became quite high-ranking nobles and government advisers under the Mongols. The primary governing administrator of that empire was a Khitan of the royal line, Yelu Chutsai, and the influence of Khitan geopolitical grand strategy soon made itself felt through this new, much larger empire (*see map 3*).[34]

The most successful group of nomads at conquering a vast empire (which was also the only one to control all of the steppes and borderlands from Ukraine through Manchuria simultaneously) were the Mongols. At its height, the Mongol Empire stretched from Korea to the Hungarian steppe and from the lower Siberian forest to the borders of India, Vietnam, and Palestine. This vast pan-Eurasian empire, while always decentralized to a certain extent, remained fairly unified, except during succession disputes in the royal family, until the reign of Kublai in 1260–1294.[35]

The founder of this empire, the previously exiled son of a slain minor chieftain, was Temujin. Temujin had worked his way up from a minor raiding party leader to eventual unifier and leader of all the Mongol tribes and a few non-Mongol allied tribes after a series of tribal wars and diplomatic integrations. At his *khuriltai* (a kind of electoral gathering to determine the next leader) he adopted the name Chinggis Khan, often rendered in English as Genghis Khan, or Universal Ruler. The Mongol document of law, the Yasa, was also written shortly after his rise to rule in the early thirteenth century.[36] It provided for religious tolerance and meritocracy (outside of the royal family, of course) across ethnic lines to those who were loyal subjects of the khan. It also guaranteed the safety of merchants, whom the government was charged with protecting during travel as well as in general. With Chinggis Khan's rule came campaigns against the Jurchen Jin state and the Kara-Khitai Khanate—the former being gravely diminished (though it was not destroyed until after Chinggis Khan's death) and the latter being totally annexed into the Mongol Empire. The Mongols could use the rights guaranteed under the Yasa to co-opt support from the Kara-Khitai, who had neglected to uphold their empire's traditional multiculturalism and thus created an alienated Muslim underclass eager to replace their rule with that of the more tolerant Mongols.[37]

Through both of these conquests, the illiterate and pastoral Mongols—who had been considering wholesale extermination for the settled peoples near them in order to expand their livestock range—came into possession of the talents of many Khitan administrators. Being the ruling class of the Kara-Khitai as well as much of the bureaucracy of the Jin, but still retaining their identity as pastoral people, they were excellent existing intermediaries for the Mongols to use. Indeed, Yelu Chutsai, a Khitan court official in the Jin Empire, was second only to the khan himself in the administration of the Mongol Empire.

Yelu Chutsai was immensely powerful. It was he who talked the Mongol ruling class out of its plans for wholesale extermination of the settled folk, arguing that dead people don't pay taxes, make works of art, or provide markets for trade. The Chinese were spared from genocide, but the nomads were unquestionably at the top of the power pyramid. The Khitan legacy was living on.[38]

The empire continued to expand at an unprecedented rate, even by the standards of the large geopolitical entities of the Eurasian steppe. After an attack on the merchants and ambassadors of the empire by the Kwarezemian Shah, the Mongols turned west. After destroying this new foe in a lightning campaign combining surprise attacks and massive military movements and deception, they entered the Caucuses and Ukraine in a reconnaissance in force that caused the subjugation of numerous minor kingdoms and tribes and inflicted a foreshadowing defeat on a coalition of Russian and Cuman military forces assembled to stop their progress. By the death of Chinggis Khan in 1227, the Mongol military machine was already a precedent-setting force of conquest on the world stage.[39]

Mongol imperialism, despite its massive scope, was predicated on the idea of indirect rule.[40] Local elites were left in charge where they could be depended on. When they could not be trusted, a loose coalition of Mongol elites, often women, took charge of regional governing. The primary objective was tax collection and securing the trade routes. As shamanists, the Mongols cared little for religious conversion and used Confucians to administer Muslim lands and Muslims to administrate China. What came from this was not empire in the more famous Roman, Chinese, or Victorian sense, but something based on hierarchy and wealth extraction assuredly, yet without either the direct political control nor the "civilizing mission" or cultural conversion attempts so common to those types of states. It was a partly parasitic but also symbiotic relationship that did not require the death or conversion of the host.[41]

Given the small numbers of the Mongols and the vast expanses of territory they ruled, these tactics may have been necessary, and they were coupled with near total ruthlessness in warfare and in dealing with rebellions. But the result was, in effect, a type of large-scale free-trade agreement and declaration of religious toleration. Perhaps (though this can be nothing but speculation) the Yasa had something to do with the relative staying power of such a large and loose geopolitical entity. In any case, Jack Weatherford refers to this height of a "Pax Mongolica" as the first true era of globalization, and of a sustainable international trading class and of interregional exchange of ideas, particularly in the sciences.[42] Amy Chua gives the height of Mongol rule an entire chapter as a supporting case study for her thesis of "hyperpowers" that rule through utilizing multicultural tolerance. Indeed, her central thesis of how the indirect rule of major powers is fostered by the accumulation of human capital by utilizing a hands-off approach to statecraft is nearly exemplified by the example of the Mongol Empire. The carrot was relatively benign governance (which could occasionally still impose massive taxes); the stick was the ruthless terror of the mobile armies.[43]

Even in the most densely populated and wealthiest of their various pan-Eurasian provinces, those of the former Jin and Sung states, the Mongols were able to graft onto the Chinese state apparatus and enforce unity (or reunification, as many Han historians would no doubt prefer), which was very much a product of Abaoji's original innovations in steppe-nomad imperialism over two centuries before. The previous states had built a path for the entire system to not only be brought to all of China, but to the vast majority of Eurasia as well. China was the economic and technological engine, and proxies—such as vast numbers of recruited Uighurs, Jurchens, and Khitans—filled out the intermediate role between the ruling class and their new settled subjects.[44]

This type of land-based empire is not usually regarded as analogous to maritime empires, but perhaps it should be. The successfully executed nomadic land empire in this era shows clearly that in the space of Eurasia, a tradition of formless flexibility brought about by nomads could exist on a massive scale and last for a significant amount of time, touching many disparate societies as it expanded. To quote the scholar Gary Seaman, "Although the Mongols created their empire with a technology of cavalry maneuver and siege trains rather than with round ships and cannon, they shared many political and strategic objectives with maritime states like the Portuguese, the English, and the Dutch, who battened off the tribute and trading systems they installed in their hegemonies."[45]

Eventually the centrifugal forces and divergent interests of the distant subkhanates began to pull this unity apart. The ascension of the controversial Kublai, who had proclaimed his desire to establish an official dynasty over China in 1260 (which became the Yuan), alienated many Mongol traditionalists and further drove the Kipchak Khanate (Siberia and Russia), the Ilkhanate (Iran, Iraq, and the Caucasus), and the Chaghatai Khanate (Central Asia) further from the new Yuan (Mongolia, Korea and China). Many of these subkhanates retained official status as tributaries, though their self-governance was never truly in question, and for a long time they still endeavored, despite the political division, to maintain the openness of the trade routes and the safety of the merchants who traveled between them (*see map 4*).[46]

Despite this overwhelming achievement, the Ulus of Jochi—a realm that was the assigned inheritance of Chinggis Khan's son Jochi before he died, was known more commonly in its era as the Kipchak Khanate, and is more famous in the West as the Golden Horde—always had a somewhat larger degree of autonomy than the other subdivisions of the empire, and also had many more semi-independent vassals rather than just lightly ruled subject populations. This was because of its faraway location from the center of Mongol power and its orientation toward Europe. Europe was given much less priority in the later Mongol Empire compared to rule over such places as Central Asia, China, and Iran.[47]

This soon-to-be-autonomous part of the Mongol realm showcased particularly well the nature of indirect imperialism and power politics common to Inner Eurasia's power relations. It also serves as a great example of interaction between Slavic and Turko-Mongolian peoples at a time when the power relations between the two were opposite of what they would be in more-modern times. Examining the policies of the Kipchak Khanate can help us understand the particular nature of flexible, steppe-based power politics and how it can affect radically different people without direct annexations or outright imperialism. This was one of the formative experiences in Russian history, and the

Russians would come to be quite the primary actors in the post-Mongol era. The Mongol Empire as a whole may have had its tradition of indirect power and formlessness in policy, but it was this westernmost outpost that, by its very nature, exemplified these principles the most thoroughly.[48] That is why it, more than any other part of the empire, deserves such a thorough exploration.

In 1223, while Chinggis Khan was still alive, the Mongols conducted a reconnaissance in force into the Russian principalities. The culmination of this first campaign was the battle on the river Khalka, which shattered the combined armies of the Russian kingdoms. The Mongols then withdrew this relatively small scouting detachment to rejoin the main armies for further campaigning against the northern Jurchen-Chinese Jin state. Thinking the danger over, the Russian principalities soon returned to squabbling with each other.[49]

The Mongols had yet to strike in true force, however. Under the reign of Chinggis Khan's successor, Ogedei, western expansion, along with consolidating and expanding gains in the Middle East, became a higher priority. From the beginning, the conquest of Russia and other lands west of the Ural Mountains was a multinational affair. The Ulus allotted to Jochi had yet to be conquered before his death, and so his son Batu set forth with a core of Mongol troops and recruited numerous Turkic, Alan, and defected Kipchak tribesmen to strengthen his forces. The Kipchaks, who later gave their name to this enterprise, were another Eurasian nomadic people who had taken up residence in the steppes of southern Ukraine and confederated with the Cuman people, who were of similar extraction. Nominally allied to various Russian principalities, they saw the Mongols as their gravest threat. This Kipchak-Cuman alliance already functioned in a flexible and amorphous way that in many ways presaged what was to come.[50]

The Mongol armies under the nominal command of Batu (the veteran general Subotai, who had already conquered large tracts of China and Central Asia, actually commanded the field battles) advanced west, deep into the Russian forest zone. This attack was conducted in the dead of winter 1237, with fifty thousand men using the frozen rivers to rapidly advance on the northernmost Russian principalities. Such provinces as Ryazan and Vladimir were the first to fall, as they were viewed as the most powerful and the ones least touched by the previous Mongol incursion. Being seen as major threats meant they suffered disproportionately, and they were not just taken and sacked but virtually destroyed. By the time Kiev fell, in 1240, the remaining Russian nobles and princelings agreed to swear fealty to the khan, even in the unconquered Novgorod Republic.[51] The Mongols went on to invade Poland and Hungary, crushing the armed forces of those countries as well as the elite Teutonic Knights (who had previously carved out their own independent realm in the Baltic during the Northern Crusades) before wintering on the Hungarian plain and withdrawing to vote in the empire's succession, as Khan Ogodei had died while they were on campaign. Although the Mongol armies withdrew from Eastern Europe, they did remain in Russia.[52]

The Mongols used spies to cite their document of law, the Yasa, as proof to religious dissenters that they would have freedom, to merchants that their trades and wares would be secure, and to peasants that they would be protected from the rich. The consequences of noncooperation, however, would be dire. In this way they were able to win support from many segments of the population, especially the important merchant and trading classes, and conclude such a vast and ambitious campaign in a little over two years.[53] Sun Tzu would have applauded this type of intelligence gathering and lightning campaigning that utilized his ideas of shock, maneuver, and deception. But the Kipchak Khanate had to be governed as well as conquered, and it was here that the principles of the Formless Empire really shone through.

The name Golden Horde, which probably comes from the yellow gers, or tents, of the royal family's entourage, is primarily a Western reference. It did not take long for the Ulus of Jochi to become known both within and outside its borders as the Kipchak Khanate. Mongols, though composing the upper echelons of royalty and hierarchy, were a minority in their new state. Most soldiers were Kipchaks or various other Turkic peoples, and intermarriage became so frequent that even the royal family itself came to represent an amalgamation of its various nomadic populations, forming a new ethnicity that came to be called Tatar.[54]

The actual organization of the Kipchak Khanate was largely the creation of Batu Khan, though it remained in place for almost a century and a half, adapting to changing circumstances but remaining fundamentally the same. One of the most unique attributes to this state was the lack of any sort of direct-rule policy toward the Russian principalities. The Mongols and Kipchaks stayed on the steppe, keeping their flexible nomadic life and building occasional cities in river valleys for administrative and trade purposes. Meanwhile, the Russians were left in their divided factions under their native rulers. Mongol tax assessors and representatives were left among the aristocracy, but for all purposes the Russians retained their lands and titles.[55] What made these princelings part of an empire was the indirect methods used to bring about their submission to the khan and his government, which was located in the new city Sarai on the Volga River.

In addition to the building of a few new cities to facilitate commerce and governing, the Kipchak Khanate encouraged the numerous peoples of its empire to migrate into these cities. Turkic peoples, more-settled Mongol aristocrats, Russians, Jews, Genoese, and merchants from many places outside of the empire came to set up new lives. With the various steppe peoples largely integrated and living a similar life to each other on the steppes, the state still derived a large amount of resources and control from having settled communities, farmers, crafters, and traders. Given the dispensation of the aristocracy, this could be done without sacrificing the mobility and military effectiveness that had made the Horde so dominant in the first place.[56]

At first, the khan of the Kipchak Khanate was officially a vassal of the great khan in Karakorum. As the empire began to fracture during Kublai's rule and the official capital of his new Yuan Dynasty was moved to China, the loose vassalage grew even more tenuous. By the death of Kublai, no one in the Mongol successor states paid homage anymore to the grand khan. The Kipchak Khanate, being naturally distant, was affected little by these upheavals back east, and it outlasted the other successor states of the Mongol Empire. Even upon its breakup it was still able to subdivide into smaller states that had quite a bit of life left in them, such as Kazan, Astrakhan, and the Crimean Khanate. The latter lasted until 1783.[57]

Part of the reason for this successful and adaptable model, which could wrest so much tribute and influence from its neighbors as well as cling to life even in decline, was the internal organization of the

Kipchak Khanate itself. The Kipchak Khanate was a confederation of vassals within further overlapping structures of confederation and vassalage. A roughly feudal structure upheld by bonds of personal loyalty and sworn fealty that was forged in the steppes of Mongolia became merged with more-official and bureaucratic forms of government picked up from previous Mongol experiences in Persia and China. Tying this together was a sort of protoparliament-type system common in the steppes of Eurasia, the *khuriltai*. It was a discussion-based forum, usually held in a grand ger, that met regularly to converse about domestic and foreign policy. The khuriltai could also nominate the successor of the empire. Although restricted to the royal family (or in dire cases a noble with some royal ties), the exact member of the monarchical lineage to be the successor was still chosen by election.[58]

This system could also be manipulated for policy and interempire goals by the khan. Batu Khan in particular was quite fond of using his indirect influence in both the Kipchak khuriltai as well as the khuriltai in the capital of the main empire (Karakorum) to bring about favorable goals for his newly conquered inheritance. Batu used the wealth extracted from his Russian vassals to fund his own intrigue. Because he was a possible successor to the throne of the great khan over the entire empire, he had much clout. But rather than gamble on trying to take the ultimate title, Batu worked to establish his personal allies in Karakorum. Ogodei's successor, Guyuk, had rocky relations with the independent-minded Batu, but after his death the next great khan was Mongke, who had served in Batu's army during his invasion of Europe and was elevated to that lofty position in no small measure because of Batu's maneuvering and patronage.[59]

The Russian princes were obligated to travel to the khuriltai as well as to pay homage to the khan whenever a new one ascended the throne or issued an edict. At great expense and with retinue, the princes made their way to Sarai (or whatever nomadic encampment the khan might be in at the time of the appointment) to offer submission and ask for support against other princes or foreign foes. At these events, the khan rewarded those princes he most wanted on his side, or those who had performed some task that benefited his regime. Often, the khan bestowed gifts, so these arrangements were not always entirely one sided.[60]

Batu had, therefore, secured his own advantageous and semiautonomous position while retaining the broader imperial links and the stable pan-Eurasian trade links forged by the empire. What he and his successors did after this point showcased further the uses of indirect power and flexibility so common to nomadic Inner Eurasian powers.

Despite the Kipchak Khanate's fearsome warrior reputation, and perhaps in large part because of it, its primary activity was commerce. The previously discussed cosmopolitan cities filled with numerous peoples from the hinterlands and periphery of the empire served to connect numerous trade routes. The Mediterranean and Byzantine world was connected with the steppe and Central Asia as well. Western merchants saw their trade routes stretch farther east than had previously been possible to directly reach Asian caravans. Sarai boomed, as travelers, traders, and ambassadors on exploration missions could pick up the route in western Russia, Scandinavia, or the Black Sea and (theoretically at least) take it all the way to the Chinese coast.[61]

Lest it be thought that this was all a great triumph of multiculturalism, it should be remembered that the entire system was, of course, built on vassalage and the payment of tribute by the conquered peoples. As the various nomadic groups in the population converged and became more equal, the burdens on the divided Russian principalities only increased. To fuel the rapid growth of the new administrative and economic infrastructure, the taxes on the peasantry and vassal kingdoms could only grow.

Tax collectors called *baskaks* were placed in the principalities, though they were often recalled once a Russian prince became a reliable vassal and more economically integrated with the Horde. Mongol emissaries and traders were the only direct Mongol presence that usually made its way into the Russian regions, as the nearby deployment of nomadic forces just across the border of the forest zone in the steppe implied the penalty for disobedience. Therefore, there was little direct Mongol imperialism, aside from the economical. The khans' influence over their nonsteppe and westerly possessions was indirect, with the army of the Horde only arriving to quash rebellions, support vassal princes, and uphold the fiscal extraction net. Despite this, the khan was acknowledged as the lord of eastern Russia. For two and a half centuries, this remained the rough system in place.[62]

As these systems were moving from outright vassalage to stratified economic unit, one principality in particular was quick to jump on the bandwagon. Seeing the prohibitive cost and risk of noncollaboration and the potential to go from backwater to forefront, Moscow was happy to become the economic and political collaborator of the Mongol overlords. When Ivan Danilovich (known now to history as Kalita, or "moneybags") ascended to the throne of Moscow in 1325, he saw an opportunity to exploit a niche as the khan's loyal tax collector and make a hefty profit for himself at the same time. By removing the Mongols from the process but still being able to render them their tribute payments, Moscow became the ultimate broker in the inter-imperial relationship between the many principalities and the Horde. For instance, when Moscow became the khan's enforcer, it often clashed with Novgorod, especially over silver payments from which Moscow took a cut. In exchange, the khan and Moscow could cooperate to keep Novgorod out of the hands of Lithuania. This served the purposes of both Moscow and the Horde.

As the runoff of this profit enriched Moscow, the city also had the good fortune to be viewed increasingly positively by the khans of the Kipchak Khanate. They in turn bestowed titles and honors on the princes of Moscow and often gave them territories captured from less loyal princelings to enrich the domain of their most thorough collaborator. In this one instance, the relationship between master and vassal became much more symbiotic.[63]

The lifeline connecting these various webs of economic activity and communication was the postal, or *yam*, system the Mongols set up. This system of postal riders, with way stations every few hours' ride away stocked with fresh horses, enabled the quick transit of correspondence, contracts, and occasionally important goods. The yam was clearly a type of soft power, constructed to economically tie the empire together and keep the disparate areas integrated. The yam was extended by the Kipchak Khanate to encompass its Russian vassals as well as their core Mongol and Turkic territories. The policy was so effective it was adopted by the future Russian state of Muscovy when it became the rising power in the region.[64]

In the western provinces, farther away from the nomadic base and its more closely tied vassals, the situation became much more complex, and by the latter part of the thirteenth century, the foreign policy use of indirect action became starkly apparent—if more convoluted.

The Republic of Novgorod, nestled deep within the forest zone and never subjected to siege or conquest by the Mongol army, found itself in a uniquely precarious situation. To its northwest, the Germanic-Baltic crusading order of the Teutonic Knights used the collapse of Russian princely power to push east. To the south, the Kipchak Khanate held sway over the remaining Russian principalities. Being a city-state whose profitable trade routes (as well as its sovereignty) were threatened, Novgorod could not stand alone. Therefore, the city elders and Prince Alexander Nevsky chose to voluntarily submit to the khan rather than become the stomping grounds of a fanatical order. To ensure regime survival, it was better to live under the Horde's loose rule than to bow before the potentially invasive and conditional Catholic-Teutonic help, especially at the cost of the local religion, which the Teutonic Knights demanded the Russian princes change to Catholicism in order to receive assistance. The greater Orthodox Church in Russia had fared well under the Mongols, being required only to pray for the health of the khan, and so the clergy feared Teutonic Knights and their Swedish allies pushing through Finland far more than the Horde.[65]

Having paid his tributes, Nevsky turned west to confront the invasion of the Teutonic Knights and their allies. At the Battle of Lake Peipus in 1242, the invaders were dealt a crushing defeat, and many of the fleeing heavily armored knights fell through the ice of the lake. Even with such a victory and a stabilized position, Nevsky turned back to the Horde and even made the trip to Karakorum to present himself to Mongke Khan upon his ascension to the throne.[66]

In the Caucasus, the newly formed Ilkhanate, another Mongol substate that Batu had even sent troops to support, became increasingly a rival to the Kipchaks. As the greater empire started to decay, these two megastates lost their unity under any kind of pan-Mongolian identity and began to compete for influence in the mountain range. They had become the largest threats to each other after having cowed their non-Mongol competition. Unlike the Kipchak Khanate, the Ilkhanate was a direct-rule system of a Mongol army and ruling class ruling over a Persian and Arabic population. The rulers there, after sacking Baghdad and killing the last caliph of Islam, were in no mood for accommodation with their Muslim subjects. Berke, the third ruler of the Kipchak Khanate, was Muslim, though his state was not, and he used his religious tolerance toward his subjects and the lack of the Ilkhanate's tolerance as an excuse for war in the Caucasus. Indecisive clashes occurred throughout the region before the issue petered out. Aside from opening up trade and diplomatic links with the primary rival of the Ilkhanate, the Mamluk Sultanate of Egypt, this issue had little impact on the Kipchak relation with Russia—except to show the vast differences between each Mongol successor state. It is relevant to note that the Ilkhanate lasted significantly less time than the Kipchak Khanate, being established in 1256 and collapsing in 1325.[67]

Farther south and west of the Kipchaks, different rumblings were taking place among the western Russian princedoms. The Grand Duchy of Lithuania, fresh from defeating its own invasions at the hands of the Teutonic Knights was on the march for expansion. Russian princes on the western periphery of the Kipchak Khanate's reach were quick to realize that an opportunity had opened for them to seek the best deal possible in exchange for their vassalage. Lithuania, the other large pagan empire in Europe at this time, sent forth similar lenient terms for vassalage to the Russian princes as the Mongols had, and now the ball was in the court of the Russians to choose who could better secure their interests. The security situation between these two jockeying powers who threatened so subsume all of Russia between them offered danger as well as opportunity.[68]

The flirtation with another regional power such as Poland or Lithuania was cause for rival princes to use large allies against each other. As Prince Rostislav of Mozhaysk, near Moscow, drew closer to Poland, Prince Danylo of Galicia used this defection of vassalage to launch a war of expansion against the former's territories. Equipping his army in the Mongol fashion, he crushed his regional opposition to become the most powerful Russian prince in the west. Once Danylo became established, he pursued a much more balanced policy of trying to keep Mongol influence at a minimum while still remaining safe from attack. This did not always work, and after a Mongol punishing expedition in 1259, he affirmed his vassalage. He did, however, marry into the Lithuanian nobility to keep his options open.[69]

Danylo was not the only one to engage in local power politics in this amorphous frontier. Princes allied to the khan expanded the vassal network of their own volition and then won favors with the Kipchak Khanate and a large amount of spoils. They were protected from counterattack from their enemies by the Mongols if they failed in these local quests to expand their power and territory. Mongol hegemony in the eastern parts of Russia could be a shield as well as a burden, but in the west, where it was weaker, large states like Lithuania could make significant inroads. But as Lithuania expanded steadily from the Baltic to the Black Sea, using largely the same grand strategy the Mongols used, events slowly came to alter this evolving indirect bipolarity. The fractured and divided nature of the Russian principalities lasted almost a century, but all the while, the star of Muscovy was rising.

Muscovy kept its collaborationist posture for almost a century, but after tumultuous times—the Horde saw the adoption of Islam as the state religion, ravaging by the bubonic plague, and a civil war over succession—this former city-state had both the wealth and influence to change the tide. Prince Dmitri (later Donskoi), a once vassal of Khan Mamai's, turned on his former master in retaliation for a lack of support for his own ambitions. Mamai had grown suspicious of the now-ascending Moscow, and his suspicions turned to truth when Dmitri gathered a coalition of princes under his lead. This development so upset the previous international order that former foe Lithuania offered troops in alliance with the Kipchak Khanate in order to keep the upstart Muscovy down. Before this could happen, Dmitri met and engaged the khan in battle on Kulikovo Field in 1380. The battle was close and hard fought, but in the end the Russian coalition prevailed. It is often portrayed as a decisive battle, but its impact was not truly known until years later. For although Muscovy was now a robust and independent nation free of vassalage, many other Russian states still submitted to the Horde, especially when Mamai was killed in a brief civil war and the tricky Toqtamysh took his place. Despite reunification, however, the temporary anarchy of the post-Kulikovo Horde had dealt the nomads a great blow to both morale and prestige.[70]

The true end of the Kipchak Empire was soon to come, though the blow was not struck from the west but rather from the east. The Horde was about to experience its demise the same way it had struck a fatal blow to Russia almost 150 years earlier. Toqtamysh may have established control over a reunified Horde, but his schemes to expand influence into Central Asia backfired when he invaded the territory controlled by his patron, the great conqueror Emir Timur. After repelling Toqtamysh, Timur drove deep into Kipchak territory in 1396, destroyed the capital cities of the Horde in Old and New Sarai along the Volga, and raided and plundered many of the Russian principalities. Toqtamysh's reunified Horde eventually collapsed into several different subkhanates, such as Kazan, Astrakhan, and the Crimean Khanate, which were separated by geography and objectives. Toqtamysh was slain while on the run, and many of his soldiers defected to Lithuania, the Timurids, or one of the new local successor khanates.[71] This was the true end of the Horde, and from this point on, Muscovy was the expansionist state to whom others paid tribute.

Once Ivan IV (Grozny, or "Terrible") had conquered the obstinate and affluent Kazan Khanate, in 1552, the way east was wide open for the settled states to take up the mantle of flexible, mobile empire—at least in the north. Farther south and east, however, Tamerlane, the true slayer of the Kipchak Khanate, had his own story to tell. The fall of the Mongol successor state hegemony and the coming of gunpowder ushered in a new era—one of increasingly modern and more-familiar looking states, but also states that were undeniably influenced by their experiences at the hands of nomadic foes or predecessors. Even as the impact of the nomads began to fade from the central position in history, their influence remained, and they still had some time as the dominant regional actors.

For those interested in the nature of imperialism in Inner Eurasia, this chapter has shown the relevance of the premodern historical precedents that were set there. It is important to establish that this nomadic style of Formless Empire was a frequently used and often effective grand strategy of powers in the history of the region. It was a natural evolution to suit the capabilities of the nomads and their goals of regime support while maintaining a distinct and separate realm for themselves. Xiongnu, Khitan, and Mongol/Kipchak people strove to retain their mobility and lower their manpower costs by keeping themselves somewhat divested from direct rule. Instead they were content to control key geographic points, roads, and trade routes, and to tie everything up nicely with a mobile, rapidly deployable combat force that did away with the need for massive garrisons and fortifications.

Many other similar empires corresponding to this period—including the first Turk Empire, the Xi Xia, and the Khazars—have been given short shrift here in order to focus on the prelude to and aftereffect of Yelu Abaoji's recorded policies and strategy directly, but they offer varying examples of nomadic power at its height.

From here on, the nomadic power stagnated, then slipped downward gradually. But as we will soon see, it did not go quietly, and it left a legacy.

THREE

POST-PAX MONGOLICA THROUGH THE TIMURID POWERS

Through me the dying house of Chinggis flares up again. . . .
When I breeze by like the morning wind, the candle of Timur
goes out as I pass.

—Muhammad Shaybani Khan

B ESIDES CONTINUING OUR NARRATIVE OF THE EVOLVING NATURE OF
empire in Inner Eurasia, the point of this chapter is to show continuity in policy even as the apogee of nomadic power that was the
Mongols began to slip away into the night. This prepares us for the
chapter that shows the mantle of the Formless Empire being inherited
by non-nomadic states for the first time since the height of the Han
and Tang Dynasties. It also shows the variety of adaptations to changing circumstances that formless geopolitics can make and shows continuity along such lines as economic and foreign policy in the Inner
Eurasian system, even while other factors begin to move in different
directions.

Also in this chapter is an admittedly unorthodox appraisal of Emir Timur's geopolitical objectives. Timur is generally regarded as a poor administrator who built an ephemeral empire on the feat of skill at war alone. I take a contrary position, more in line with John Darwin or Beatrice Forbes Manz, who are cited heavily in the coming pages, that Timur's actual empire was much smaller than the realm of his conquests, and that his objectives were much more about enrichment of a core at the expense of a periphery than about creating a massive and cohesive state under one law, as was the Mongol Empire at its height. This aspect of Timur's career has been largely overlooked, and hopefully, redressing the balance can show the importance of the Timurid legacy to our topic.

Following the Timurids, we will look at the dynastically related Mughals, who took the formless geopolitics of Inner Eurasia out for a spin in the foreign territory of India with mixed results. They are an illuminating example for land and maritime powers alike, and they illustrate the process of acculturation that often occurs in states with flexible nomadic ruling classes. The chapter then finishes with an examination of postimperial Mongolia, its adaptation from being the first and only supreme hegemon of the entire region examined in this book to being a relatively insignificant nation on the margins of the various civilizational cores that reemerged after Mongol collapse (*see map 5*).

The Chaghatai Khanate warrants a look because at this time it overlapped more with the states of the post-Mongol era than it did during the Pax Mongolica. In addition, like the Kipchak Khanate, it remained a steppe-based enterprise with a clear delineation between nomadic ruling class, warrior elite, and townspeople and farmers. While the Yuan and the Ilkhanate soon acclimated to local systems and the Yasa became less important for how they conducted domestic affairs, Mongol tradition persevered quite strongly in these two other successors.

Perhaps owing to its central location within the trade networks and Mongol-ruled realms, the Chaghatai Khanate was the most peaceful of the subkhanates. Despite its gradually increasing domestic autonomy in the late thirteenth century, it generally behaved in foreign affairs as a loyal vassal to the great khan in Karakorum (and then after Kublai's ascension in Beijing). By the reign of the third khan, Mongke, the khanate had a great deal of autonomy in foreign policy relating to more-westerly nations such as the Mamluks in Egypt and the Byzantine Empire.

Most people in the Chaghatai Khanate lived in a rural fashion, with a strong agricultural base provided from the Turkic and Tajik peasant populations. The ruling classes intermingled with many of the preexisting nomads, making this segment the second-largest element of population and by far the dominant one. The cities of Central Asia were a fusion of these interwoven populations, though this merger was only part of the state in its beginning. Much like the Kipchak Khanate, the rulers maintained a detached and hands-off approach to governance. Despite the fact that most of their subjects were Muslim, they did not even convert to the local religion until 1326, when the last khan who controlled the state's core territories tried to keep the decentralized state on a more unified path by adopting Islam. After this khan's death, however, the area containing most of the trading cities of Transoxiana broke off into a complex mosaic of feuding local warlords.[1]

This situation of partial fragmentation eventually enabled the rise of a new dynamic and expansive state that built on the core left by the Changhatids, as the khanate would be known to posterity.

Like a phoenix rising from the ashes only to burn out again soon after, the rise of Timur (commonly known in the West as Tamerlane) not only gave the core area of the Central Asian trading cities its last truly homegrown and powerful indigenous son but also made them the center of a new political reorientation. Rather than being tax-collection depots for foreign nomads and distant interlopers, the cities were the core of this newest nomadically driven enterprise. The short duration of the Timurid Empire is well known, but what is not so well known is its relevance in the evolution of Formless Empires and geopolitical strategy. Because it represents the beginning of a transitional phase and left important dynastic and economic legacies, it deserves to be looked at in depth in order to establish when things began to change into something more understandable as geopolitics from a contemporary perspective.

Timur was a minor aristocrat in the peripheral Barlas tribe, which was located in present-day Uzbekistan. At the time, the Chaghatai Khanate was increasingly becoming known as Moghulistan because the Mongol ruling class was integrating more and more into the local culture. Timur entered the feudal service of Moghulistan's Khan Tuglug-Temur in 1360, but he rebelled by breaking subservience to the khan when overlooked for a promotion. He then entered an alliance with the khan of Khorasan and soon after received the arrow wounds to his right arm and leg that led to his being called "the Lame," or Timur-i-Lenk.[2]

In the fractured realm of posthegemonic Chaghatai decay, the numerous independent rump states offered great opportunity to the ambitious chieftain, and soon he was the chief power broker of the region's cities, such as Samarkand and Bukhara. With a few strategic marriage alliances into the Chingisid line (of Chinggis Khan) and a simultaneous commitment to both the settled and nomadic cores of his power base, Timur rose to control most of the territory that had fractured off the western edge of Moghul control. According to Hilda Hookham, "Timur was active in plunder, pillage and spoliation, and gathered supplies and collected resources and won to his side the common people and the leaders alike, who obeyed whether they wished to or not. . . . So he gained the realms of Transoxiana and sub-dued the population by force and compulsion."[3]

As a nomadic tribesman whose capital was a city and who was a patron of the arts and infrastructure as well as the trade of his core cities, Timur was already moving in the direction of a different kind of conqueror—albeit one still firmly rooted in Inner Eurasian traditions.

Timur's empire has acquired a fairly negative reputation based on the massive devastation he inflicted on places such as the Caucuses and Iran. He failed to administer the areas he conquered, resulting in breakaways and rebellions that necessitated his return to campaign in the regions again and again.[4] But considering that Timur's primary objectives were domestic, these peripheral lands should be considered less his territories than his unfortunate neighbors and perpetual raiding grounds. Timurid campaigns were not for territorial aggrandizement outside of Central Asia but rather for the accumulation of wealth and prestige for cities like Samarkand and Bukhara. In addition to this objective was the added benefit of taking potentially rebellious and predatory Chinggisid nobles out of Transoxiana and into foreign campaigns, where they could share in Timur's prestige and looting. This removed the displaced former rulers and regional aristocracy from Timur's unguarded rear and also gave them something of a stake in the current political system. In addition to this, the policy also prevented the predatory nomads (who were no longer the sole tax collectors of Transoxiana) from raiding the locals of their own nation in order to supplement their incomes.[5]

To use a more modern term that is generally not applied to these eras, Timur was a patriot. Not to the Changhatai Khanate, which he largely usurped and relegated to secondary status within its own realms, but rather to the region of Transoxiana at large. He was de facto emperor (or emir, his preferred title) of Transoxiana, and it was up to him to restore, through wealth, prestige, and art, its central location in Eurasia both culturally and economically. His objectives were to wreck rivals, redirect trade, and balance the concerns of his nomadic and agrarian core constituencies.[6] With this in mind, a further exploration of his career and his likely purposes can show his critical, if brief, role in the evolution of the Formless Empire in Eurasian geopolitics. No longer did grand conquerors in the region dream of uniting the entire steppe and its periphery around their personal rule; rather they sought indirect hegemony through targeted campaigns with economic and status-related motives.

Though Timur may have been moving, however unconventionally, in the direction of having a centralized state and being a cosmopolitan patron, his army was still a cavalry-based nomadic force of Turks, Mongols, and others of a similar lifestyle. Whole families, including warrior women, accompanied the army on campaigns and lived as if on a giant migration, setting off on deep campaigning abroad with little to no need to establish supply lines. According to Arabshah, Timur's often-hostile contemporary historian, the army (despite being part of a now almost uniformly Islamic Central Asia) contained many pagan and foreign elements, as itinerant warriors from all over the continent flocked to join up with the successful emir.[7] Once again, nomadic steppe toleration helped further the goals of geopolitical control.

With his actual hegemony secure in the core and his de facto hegemony now extending out into the Middle East, Timur turned to his northern frontier. With his help, the outcast warlord Toqtamysh (mentioned in chapter 2) was placed as a Timurid ally on the throne of the now-declining Kipchak Khanate. Barely any time passed, however, before Toqtamysh turned on Timur and sacked Tabriz while he was away campaigning elsewhere.[8]

After returning to the front and thwarting further damage from this raid, Timur negotiated with Toqtamysh to reacknowledge Timurid supremacy. Timur then went on to bring the remainder of outlying Central Asia and Iran under his control. He also pushed up to the southern borders of the Kipchaks by reducing Georgia and its neighbors to vassalage. It was at this point in 1388, while Timur was largely mopping up small fractured states, that his most dangerous enemy, who was apparently unchastised from before, struck once more from the back.

Toqtamysh's objectives may not seem apparent, but this was after he had temporarily reestablished hegemony over the Russian states in the post-Kulikovo world, and he was clearly trying to reestablish the Kipchak Khanate outside of Russia as well. The disputed pasturelands north of Iran were the perfect testing ground for the finicky khan to bid for supremacy against Timur. By 1387 he was already deep in Timurid territory, encouraging the revolt of various nobles recently coopted into the Timurid Empire.[9]

Rather than rushing to engage Toqtamysh, Timur saw the threat posed by this third column of disgruntled nobles and made sure his various campaigns to establish hegemony in his outlying areas were not interrupted. Only after he had finished rooting out potential problems among the nobility—more than a year later—did he turn to engage with the forceful annexation of his northern frontier provinces by Toqtamysh. In the meantime, Toqtamysh had sent envoys to hammer out a peace deal. Apparently, Timur's response to them was dismissive, according to a scholar named Sharaf al-Din Yazdi:

> When your master Toqtamysh was wounded and fled the enemy, I received him like a son. I took up his cause and made war on Urus Khan on his behalf. I sacrificed my cavalry and

equipment, which were lost to that hard winter. However, I continued to support him, and placed this country in his hands. I
made him so strong that he became Khan of the Kipchaks, and
he mounted the throne of Jochi. But when fortune began to
smile on him, he forgot his obligations to me. He chose the time
when I was occupied with the kingdom of the Persians and the
Medes to betray me, sending troops to ruin the borders of my
realm. I pretended not to notice, hoping he would be shamed
into regretting his action. But he was so drunk with ambition
that he could not distinguish good from bad; he sent another
army into my country. It is true that when we marched against
him his advance guard turned tail at the very dust of our
approach. Now, when Toqtamysh has heard of our approach,
he craves pardon, not seeing any other way of avoiding the punishment he deserves. But since we have seen him break his
word and violate his treaties so often, it would be imprudent to
trust his word.[10]

The titanic clash between jilted master and tricky protégé for the
two most powerful Inner Eurasian states of their time was about to
come, and it would have a resounding impact on the history of both
Central Asian peoples, and perhaps even more critically, on the agrarian players who so far had been victims rather than conquerors in the
system.

Emir Timur's force struck into the Kipchak Khanate via the eastern
Siberian approach, circumventing the mountains and well-defended
Caucasus to approach Sarai and New Sarai from the east. The vast
expanses of Siberia, however, were not ideal for provisioning Timur's
massive army, and Toqtamysh was sticking to the tried and true steppe
tactic of constant tactical withdrawals and leaving behind nothing but
scorched earth. Periodically, Timur had to stop his army even when on
the verge of engaging the Kipchak Khan and organize giant hunts to
acquire the food his army needed. This, of course, exposed his forces
to harrying counterattacks.[11]

Toqtamysh had now moved so far north that he ran out of steppe
and had to retreat into the taiga forest of Siberia before wheeling west
into the northern Caucuses after being thwarted in an indecisive battle. This slowed his flight immensely, and Timur's scouts soon detect-

ed signs of the enemy camp in the Terek River valley. In June 1391, the armies engaged. After Timur had changed his observed battle formation in the night to something less predictable, he charged the slightly numerically superior Kipchaks. The fight was desperate; at one point Toqtamysh, in a rare showing of fortitude, charged his guard straight through Timur's army, temporarily dividing it. This potential rout was only stopped (so it was said) because Timur ordered his grandson to start preparing a meal in a nonchalant fashion to which they would leisurely sit down to eat. This would let his reserves know that they would neither be leaving the field nor retreating when so deep into enemy territory. With this in mind, Timur's reserves charged at the now overextended Kipchak forces and put them to flight. Toqtamysh fled into exile in Lithuania as the remnants of his army were chased down and slaughtered for miles across the region. Thus ended the threat posed by Timur's most erratic and wily foe.[12]

Although Toqtamysh survived (and even outlived Timur by a year), he did so as the auxiliary to Lithuania's interests in the east. He was eventually killed by the joint Timurid and puppet Kipchak forces in an inglorious manner in 1406 after attempting, in alliance with Grand Duke Vytautus, to recapture his position in the now-shattered Kipchak Khanate.[13]

Before leaving to go back south, Timur returned to his strategy of plunder and proxies rather than formally take any additional territory from the Kipchak Khanate. After thoroughly devastating both of the Sarai cities, he sent forth his units to plunder to their hearts content while he placed a puppet khan on the Kipchak throne. Having uprooted the various links in the still-functioning trans-Eurasia northern Mongol trade network, Timur not only accomplished the immediate enriching of himself and his army as payment for their service in the rigorous and difficult campaign, but he also restored the Central Asia-oriented trade routes of the south to their former preeminence in the economic system of Eurasia. Once again, Timur was not building a giant empire or waging wars of conquest; he was sabotaging neighboring states to restore economic and political preeminence to the trading cities of Central Asia.[14]

With his chief rival now removed from the equation, Timur could turn to ravaging softer targets to the south and indulging in the patronage of his beloved Samarkand. Public gardens and large mosques shimmering with blue tile rose up, and his people were often exempt from increased taxation to pay for these power displays. The reinvigoration of the trade routes through their lands coupled with the massive spoils brought back by Timurid and Chaghatai nobles into the kingdom made such lavishness possible and likely justified in the eyes of their subjects. Indeed, the growing suburbs of Samarkand were named after the other great cities of the Islamic world in order to show the subordination, at least symbolically, of those cities to Samarkand, with the new neighborhoods of Damascus, Baghdad, Shiraz, Cairo, and Sultaniya leading the way. Within these new areas were fountains of iced water. Outside the walls, for the first time, an avowed nomadic state founder was constructing fortresses while his army was still nomadic and his territories mostly still steppe.[15]

Timur went on to invade the Delhi Sultanate in northern India. It became his most profitable campaign of all. He drove the war elephants of the sultan back on his own armies through the use of caltrops, putting the massive armies of that state to inglorious flight. This time no puppet leader or any other pretense of vassalage was even considered. It was simply a raiding expedition for the wealth of India, and once enough of it was pillaged, Timur's armies departed west to subjugate Mamluk Syria and move deep into Anatolia to confront the nascent state of the Ottoman Empire. Of this five years of whirlwind wars around the periphery of Inner Eurasia, Hookham says:

"The Campaign of Five Years had, in fact, destroyed in four seasons the one opponent capable of offering decisive resistance to the Lame Conqueror. It had secured the vital centers and stages of the trade routes of the Levant, as well as the plunder of the provinces from the Caucasus to the Persian Gulf and the Indian seaboard. It had brought Timur's conquests to the marches of Arabia, thus challenging the dominion of Bayazid the Ottoman Turk."[16]

And so Timur's final challenge (though he had no way of knowing that at the time, of course) was Bayezid "The Thunderbolt," the Ottoman sultan and decisive defeater of an elite pan-European crusader army outside of Nicopolis. On the verge of being the conqueror of Constantinople, Bayezid first had to face down the onrushing hordes of Timur's army, now augmented by elephants with Greek fire projectors on their backs. Hastily, Bayezid and Timur, after an exchange of increasingly acrimonious letters, rushed from their respective directions to meet in battle on a plain near modern-day Ankara. Timur, knowing he would be going farther from his base of support than his opponent, had numerous spies, paid travelers, and traders go ahead and report back to him. Thus he was able to secure the favorable terrain, including the wells, for his army before Bayezid.[17]

Bayezid was the first truly skillful general Timur had faced since Toqtamysh, and he had a professional army that rivaled Timur's. However, it was augmented by auxiliaries of Tatar extraction of dubious loyalty, and before the battle, Timur had used the tendrils of his intelligence network to secure their betrayal of their Ottoman master. It was this treachery, in the pell-mell and closely fought battle, that turned the tide, as the more-nomadic Tatars turned on their partially settled Turkish allies and gave full victory to Timur. Bayezid was captured, and his exact fate remains unclear to this day, but he eventually died in captivity. The Ottoman siege of the rump Byzantine Empire was called off as a bloody succession struggle picked up in the vacuum. Timur returned home in triumph only after a brief excursion to the coast of Smyrna to wipe out the last crusader stronghold in the region (thus doing his service as a *ghazi*, or holy warrior). His grim parting blow, as the remaining knights rowed away into the sea, was to catapult the heads of their fallen companions toward them.[18]

Timur now planned on his most ambitious campaign yet, one to the still-young Ming Dynasty, which had supplanted the Mongol Yuan with a native Chinese dynasty. However, after setting out to cross the mountains on his way to Xinjiang, he became ill, and, far into old age, died. The campaign dissipated, and soon after, the outlying regions of the empire began to fall away.[19]

Timur enriched his home region and decorated his cities as monuments to triumph, but we are less interested in the immediate impact of his campaigns and more concerned with what came next. For the first time since the Han Dynasty in China, someone had blended the grand strategy of a state primarily agrarian in character with the tactics and the abilities of the nomads. The division between nomad and settled was becoming less clear, and Timur had opened the door to a new transitional era. It was an opening through which many others followed.

The Timurid Empire is often understood to have effectively collapsed soon after Timur's death, but as has been demonstrated by the nature of Timur's campaigns, most of what was immediately lost to rising factions like the Ak Koyunlu tribesmen and regional Turkic rulers in Iran was not really part of the Timurid Empire but rather its stomping grounds for raiding. The core territory of the Timurid realms, the traditional cities of Central Asia, remained for a few more generations under Timurid rule, along with parts of northern Iran.[20]

Shahrukh, Timur's first successor, faithfully governed according to the Yasa of Chinggis Khan. Under his administration, as under the dynasty's founder, nomads were given more regional autonomy than settled people, though both communities had a significant measure of self-governance so long as they stayed loyal to the head of state in Samarkand. In fact, the level of decentralization was so great that the many tribes and cities soon became as much a hindrance in their autonomy as they were a decentralized, cost-cutting measure.[21]

Despite the eventual rule of the enlightened astronomer Ulugh Beg, the military weakness of the state and its gradual disintegration were becoming more and more apparent as the fifteenth century wore on. The increasingly disloyal subordinates had to be kept in check with divide-and-rule tactics. Eventually, though the wealth and prosperity of the Transoxianan cities still gleamed, the political power unraveled and split. Minor princelings held on to some territory, while the Uzbeks (themselves refugees from parts of the collapsing Kipchak Khanate) invaded from the north. Muhammad Shaybani Khan, a Chinggisid, was able to reestablish power over many of the Central Asian cities, and so it seemed that Toqtamysh had his posthumous revenge. But the story of the Timurids and their attempts to adapt to a changing world was not over.

To chart the rise of the Mughals and, thus, dynastically, also the resurgence of the Timurid line, historians are fortunate to have an indispensable source that is not only primary but autobiographical. The founder of a new empire, Zahir ud-din Muhammad Babur, best known by his nickname Babur (Farsi for "tiger"), kept a detailed journal from his youth in Transoxiana to the establishment of his rule across much of northern India. Using this as a guide to the formation of the Mughal period offers a glimpse not only into the actions of someone engaged in Inner Eurasian geopolitics at an important transitional moment but also a view directly into the conscious decision-making processes of one of its most pertinent driving actors.

Born in 1483 to the royal lineage of the Timurid line, Babur rose at age twelve to the kingship of what effectively had atrophied to a Samarkand city-state. His unstable rule under his mother's influence and advice weathered numerous upheavals, including a revolt by the knightly Tarkhan class of elite warriors, tribal warfare among the other cities and countryside of Transoxiana, and divided factions within his own realm.

This was not the ideal situation to learn the art of statecraft, and the boy and his family were soon evicted from their territorial inheritance. Despite this, young Babur learned quickly and retaliated, temporarily seizing back Samarkand from the usurpers and exerting enough authority to stop his army from looting the population. But his second reign was even shorter than his first. Once Babur left the city to take Andizhan, he lost it to the ever-southward-expanding Uzbeks under Muhammad Shaybani Khan. Deserted by all but two hundred warriors and his immediate family, Babur fled south in 1498 at age fifteen.

Babur began to notice a certain acceleration of changes that presaged a new geopolitical era in Inner Eurasia. As he continued his flight south, he remarked on the noticeable physical changes to the landscape that were starkly manifested in the massive amount of fort building: "Because of the Moghuls and the Uzbeks not a single village is without a fort." After yet another failed sojourn to recapture part of the lost Transoxianan lands, Babur entered a dejected exile in Tashkent, composing a few lines to describe his sorry state of affairs:

> No one remembers anyone in tribulation,
> No one gladdens anyone in exile.
> In this exile my heart has not been gladdened,
> No one can be comforted at all in exile.

After gathering enough patronage to be able to reconstitute a following, Babur moved into Kabul, an independent city whose previous ruler had died heirless. Babur placed Kabul under his own rule. His following there, as well as his wealth and relative power, grew, and he now could launch raids into Hindustan, or the Indian subcontinent, with ease. The booty proved both lucrative and helpful in building up a new army.[22]

Soon, at the gates of Herat, just west of Kabul, the Uzbeks were finally stopped by Babur's forces, and their southward expansion was halted. Shaybani Khan (whom Babur had taken to calling "Wormwood Khan") may have been contained, but he had won the struggle for the cities of Transoxiana. The Uzbek position in the lands they had overrun was secure. Returning to the north looked like an increasingly futile enterprise, and so Babur sated his lust for a kingdom elsewhere.[23]

Despite all the losses, Babur and his army were stronger for them. He had adapted well to learning at the hard end of conflicts. His small force, which he led into India to replace the Afghan Lodi Dynasty sitting on the decaying Delhi Sultanate, was well equipped with matchlock firearms in addition to its more traditional Central Asian military equipment, such as recurve bows and sturdy horses. Meanwhile, the Lodi Dynasty had technologically stagnated and divided along sectarian lines of Afghan rulers and disgruntled Hindu nobles. Though outnumbered, and with a so-far-unimpressive record, Babur saw this as the time to strike south and take in India what he had lost in Central Asia.[24]

It was time for India to get a taste of the Formless Empire. While past steppe invaders had built a plethora of empires in India's northern reaches in previous eras, now the Timurids were coming with accumulated experience, as they had already been an empire elsewhere. In an experience reminiscent of the Khitan exile and rebirth, and with the merged historical and political influence of both Mongol and Timurid lineages, a geopolitical tradition begun by Abaoji now entered new territory.

In 1525, Babur made it to the outskirts of Delhi, where a massive yet hastily collected Lodi force under Sultan Ibrahim Lodi waited for him, equipped with war elephants and daring the much smaller invading army to attack. Rather than do this, Babur drew up a defensive line in Panipat, a town to the northwest. There his flanks could be secured by the town on one side and hills on the other, allowing for a funneling effect of the enemy should it come for him. A trench was dug across the front and—something new for an Inner Eurasian army— acted as the lynchpin of the defense lines of matchlock-armed infantry behind a field fortification. This innovation was paired with traditional horse-archer and heavy-cavalry formations that went out nightly to raid Lodi's army and kill stragglers to inspire fear.

Having an upstart enemy so closely camped to his capital meant Lodi had to attack, and so he did. As Babur had anticipated, he rushed into a headlong attack, thinking to use his elephants to maximum advantage. Babur's cannons and matchlocks made short work of this charge, causing panic and confusion among the massive host. The cavalry then swooped in from around the flanks and completed a near-perfect encirclement of the enemy forces, who suffered massive casualties. Sultan Ibrahim and half of his army were slain, and the Timurid army moved into Delhi. The plunder from this single campaign alone solidified the nobles behind Babur and allowed him to constitute a new empire. This empire was seen as a successor to that of the Timurids, but it went down in history by the name the Indians gave it—the Mughal Empire, based on their pronunciation of the word *Mongol*.[25]

Babur went on to secure most of northern India in the next few years, winning further impressive victories over the Hindu noble Rajputs at Khanwa and stopping a Bengali counterattack in the east. In all of these cases, his small mobile army packing superior firepower was able to choose the location of the battle and react to changing circumstances faster than the larger and more-cumbersome hosts of his foes.[26]

Babur did not have long to enjoy his final success, for despite still being relatively young, he died of illness in 1531. His son, Humayun, was outmaneuvered by powerful nobles and had to flee the country, entering the protection of the Safavids in Iran. This left the Afghan Sher Shar Sur in charge of the empire. This usurper turned out to be quite capable. He built the Grand Trunk Road, the longest road in India, to better facilitate commerce and communication through the new empire. But when he died in a gunpowder explosion and his heir did not last long in the aftermath, Humayun returned and reestablished the legitimate succession to the Mughal throne. Humayun died the very year of his joint revenge and triumph, however, and so the throne was open to his son Jalal-ud-din Muhammad Akbar. In many ways, his reign embodied the height of Mughal rule and the geopolitical traditions of the Formless Empire when exported out of its natural habitat and into the agrarian littoral.[27]

Akbar, like his grandfather Babur, was established as ruler of the Mughal state at age twelve, but fortunately for him, the circumstances of his coming to age in rule were much less harrowing. His first major challenge was to deal with the Rajput threat, which he did. In 1564, the major Rajput areas had been cleared, and during the fall of the city of Garha-Katanga, many of the noble women committed self-immolation en masse. Despite this dramatic act, Akbar saw an opportunity to solidify his rule in a way that would set the Mughals apart from the Afghans. The Mughal Empire would not merely be ascendant; it would also be an attractive place to live, regardless of the faith of the subjects. This kind of toleration would not only solidify Akbar's reign with the masses but also ensure the relative weakening of Afghan, Uzbek, and Timurid nobles who had already proved the consequences of their influence by deposing his father.

Given the previous encounters between Muslims and Hindus in India, it perhaps seems remarkable that the Mughals could so successfully co-opt the Hindu aristocracy for its state, but Rajput warrior ethics were actually a fairly good match for the Mughal-imported Central Asian system. Generations of Rajputs would serve the Mughal state along with the imported seminomadic cavalrymen who were the core of the original army. As expansion continued, more emphasis had to be put into infantry and sieges as a proportion of the military when the army started having increased difficulty in the more broken and swampy terrain of the Deccan and Bengal.

Akbar drew upon influences the Timurids had picked up from their Central Asian background as well as their time in exile in the

Iranian court to create a system in India that reflected the kind of strategies of rule and foreign policy that they were familiar with and adapted to the Indian circumstances. As Jon F. Richards writes:

> Buoyed by conquest and plunder, Akbar and his advisers built a centralizing administration capable of steady expansion as new provinces were added to the empire. The Mughal emperor presided over a system that moved money, commodities, men, and information freely across the empire. The emperor and his advisers were rigorous managers who creatively adapted and responded to changing circumstances. Building on this foundation, Akbar's successors oversaw steady growth in imperial effectiveness, power, and resources through the seventeenth century.

Keeping this "heterogeneous body of free men" that was the Mughal nobility as a unified force was facilitated by constant territorial, economic, and cultural expansion.[28]

The Inner Eurasian heritage of the dynasty was the direct precursor to Akbar's style of rule, so rather than being seen as a uniquely visionary ruler who tried to bridge divides in culture and tradition, perhaps Akbar should be seen in the context of where his family came from and the techniques of statecraft they inherited:

"The Mughal Khan—the Great Khan—was different from the Khalifa of Islamic theory. The Great Khan was purely a political and military and not a religious leader. It was no part of his duty to enforce a well-defined and immutable code of divine or quasi-divine system of law as was the case with the Khalifa ground by the Shari'at. The Mughal sovereign had no such limitations. He was a political sovereign pure and simple."[29]

Even in a place as foreign from its origins as India, the Formless Empire was a workable model for those with the speed and adaptability to use it.

Akbar's searching for religious syncretism and abrogation of traditional Islamic religious laws, which advocated greater taxation of unbelievers, showed his tolerance and enlightenment regarding his diverse subjects. He also had the fortunate circumstance of ruling at a time of regional economic expansion. As trade routes around the world became more integrated because of European exploration and expansion, the vast markets of the Mughal Empire and its many exports found new markets, and New World silver flowed in from the Americas to greatly enrich the state. This influx of cash initiated a market-driven, rather than state-directed, capitalist expansion in the early seventeenth century. This led to the empire becoming perhaps the largest and wealthiest economy in the world. Before the coming of the British, arguably before the capitalization of any nation save the Netherlands, the Mughal Empire had become a monetized and capitalist giant.

Akbar's eldest son, Jahangir, rose to the throne in 1605, after the death of his father. His reign marked the largest territorial extent of the empire, but also the seeds of its fall. This could be seen in both military and domestic political factors.

This process was, of course, a more modern version of what people like the Khitans and Kipchaks before had tried to avoid by remaining connected to their nomadic roots, with various levels of success. The Mughals, increasingly integrated through their own policies and also more and more cut off from Central Asia, had not retained their military and diplomatic flexibility. They were well aware of the threat that someone could do to them what they had done to those who came before. Central Asian security became an increasing concern. But rather than flights of fancy regarding restoring Transoxiana to Timurid rule, this was a defensive and fear-based concern.

The Mughal Empire had continued to follow its successful gunpowder-based model, but the large siege weapons used in the south and east lacked the portability of the lighter field pieces used elsewhere, and the well-armed infantry had increasingly dislodged cavalry as the decisive arm of service. Furthermore, the erosion of the Central Asian concerns and lack of direct naval connections meant that the state was losing out on technological advancements being made in the rest of the Turkic world, particularly the Ottoman Empire.

On a campaign north to secure the frontiers of northern Afghanistan (itself barely a part of the empire anymore), the ponderous Mughal host, which came to resemble something akin to a better-armed mob from the Lodi period, overwhelmed its Uzbek foes with firepower but never caught or outmaneuvered them. The Mughals ended up being led around the country from frustrating action to fruitless pursuit. Finally, two years later, they gained two marginal provinces at the cost of 40 million rupees. The annual income of these provinces was only a few million combined. Meanwhile, the once-friendly Safavids had seized the opportunity of the Mughals' embarrassing quagmire and driven into western Afghanistan, taking Kandahar and holding it against massive Mughal counterattack with superior artillery. Combined with an army breakdown in the Himalayas, the rule of Jahangir seemed to show the beginning of the reversal of previously ascendant Mughal power.

It wasn't just the military failures that were a problem. For a country that had lost touch with its roots, the domestic policies of Jahangir and later Aurangzeb played a decisive role in ensuring that the Mughals' inroads into being integrated into India would not work either.

The one front where the empire was still expanding was to the south. It reached its maximum southward extent under Aurangzeb, though at that point it was largely expanding for reasons of capturing a monopoly on the regional textile trade with the Europeans and Persian Gulf merchants rather than for the glory of its upper classes and tribute system. Aurangzeb, however, was much more totalitarian than even his increasingly conservative predecessors. He reinstated harsh taxes on non-Muslim subjects, attempted to remove powerful non-Muslim nobles from positions of power—angering the core Rajput constituency in the process—and curtailed the freewheeling economic system that was at the center of Mughal economic might. State censors, who were agents to enforce sharia-type laws on the populace, crawled through the marketplaces making sure nothing forbidden was on sale.

Having a trained but now unemployed cadre of military Buddhists and Hindus was bad enough, but internal trouble brewed on the opposite front as well. The more traditionally inclined Timurids resented the erosion of their cultural ties, as well as the loss of power by the traditionally influential females of the Timurid line. So while the empire began to crumble around the periphery for betraying the flexibility and dynamism of Babur and Akbar, it also rocked from dynastic revolts from within for much the same reason.[30]

Despite Aurangzeb's attempts at centralization and homogenization, his reign, which ended in 1707, had the opposite effect, as more and more provinces became de facto or even outright independent. The previously societally indifferent government had created a consensus that even European merchants felt at home in, but the reactionary tone of the Mughals into the eighteenth century, as well as the evident decay, did little to slow the decline of the hegemon. A rising group of Hindu nobles, the Marathas, was fast becoming the new power. From their base in the west, they harried the ponderous and increasingly backward Mughal forces with light cavalry, guerrilla tactics, and mobile strikes. The mantle of the Formless Empire had moved once again, and soon what little that was left of the Mughal Empire was a rump state based in Delhi whose detritus was fought over like scraps between the Marathas and a succession of Afghan warlords. This lack of political and military power, coupled with still having some of the richest ports and merchants in the world, made much of post-Mughal India a tempting target for new colonial powers coming not just from the land but the sea. With the sacking of Delhi by Nader Shah in 1739 (discussed in chapter 4), the floodgates were open to the Dutch and, above all, the British.[31]

So ended an era where the Formless Empire met India. Other Central Asian empires had come to India before, but the impact the Mughals had, especially financially and culturally, marked them as among the most memorable of invaders. For two hundred years they were the regional power, and they considered only the Ottoman Empire as equal.

In absolute terms, the Ming Dynasty in China probably outclassed them both, but as the Mughals' trade was overwhelmingly directed west rather than east, it hardly mattered to them. Their mark on the Indian economy and society was so pervasive that the British chose to co-opt Mughal-style governance and fiscal policy rather than introduce their own, at least initially.[32] Elements of the Inner Eurasian style of governance matched, rather than clashed with, the flexible, mobile, and mercantile nature of sea power. It was an omen of a general geopolitical trend to come in which maritime nations would surpass the land states with technology that brought the mobile firepower of the steppe to be even more effectively wielded from the sea.

Back in the homeland of the Mughal Dynasty, events had continued to unfold in their own way as well. Shaybani Khan could have taken the Uzbeks to new heights after his expulsion of Babur in the early 1500s, but it was not meant to be. He overreached himself in wars with the Safavids and was killed at the Battle of Merv shortly after his greatest triumph. "Wormwood Khan" met his end because of his aggression, but not at the hands of the Mughals. The legacy he left behind was a mixed bag. He reinvigorated post-Timurid mercantile culture by importing Indian merchants, even while allocating formerly Timurid domains to his nobles through redistribution.

Despite its briefness, Shaybani Khan's reign was important for a variety of reasons. Uzbeks, themselves migrants from the various khanates that sprang from the now-defunct Kipchak Khanate, made up a large proportion of the population ethnically, but at this point they seemed much more willing than before to start settling down among the farmers in significant numbers. This led to an explosion of productivity in the cotton production of the region, which was only starting to expand. This further sped up the process of formal bureaucratization as farming and production started to replace the centrality of herding and trade.[33]

Shaybani Khan's death, however, heralded the loss of many of the briefly held Uzbek domains. Bukhara became the rump state of the Shaybanid Empire, and Kokand and Khiva broke off to become de facto independent city-states. Bukhara's awkward attempts to restore unity, plus Khiva's incessant raiding on its neighbors, only exacerbated what became full-scale and lasting division.[34]

In addition, most of these states were divided by internal family feuds and rivalries that tore apart any kind of cohesive foreign policy. Small, weak, and divided, these post-Timurid statelets were only saved (for a while at least) from the aggressions of others by their remote and distant location. The turning back of an antiquated Mughal army by the Uzbeks (as mentioned earlier) was one of the last large-scale triumphs over people from outside Transoxiana they would have. Eventually this constant strife culminated in a large, draining, and indecisive war between the various khanates in the region, after which many of them simply retreated into slave raiding Russian settlements and jealously guarding their increasing insularity. This spurning of traditional Inner Eurasian cultural and political openness and flexibility had dire consequences in the centuries to come. Soon, the once-colonized Russians appeared on the scene and turned the tables decisively on the region, and these once-roaming nomads and traders who had appeared so omnipresent and adaptable had no inkling of what was to come.

This time of transition did not pass by the original birthplace of the Formless Empire either. Mongolia, the genesis (or at least frontier) of so many of the case studies examined here, had one last indigenous hurrah before the era of nomadic power and formless steppe empire started to come to a close. Mongolia's rump empire experienced both division and rejuvenation as the powerful native Ming Dynasty in China rose to be the primary power broker in the region.

The premodern example was pioneered by a later Mongol leader who emphasized the indirect and flexible nature that has been discussed yet did so from a stable territory with little need for direct expansion into other nations. She was Queen Manduhai, or Manduhai Khatun.

As noted earlier, the once-unified Mongol empire started to disintegrate after the civil war of succession and the rise of Kublai. The universal laws, trade regulations (or lack of them), and tax policies inherited from preimperial steppe practices were applied consistently. At the time of the empire's height (and its last phase as a truly unified entity) during the reign of Mongke, the government exchequer contained so much wealth that slipped away from the main Transoxiana bureaucracy that individual regions could keep enough for their own domestic investments.

The process of change from Mongolian to more regional bureaucratization was one of profound impact, particularly in the era of the Yuan Dynasty. Kublai began that process to strengthen his case as he campaigned to get the remainder of southern China under his rule. After he died, the Yuan rapidly became more and more Chinese in character. As this was happening while Kublai was still alive, economic development sprang up along the margins of the steppe, drawing massive Mongolian immigration into new market towns in what eventually became Inner Mongolia. This was useful for Kublai, as he was using the support of his settled constituency to fend off more traditional steppe rivals such as Ariq-Boke, and it may have even been an intentional strategy to integrate populations on behalf of the Yuan government in later eras. This process eventually led to Mongolia being given civil and provincial administration in 1307 under the Chinese-style title of Greater Yuan Province.[35]

When the dynasty collapsed in China because of internal revolt and the native Ming administration took power over all of the remaining provinces of China proper, the Yuan court fled north to Mongolia.[36] However, the Yuan found that while they had never truly become Chinese, they had also ceased to be Mongolian. The court of the self-proclaimed Northern Yuan quickly sank into irrelevance. Factionalism reigned supreme on the steppe, and the dynasty's repeated, tired claims of lordship over China seemed increasingly pathetic in the face of Ming expansion and the loss of territory to Turkic warlords in the western steppe. In fact, many Mongols stayed in the now-Chinese-ruled areas they had migrated to as the Ming offered more prosperity and security than the deluded Northern Yuan. This division remains in force today as the distinction between Inner and Outer Mongolia, and Inner Mongolia (the province of China) remains the more populous of the two. As Jack Weatherford says in most artful terms about the Northern Yuan:

> No heroes came to recharge the energy of the sapped nation. No new allies came to join them. No armies set out to expand the decaying Mongol rule over China. Throughout the fourteenth century the Mongol leadership, especially the Borijin [Chinggisid] clan deteriorated. Each generation proved less competent and knowledgeable, as well as more isolated and corrupt, than the last.

In this vacuum, the descendants of Ariq-Boke (Kublai's defeated rival from the civil war in which he seized power) returned to Mongolia and became one of the ascendant clans. They had not squandered their political capital on becoming perfumed and obese aristocrats. However, there was no resurgence of the clan overall, and this potential soon frittered away into just more division. The Northern Yuan were now so weak and insecure that Mongols in the employ of the Ming and mobile Ming cavalry units of Chinese soldiers alike raided with near impunity, or looted their own trade with Beijing and blamed the loss of valuables on Mongol raiders—which only increased the raiding, of course.

Manduul Khan, ruler of Mongolia (if largely in name), was assassinated in 1479, opening an entirely new lot of claimants and creating the potential for a many-sided civil war. It was onto this dire stage that a woman named Manduhai tentatively stepped.

Manduhai had been Manduul's young wife. She was now Manduhai Khatun, or female khan. Her position was vulnerable. The Ming still campaigned, and the Xinjiang-based warlord Ismayil was attempting to place his own puppets in power in the Mongolian court. In a society where women may have been traditionally powerful but never the head of state (at least officially), the circumstances did not bode well for the postimperial Mongol nation.

Fortunately, Manduhai found a legitimate Chinggisid heir—a small, sickly boy with the extremely royal Mongolian name of Batu Mongke. Unfortunately, Ismayil had already found out about this family line and had abducted the boy's mother. Queen Manduhai and her warriors rode to snatch the boy before the same fate befell him and took him back to her primary encampment. In a formal ceremony there she installed the boy as joint ruler with the title Dayan Khan, and soon after she married him officially. No one could now dismiss the khatun; she had shored up her position.

Before confronting her two biggest threats, though, she had to clean house in the north. The Oirats, a tribe of Mongols no longer under Chinggisid authority and from a bit farther northwest, had begun to migrate into Manduhai's territory. She turned her forces and, with General Une-Bolod, struck a series of defeats against the tribe, which had sought to capitalize on her nation's weakness. The Oirats were driven from the field and from the lands they sought to claim for themselves, and so the disruption was ended. This show of strength from the new ruler made it apparent to her enemies that she was not to be underestimated, and so they began to gear up for a showdown with the khatun. She dealt with them in different ways, but both methods showcased the dynamism of formless geopolitical policy in ways reflective of its evolution up to that point in history and familiar to us contemporary viewers.

The Chinese general Wang Yue increased tensions on the border by luring Mongols into traps with defenseless-looking caravans and then launching ambushes on them while they pillaged. Though this tactic was successful, it led to casualties and expenses that detracted from the overall purpose of the Ming government, which was the rebuilding and reconstruction of the Great Wall. Chinese internal politics had bought Manduhai a reprieve from one enemy, so she could focus on another.

The warlord Beg-Arslan was killed in an ambush by Manduhai in 1479, but the bigger problem, Ismayil, remained. He still had Dayan Khan's mother, and now that the khan was a teenager, the shame of this slight could no longer be put aside for the sake of expediency. Besides, Ismayil had been interfering with Mongolian politics for decades. Manduhai had had enough, so she selected a small strike force of her best warriors and sent them west over the treacherous territory of Uighuristan on a twofold mission: assassinate Ismayil and return the khan's mother.[37]

The strike force was lucky to come upon both objectives in the same place, and by surprise. Ismayil rode out to see who the small party of new arrivals were and was instantly shot dead by the expedition leader. The party looted Ismayil's camp of its wealth, driving off his nearby supporters in the process, and took the khan's mother back when it departed. She had lived a long time with Ismayil and had grown accustomed to the change. The reunion of the young khan with mother was complicated and bittersweet, but the job was done and Manduhai's territory now stretched west into Uighuristan. This left the Ming challenge as the only major stumbling block to the newly invigorated nation.[38]

The Ming could not be so easily dispatched, so Manduhai tried a softer approach. The Ming knew she could do immense damage to their frontier settlements and rob them of wealth if she so chose. This path was dangerous for the Ming, but also for the Mongols. With this in mind, Manduhai reopened official relations with the Ming. In exchange for the Mongols' renouncing all claims on the people of China and stopping the regular raiding in Inner Mongolia, Manduhai demanded full recognition of the Mongols as a sovereign entity with equal diplomatic status in negotiations with the Chinese and a resumption of trade between the two. Even upsetting the traditional order of the Confucian state system was worth security on the northern frontier, so the Ming acquiesced to the proposal in 1488.

Manduhai issued a decree recognizing all who lived the pastoral lifestyle in Mongolia as equals and part of the Mongol identity. She was, of course, harking back to Chinggis Khan's Yasa, and in so doing she made sure that the various ethnicities that had migrated to the Yuan court back in the days of empire were integrated into the nation. These included Turkic peoples, Kipchak refugees from the breakup of the Kipchak Khanate, Uighurs, and even the descendants of Ossetian bodyguards that the khan of old once had used. To build on this reconciliation, she also reiterated the old Yasa edict that the state would have no official religion. Like the Khitans, she also created mobile flying base camps that rotated around the periphery of the empire securing the trade routes and holding hostile tribes at bay.[39]

When Manduhai Khatun died in 1510, Dayan Khan became sole ruler. He continued her policies, as did several generations of his descendants. This small nation sharing borders with a great power and hostile neighbors endured until the rise of the Manchus in the seventeenth century. This had important implications for the future states of the region, nomadic or not. Weatherford sums up Manduhai's reign and political system from the perspective of a historian, though his observations are just as pertinent to the study of Mongolia in international relations, as well as the general concept of the Formless Empire we are examining:

> In contrast to the expansive territorial acquisition favored by prior generations of steppe conquerors, Manduhai pursued a strategy of geopolitical precision. Better to control the right spot rather than be responsible for conquering, organizing, and

> running a massive empire of reluctant subjects. . . . Now, rather
> than trying to conquer and occupy the extensive links of the
> Silk Route or the vast expanse of China, she sought to conquer
> just the strategic spots from which to control them [indirect-
> ly].[40]

Previous iterations of the Formless Empire had been large and dynamic but often lacked long-term staying power. Manduhai showed that nations, rather than empires, can not only play the game of formless strategy but can become powerful actors outside of their normal scope by doing so. In following the policies she put into place, Mongolia was a preview of a more modern period in the history of Inner Eurasia. But before that era could come, the geopolitical formlessness of the region would be first diminished, then seemingly destroyed forever by the encroaching technological power and expansion of the settled states and their burgeoning populations who had suffered at the hands of nomadic people for a significant portion of recorded history.

This chapter has covered a period of time in which the Formless Empire, usually dominated by nomadic or seminomadic peoples, began to integrate across civilizational boundaries more often. This process was accelerated by the changing nature of technology and economics, with the more-maritime states now overtaking the land-based ones. The early Ming voyages of exploration into the Indian Ocean by the massive ships of Admiral Zhung He, temporary ventures though they may have been, were just a glimpse of what was about to happen with the nations of Europe. Whatever the cause, though, at the end of the era, the balance of power had already started to blur, and the definition of what was formless politics started to change.[41]

Not only were the nomadic peoples adapting and accommodating to the settled states, but the settled peoples were learning their own lessons in turn, or relearning them. This soon bore terrible fruit for the nomads, as the pace of technological change accelerated.[42] Timurids maintained the separation between nomadic military and civil governance while running a massive trade-redistribution racket across Eurasia. Plunder fed the army, and what can only be called economic redistricting fed the cities. It was a symbiosis along uniquely Inner Eurasian lines.

Meanwhile, the Mughals left the realm almost entirely (if not by choice), and over the course of time became more and more like the people they conquered. Seeing the shifting winds of trade and priority, they soon abandoned their Central Asian possessions and refocused on developing Indian and maritime commerce, evolving into a different kind of state through gradual adaptation.

The Central Asian states began to break up and decline. Timur had brought their prosperity a new lease, but long after his death, the trends of global change started to pass the region by. Once a center of culture and commerce, the various rump states of Transoxiana deteriorated into a succession of squabbling and increasingly impoverished backwaters.[43]

From a contemporary perspective, Mongolia had the most interesting adaptation to the changing times and increasing power of the settled states. It effectively abandoned dreams of direct empire and went full force down the path of indirect control. As has been shown, this was not new to Mongol policy, but previous examples of Mongol indirectness usually involved direct conquest, at least initially, and expansion. Manduhai Khatun showed that in light of changes in the balance of power, Mongols could adapt and use the strategies they had perfected for defensive as well as offensive purposes.

No matter the geographic and circumstantial divergence that made these examples of an era in flux apparent, they shared one thing in common: the situation was changing and the settled littoral states were on the rise. This reversal in the balance of power reoriented Inner Eurasia—but not without a fight.

FOUR

THE RISE OF STATES
AND THE TRANSFERENCE
OF A GEOPOLITICAL LEGACY

Military strategists say: Those who show force arrogantly will lose; those who do not know the other will lose. Our army has committed all these mistakes. . . . We cannot predict the day when I can wipe away this shame and take revenge.
  —The Yongzheng Emperor's Edict to General Yue Zhongqi regarding a Zhungar defeat of a Qing frontier army, 1731.

The vanquished always seek to imitate their victors in their dress, insignia, belief and other customs and usages. This is because men are always inclined to attribute perfection to those who have defeated and subjugated them.
  —Ibn Khaldun

W HEN THE END CAME FOR THE FORMLESS EMPIRES OF THE nomadic confederations and armies of the steppe, it was not so much because of the failure of their own system but rather because of its large-scale adoption by the settled agrarian states that were so often their foes. We have already examined the varying degrees of integration of the Han Dynasty and early Muscovite Russia within the systems of previously nomadic powers. Moving into the post-Mongol and Timurid eras, a large change begins to occur at a critical technological juncture: settled states partially adopt formless geopolitics. The use of gunpowder and mercantile innovations, which were scattered throughout Eurasia because of the Mongol conquests and administration of their vast domains, took root in the vastly populated and often militarily beleaguered agrarian societies and bureaucratized states.

Over the course of what is often termed the early modern period, the military and commercial balance of power gradually shifted to the settled states. The Mughals and their earlier Timurid ancestors were seminomadic elites who eventually became more and more sedentary, creating a type of transitional bridge between the nomadic Formless Empire and the more conventional state's practice of similar strategies. In this chapter, the focus moves to two states that are still with us today as originators of and actors in contemporary geopolitics and that thus mark a direct lineage from this charted past: Russia and China. Iran, too, makes an appearance.

But first, it is worth looking at the general strategic and tactical changes that occurred to make these states, which suffered most from nomadic peoples, turn the tables so decisively, though in the case of Iran only temporarily.

In the previous chapter, we discussed the influence and changing nature of a state's tactical options, and touched on the adoption of gunpowder weapons in Mughal armies. This military evolution gradually increased, especially among the littoral states. This new advantage, combined with greater mercantile and agricultural productivity and increasing naval technology, enabled many more trade routes to become redirected to the maritime realm, and the previously victimized settled states saw a logistical upgrade to complement their increasing military capacity. Even so, they did not attain true military dominance on the whole until the eighteenth century, when both Russia and China entered the real core territories of their longtime nomadic rivals for more than temporary excursions.[1] But this increase in the relative power of the more conventional and settled state was not untouched by its interactions with the nomadic foes it so desperately tried to destroy.

Gunpowder weapons, now in the service of a more sophisticated and resource-rich societal apparatus, would be a decisive element of nomadic downfall, but even that paled in comparison with the new and more flexible understandings of geopolitics that were being developed in both China and Russia (and indeed, elsewhere). It is now time to examine how the settled states brought an end to the formless geopolitics of before and also brought about its new beginning. From the perspective of Eurasian land powers, the vast spaces still called for the utilization of proxies, ambiguous space, and unrivaled mobility (*see map 6*).

It was the Qing dynasty, the last imperial dynastic age of China, that most clearly came to define contemporary Chinese border and foreign policy in both its nature and its physical shape. Like the Khitans, it was born in a foreign land, but unlike them, it shaped the entire destiny of what we now call the unified Chinese state, including its present-day borders.

The Jurchen people evicted the Khitans from their first empire and established the Jin Dynasty. That was in turn destroyed by the Mongols, but the Jurchens did not completely disappear. Like the Khitans, many of them were co-opted into the Mongol ruling apparatus. Unlike the Khitans, however, they stayed in their Amur River valley area. With the collapse of the Mongol Yuan Empire in China, the Jurchens could reassert sovereignty. At this point, there were groups of Sinified Jurchens, "wild" northern Jurchens, and Jurchens who maintained close contacts with Mongolia and China. The Mongol yam postal service remained in service throughout the Jurchen realms. The Ming Dynasty often projected military power into the southern realms of Manchuria to make sure the Jurchen people remained cowed. With the construction of numerous fortresses along the frontier, the costs of this policy eventually spiraled into a liability for the Ming, and they abandoned the project and withdrew their frontier farther south in 1435.

The Jurchens experienced much of the Chinese culture, which they had spent centuries out of direct interaction with, through a type of Mongolian filter that influenced many independent chieftains to consider rebuilding their Eurasian-style decentralized confederacy. In the late seventeenth century, this desire to be more than a few disparate tribes fighting for the scraps of what trade the Ming gave them grew.

In the Aisin-Goro clan of the Jurchen was a young warrior who sought revenge for the death of his father at the hands of a rival tribe. He had had a Ming Chinese tutor and was both literate and aware of the Chinese ways. He had also been raised to be a proper horseback warrior. This was Nurhaci. As his quest for vengeance unfolded, he won battle after battle against the other tribes. His primary foes fled to the Ming, where that declining dynasty, fearful of the new power held by the Jurchens, acquiesced to demands by Nurhaci to put these exiles to death. It is around this time that a proper unified nation began to emerge for the first time since the old Jin Dynasty of the twelfth century. The term *Manchu* started to replace *Jurchen* around this time, describing this rebirth of the Jurchens as a power.

Though his state was fragile and he dared not yet strike south for full-on war with the Ming Dynasty, Nurhaci decided to occupy his warriors by moving west and incorporating the eastern Mongol lands into his domain. As justification he is claimed to have said: "The languages of the Chinese and Koreans are different, but their clothing and way of life is the same. It is the same with us Manchus and the Mongols. Our languages are different, but our clothing and way of life is the same."

To make sure he had the right amount of sinew holding together this new and flexible state, Nurhaci organized the banner system. The ultimate combination of budding modern bureaucratic state with traditional Inner Eurasian decentralized organization, the banner system was a way for warriors of all tribes and ethnic backgrounds to retain cultural autonomy with regard to the state apparatus while being loyal to the emperor/khan (depending on whom was being addressed) personally. Loyalty was ensured by making an elite warrior rewards system that valued prestige from battle and brought the promoted warriors closer and closer to the Manchu ruling establishment, which they now had a stake in.[2]

Having secured his kingdom, Nurhaci turned on the Ming, but the fighting was inconclusive. The raids on the Ming redirected trade and tribute to Manchuria, and the Ming counterattacks were largely ineffective. Nurhaci seized the critical Liao River valley in the south, where the Khitan Liao had once ruled, and thus finally had an agrarian base from which to farm surplus food. Soon after this success, however, Nurhaci died, in 1626.[3] It was a testament to his state-building abilities that the empire he founded and the dynasty he propagated not only long outlived his death but became symbols for formless geostrategy in their own ways.

When the Manchu people swept south to claim the reins of the collapsing Ming state and set up their own dynasty, they did so using a combination of the mobile warfare of their seminomadic society and the technological ability of China itself. Well-armed with gunpowder weapons and avoiding fixed positions that could be threatened by sedentary Ming forces, the Manchus were able to skillfully maneuver their way to power in both war and diplomacy despite being massively outnumbered by even the remaining forces of the old Ming Dynasty.

Once they were united by Nurhaci, the Manchus dominated the mixed forest-steppe zone of the Manchurian and maritime Siberian frontier and abutted the lands of the Mongols and the northern edge of the now increasingly decrepit Ming Empire. They soon co-opted many of the remaining independent Mongols into their imperial scheme as well and thus could exert control over the northern and western steppe through proxies, particularly their Eastern Mongol allies. Combined with their widespread adoption of firearms, their mixed semipastoral and semiagricultural base, and their many Mongol allies, who had an almost equal status in the regime as Manchurian peoples, the Manchus seemed to be well on their way to rebirthing the Liao Dynasty by creating a confederated counterpoint to Chinese civilization in the north.[4]

Manchurian rule was in some ways a successor of their ancestors the Jin and the continuing influence of the Mongols, as stated by Peter Perdue:

> In short, the Mongols contributed a great deal to the early Manchu state. They provided military allies, horses, and a tradition of legitimation reaching back to Chinggis Khan. Along with the Yuan official seal came the concept of a universal empire encompassing many peoples, an ideal of rulership that vastly transcended either the state of the Manchu's ancestors, the Jurchen Jin, or that of the Ming."[5]

The Manchus had much greater success than the Khitan Liao—
more akin to duplicating the Mongol achievement in China, but with
its own key differences.

Fortunately for the ambitions of this new Manchurian power, the
late Ming were crippled with corruption and shaken by the cost of having to fight off a Japanese invasion of Korea in the late sixteenth century. The state had undertaken the rebuilding of the Great Wall as a
result of the post-Yuan Mongolian resurgence and was nowhere near
as able to defend itself from nomadic attack as it once was. After a
palace coup and the collapse of the Ming government due to rebellions, the mayor of Beijing invited the Manchus to fill the power vacuum, which they and their armies were more than happy to do in 1644.[6]

Horsemen used gunpowder weapons and superior maneuverability to breach the Great Wall. Charging south, they removed the last ves-
tiges of the Ming Dynasty in Beijing and quelled the uprisings that had
started in the power vacuum caused by the collapse of the dynasty. To
make the process of conquest as smooth as possible, the Manchus
adopted a general amnesty program for any Ming officials and literati
who submitted to the new order.[7]

After the southern Ming and their de facto leader, the pirate admiral Coxinga, established control over northern China, it seemed they
might hang on. But the Manchus, unlike the Khitans, made sure to
fully build a centralized state in the Chinese-dominant provinces to
better harness the resources there, and they were able to bring the full
realm of China under their unified rule. Legitimacy was conferred on
the Manchus by adopting an official dynasty name, Aisin in
Manchurian, Qing in Chinese. Several decades of war in the south
ensued, culminating in the unification of the former Ming realms
under the absolute control of the part-Mongolian, part-Manchurian
Kangxi Emperor in 1678.[8]

The Qing Dynasty was born, and with it came economic revival, a
reassertion of military power, and a grand strategy that hybridized
Chinese security concerns and Manchu expansionism. The western
frontiers were, however, not yet pacified. And while the Manchurian
rule of China became quite conservative and effectively Chinese, its
foreign policies and grand strategies took their own mixed path.[9]

After a brutal western campaign utilizing Chinese know-how and Manchu military skill and frontier adaptability, China's modern western borders were finally formed. Nomadic and non-Chinese people were often integrated into the ruling elite, much like the Mongols in the north, and a mixed regime was adopted to pacify the border. There were two major differences between the Qing and their nomadic forebears.

First were the technological and economic advantages enjoyed by more-settled (or in the case of the Manchus, conquest-settled) people over the famously intractable nomadic peoples. Thus were laid the foundations of the more-modern and conventional state, which could establish inroads into the far more amorphous political realm of peripheral frontiers such as Siberia and Central Asia. But the new Qing state was itself a modified child of formless policy.[10]

Second was the northern border itself. Because while China in all its various dynastic forms had always been the land power hegemon in its region, it was about to meet its first real settled-state foreign competition—a nation whose expansion from the opposite direction mirrored the vigor and ambition of its own.

Russia's own version of the formless grand strategy was to use space as both defense in depth as well as power projector. Once Russia, like the Manchu Qing, adopted the mobility of nomadic cavalry coupled with the technology and logistics (especially in the realm of firearms and cannons) of the rapidly developing settled societies of the seventeenth century, it was on course for formless expansion. The principality of Muscovy was the dominant city in post-Mongol Russia, largely owing to its collaboration with the Mongols against the other city-states. Rather than constructing a circular buffer zone around the core, as the Manchu had done, Muscovy (which eventually became the Russian Empire) embarked on an unprecedented landward expansion of colonization and conquest.[11]

None of this is to say that the balance of power had shifted so dramatically as to make Russia's territorial growth a cakewalk. In fact, the composite bow used by steppe nomads remained the superior weapon over gunpowder until the nineteenth century. But it required a massive time investment to learn properly. Firearms, on the other hand, were relatively easy to use. That fact and the larger population base of the settled societies created an overwhelming combination against the far less populous nomadic peoples. Russia outnumbered much of its eastern opposition by a significant margin; now it could go into battle on a more-even qualitative level as well.

Because of its previously discussed rise as the Golden Horde's tax collector, Muscovy had consolidated its dominance as the first among many Russian principalities. After the crushing of resistance of Novgorod and other potential rivals, Muscovy was the sole indigenous Russian power. It was not, however, the sole Inner Eurasian power. Owing to its command of resources and military abilities though, Muscovy was arguably now the dominant Central Asia-connected fulcrum power west of China.[12]

This was largely evident after Tsar Ivan IV of Muscovy (whose Russian nickname, "Grozny," is often translated as "Terrible" but actually means something more like "Fearsome") opened up Siberia to Russian expansion. His campaign against the Kazan Khanate to the east was the decisive moment. The khanate, a remnant of the old Golden Horde/Kipchak Khanate (as well as the even older Volga Bulgars), was split among Sibir, Astrakhan, the Crimean Khanate, and Kazan. It stood at the gateway to the Urals. East of it, throughout the Siberian forest and north of the steppe, there was no other significant state entity all the way to the Pacific Ocean. Though it had been occupied by Russia before, under Ivan III ("The Great") it had merely been lightly vassalized, and it soon regained its independence. While it is unlikely that Ivan IV was aware of exactly how little resistance lay east of the khanate, the Russians soon discovered it for themselves. It is certainly possible, given Muscovy's integration with defecting Tatar elites and military units, that they had some inkling of this fact, but either way the campaign to crush this meddlesome surviving appendage of the old Horde was launched in 1552. It took only a few months for the city of Kazan to be breached and its surrounding lands to fall to the Russians.[13]

What may seem like a highly conventional conquest was in fact highly tinged with the formless legacy of the geopolitical region the Russians were entering. Even though they were now the conquerors rather than the conquered, and their society, outside of the military, was quite divergent from that of the Turko-Mongolian peoples, Russian postwar policy was decidedly more reminiscent of the Kipchak Khanate than any more typical western equivalent. For example, though initially the Russians behaved in the typical medieval and early modern pattern of Christian vandalism and forced conversion of non-Christian subjects, the peace settlement for the newly annexed Kazan was soon codified to be religiously plural. The Muslim Tatars and pagan hangers-on were soon liberated from the initial religiously overzealous actions of the conquering army by royal decree, and initial missions by priests to the new territories were curtailed on order of the central government in Muscovy. In order to better take over the people and trade routes of the Upper Volga without the threat of continuous rebellion or economic disruption, it was determined that it would simply be easier to accommodate the new ethnic minorities with a more decentralized policy.[14]

Farther west, one fragment of the now-defunct Kipchak state, the Crimean Khanate, was being reinvigorated, rather than weakened, by its full independence from any Mongol/Tatar successor state. Being able to geographically reorient its priorities to the Black Sea region, and taking advantage of the chance to forge an alliance with the rising Ottoman Empire, this subkhanate under the Giray branch of old Kipchak nobility retained its steppe-style military, raiding and plundering its northern frontier with Lithuania and Muscovy while at the same time becoming a maritime trading power with its new ally across the sea. Slaves and goods taken from these northern and western raids could be sold directly to Ottoman merchants (previously it was Genoese) on the Crimean Peninsula, which was where the new capital of the state was located.[15]

In a series of conflicts, the Crimean Khanate gave as well as it got against the rising Russian state, but time was not on its side. As allies like Astrakhan and Kazan were crushed by Ivan Grozny, and Russia's resources and technology began to surpass that of the Tatars of

Crimea, over the course of centuries the khanate weakened, eventually seeking safety by entering an unequal vassalage with the Ottoman Empire. But even this step could not save it. By the eighteenth century, the situation was irreversible. After a victorious war against the khanate and the Ottomans, Tsarina Catherine the Great's forces compelled an end to the old alliance, which was followed shortly after by the Russian Empire's full annexation of the khanate. The Kipchak Khanate ended in 1783. Its final khan fled to the Ottoman Empire for refuge, only to be beheaded in exile by his patrons for his failure. As Rene Grousset states, "Thus on the eve of the French Revolution, the last Jenghiz-Khanite of Europe met his end."

Once the splintered leftovers of the Golden Horde were swept aside, there was no effective barrier, aside from daunting climate and distance, to keep Russia from expanding its economic base (largely through the fur trade) and its territorial control all the way to the Pacific. These borders, which grew at first so they could be contracted for defense, were spread by Cossack horsemen who used much of the mobile tactics of their ersatz Mongolian overlords to expand. Unlike those former power brokers, however, they left forts and settlements in their wake. The Cossacks were largely composed of stateless brigands, dislocated Tatars, Russian peasant runaways, and anyone else from the region who joined up. In exchange for their domestic and regional autonomy, they served the Russian state in Ukraine and Siberia. As time went on, they were largely deployed on any front as the seminomadic cavalry force of the settled Russian state. They used many of the same military methods as the Turko-Mongolian nomads once had, but they had the additional benefit of cutting-edge gunpowder technology to augment their personal arsenals.[16]

This is not to say that Russia, like China, used expansion purely for security. Defensive security concerns could hardly account for the massive explosion of Russia's frontiers, which made even the Manchurians look modest in their epic scale of hegemonic conquests. A key difference fueling Russian expansion was simple profit. The fur trade was a great opportunity to make copious wealth, and so unlike the Qing, Muscovy/Russia was not content just to create a buffer zone, and the fur trade had to keep growing for the benefit of the state. The fur supply often became depleted, and the natives either hired or enslaved to do the hunting and trapping often fled or died in the process.[17]

The blurred line between Siberian natives and new Russian settlements, exuberantly expansionist as they were, was itself a unique and formless method of expanding geopolitical power. After all, the Russians kept to the forests until the mid-eighteenth century, when their greater population numbers and access to technology allowed them to take on in direct battle the steppe tribes that still existed in the plains to the south. Before Russia could exercise its new dominant colonial role, however, it came into conflict with the other settled behemoth of Eurasia.

The Formless Empires of the Qing and the Russians were about to meet in a way that not only exposed both powers' similarities and differences to each other but also set off another round of battle as the last remnants of the autonomous nomadic actors struggled to survive the coming end times for their way of life as it was crushed to pieces between the two advancing hegemons.[18]

The collision of Chinese imperialism by proxy through the Manchus and Russian imperialism by proxy through the Cossacks finally occurred in the Amur River valley, which lies within contemporary Primorsky Krai in the Russian maritime east. A Cossack fort had been constructed to claim the river basin, but the Manchurian leaders of the new Qing Dynasty found this uncomfortably close to what they regarded as their ancestral homeland and launched their forces in a counterattack in a rare display of power northward, rather than westward or southward.

The beleaguered Cossacks were soon surrounded, under siege, and decisively defeated. Russian forces in southeastern coastal Siberia surrendered to peace terms dictated by China, and a solid border between the two Eurasian giants was codified in the 1689 Treaty of Nerchinsk. This kept Russia far north of the Amur region until the mid-nineteenth century, when it was able to capitalize on the instability and increasing weakness of the Qing regime after the dynasty entered a period of terminal decline.[19]

Now that the two giants had met, the former and current nomads between them became endangered societies. The seventeenth and eighteenth centuries were times of increased settlement of Siberia and the steppes by Russians and the border regions of Manchuria by the Chinese. Despite the formless Inner Eurasian influences adopted by both powers, it seemed possible that the formless borderlands had been forever crushed between them as their expansions finally brought them together. It would have been premature to celebrate the death of those people who played a large role in inspiring the methods of expansion used by both settled powers who were now on the rise, for there were still a few rounds to go before the new order could be stabilized.

Most threatening to the new Qing (and, indirectly, Russian) order were the battles against Galdan Khan, a Mongol warlord of the Dzungar tribe in the west who tried to unify the Mongol tribes into a power once again. His numerous campaigns to create a Dzungar-dominated Mongol state represented the last gasp of relatively large nomadic resistance to the new waves of settlement and conquest by the Qing Dynasty. His ruthless policies of pursuing state creation had almost the opposite effect by increasing the dissatisfaction among more peripheral tribes of his confederation. To groups like the Khalka and eastern Mongols, the non-Chinese origin of the Qing Dynasty and their battlefield prowess made them just as legitimate overlords as Galdan and his distant Tibetan allies. The Qing decided to nip this potential threat in the bud by harnessing this internal discord and showing off to the western tribes how open they were. The military banner system founded in the Manchu state before it took over China, which consisted of numerous ethnic military divisions with significant social and cultural autonomy and great prestige, was ideal for recruiting these disaffected Mongols and using them to claim that the Qing had just as much right to the western steppes as Galdan Khan did. It also served to stipulate in their terms of service that they had to cut any homage or obedience to the Dzungar-allied Dalai Lama.[20]

With his own polyglot and seminomadic army, Emperor Kangxi set out on campaign in 1688 to end the rise of Galdan and establish Qing hegemony deeper into Central Asia than had been done before. At first Kangxi was happy to allow submitted oasis city-states and nomadic tribes along the trade routes to submit and keep their domestic autonomy, as was common with policies of Eurasian geostrategic formlessness. Galdan proved more effective at this indirect type of warfare, and he often withdrew into the steppe, reemerging when the Qing forces had left only small garrisons as they moved on and bringing the region under his control.

Kangxi saw the futility of engaging his more mobile foe in this way and adopted his own version of a false retreat to use on Galdan. He claimed to have been tired of fighting and offered to sign a treaty of peace if Galdan would come to Beijing. As Galdan's forces moved east and closer to Beijing to what they thought would be a peace settlement, Kangxi attacked. Galdan lost many of his warriors, and the Manchus chased his shattered forces back into Central Asia. Eight years later he was beaten again, with the Qing mobile artillery (small cannons mounted on the backs of camels) playing a decisive role in decimating the trapped Mongols. After this second bout of carnage, Galdan and a few of his followers fled into exile, where he soon died.

The Dzungars were not quite finished, however. Half a century later, a second khan who also went by the name Galdan took a more independent path toward the Qing than had been established in the peace following the original Galdan's death. This necessitated a new campaign, which finally finished off the Dzungars for good in 1745. The divided Dzungar tribes lost their religious legitimacy that year when a pro-Qing government was installed in Tibet and the religious institution there withdrew from the alliance with the western Mongols. Only then did the Dzungars finally and truly submit to the Qing.[21]

This enabled large Qing armies to advance farther west than ever before, prompting the eventual capitulation of the tribes and independent cities in what has become China's western border region. With the Manchu rulers also came Chinese settlers and farmers, as well as economic policies to solidify state control. This disruption of the order, though tying the frontier much closer to Beijing, upset the trade- and mobile-commerce-based economy of the region to such an extent that this once wealthy part of Eurasia became a backwater subsidized by the central government and largely held for security, rather than economic, reasons.[22]

It is worth noting that Galdan Khan was aware of the endangered nature of his type of state on the Eurasian stage as well as the emerging bipolarity. On numerous occasions he made overtures to the Russians for weapons and support to help him resist the Qing advance. Russia was too weak in the east at this point to help, even if it had wanted to. Also, both the fur trade and the links with the Qing were profitable, so Russia rebuffed his diplomatic advances. He was crushed by the Qing with tacit Russian approval.[23] The Treaty of Nerchinsk held strong as both powers seemed more concerned with ensuring control over their expanded borders than interfering with each other.

This border insecurity was about to show itself in another way. Galdan may have been gone, and so eventually his empire, but the need for mobility and pasturage still drove many people on the steppe. With an unprecedented amount of control finally seeming to have descended on the region, the various peoples there who were still comparatively nomadic used confusion over which empire they belonged to in order to retain some amount of autonomy and freedom. Therefore, even during the process of making the borders more defined and solid, the people who lived in those areas found ways to blur the lines imposed on them, for their own self-interest.[24]

Arguably, this was not always in contrast to the interests of the now-dominant settled states, which could use claimed overlordship of some mobile ethnic group of people to claim a new region. Qing policy toward many regions of its frontier post-Galdan retained this general attitude, as did Russian policy south of the Siberian forest belt and toward the Eurasian steppe. The best example of this was a tribe that was trapped between both powers: the Kalmyks.

Robbed of the power over their settled periphery by the rise of the new Eurasian states, the Kalmyk peoples still showed an amazing amount of formless adaptability in the confining spaces between the Russians and the Qing. Originally known as the Oirat, an eastern Mongolian tribe, the Kalmyks were a subbranch that migrated west to flee internal disputes among the Oirat as well as the Qing conquest of Mongolia. They and their herds traveled all the way to the Volga in the Russian Empire, where they began raiding outlying Russian frontier settlements and settling in the region. By the mid-seventeenth century, they were established in a new region, seemingly free of the new Qing regime on the less secure frontier near the Urals.[25]

Rather than take the time to expel them by force in this still-periph-eral region of the empire, the Russian government decided to co-opt these people into its sphere of influence as a buffer against other, still-roaming nomads. The Kalmyk Khanate made itself wealthy by con-trolling the vital trade routes between the Russian and Chinese fron-tiers and did its best to maintain alliance and kinship networks with the other still-nomadic people. This system, and this uniquely major-ity Buddhist political entity in Europe, lasted for a century in the same region where the Kipchaks once held court in Sarai.

But with the centralizing policies of Catherine the Great and the increase in Russian and Germanic settlement in and near Kalmyk lands, the situation began to reverse itself from a favorably exploited niche for a remnant nomad people to a more precarious one. Fearful of losing their semiautonomy, many Kalmyks decided to return to the eastern steppe and western Mongolia. In 1771, with the flight of so many reversing their original epic trek across Eurasia and back to the now Qing-dominated lands they once fled, Empress Catherine abol-ished the khanate and formally reintegrated the lands back into Russia proper.[26]

It wasn't just the borders of the settled states that expanded into Eurasia—it was in many cases their way of life as well. The seeds of this change in lifestyle were laid out in the original and regionally seminal 1689 Treaty of Nerchinsk: "After 1689, refugees, deserters, and tribes-people had to be fixed as subjects of either Russia or China. Maps, sur-veyors, border guards, and ethnographers began to determine their identities internally and externally by stabilizing movement across bor-ders and enabling the suppression of groups who did not fit imperial definitions of space."[27]

The destruction of the ways of life of many of the indigenous inhab-itants of Inner Eurasia wreaked by these policies was immense. The free-flowing caravan and trade system that gave the region much of its prosperity was terminated by the border and customs agents of the new bureaucratic state. The freedom to move from pasturage to pas-turage was severely curtailed by the construction of fortresses and new towns of farmers, often from the center of the new regime.[28] Chinese and Russian peasants and their subsidiary agrarian peoples were the makers of the economy from now on. The agrarians who migrated inward into formerly nomadic lands to exploit the new niche opened up the great reduction, if not outright elimination, of the nomadic threat. After thousands of years of being on the shorter end of the military and often the political equation, the settled people finally appeared to have achieved total victory.[29]

Nomadic pastoralism had begun an inevitable decline for people inside deep Eurasia. But the geostrategic practice that had been so well honed by the peripheral nomadic and seminomadic peoples of the heartland did not disappear into the sunset with them. We have examined how the settled states gradually adopted more and more of the nomadic methods of diplomacy and warfare to at first keep them at bay and then supplant them entirely. But the geopolitics of formless space would not be totally disregarded merely because their main antagonists had secured the frontier. Such political systems were also useful against other settled states. After all, the geography of Eurasia had hardly changed, even if the political and economic elements that evolved on it had. An example of this involved neither Russia nor China, but it lurked quite near another front of the expanding Russian state.

Unlike Siberia, the Caucasus did not represent much of a settlement opportunity for Russians, not comparatively anyway. Most of the people there were already settled and agriculturally based. What inroads were made by the empire tended to be by co-opting local ruling elites as independent vassals of the Russians.[30] If the Ottomans could be influential through regional proxies, so could the tsar.

Also, compared to its Siberian expansion, Russia did not drive deep into the region until much later. This was largely because of the existence of both the Crimean Khanate—still hanging on all this time since the breakup of the Kipchak Khanate but now as an Ottoman dependency—and the Ottoman Empire itself. Largely indirectly, the Ottoman Empire was surely the most dominant power in the region, and the mere threat of its involvement kept Russia far away from too much southern movement, at least until the mid- and late-eighteenth century. Looking at the situation from an Inner Eurasian perspective, the power of Russia was not yet apparent. The Ottoman Empire was still the dominant power on the western half of Eurasia, and Russia was tied with Iran for second place. That balance would tip in favor of Russia before its hegemony would really be felt.[31]

Before we move on to the further Eurasian dominance exerted by Russia and China in the modern era, it is important to investigate the flash in the pan where the mantle of the Formless Empire was passed, if ever so briefly: Iran.

Outside of the normal geographic scope of this book, another blending of steppe military tradition with that of an established agrarian state was occurring, one that showed just how effective such a strategic marriage could be. It is worth taking a detour to see this stunning example.

The Safavid Dynasty of Iran was a peripheral player in formless politics to a certain extent ever since its founding in 1501. Its military aristocracy was dominated by Turkic and Caucasian tribes and semi-nomadic warrior peoples who had come to call the area in and around Iran a home of sorts in the wake of the Mongol and Timurid conquests. Trapped between the behemoths of the Mughal and Ottoman Empires, and with an economy still shattered by the many predatory depredations it had been subjected to, Iran found itself less of a power projector and more of a struggling entity outshined by its neighbors and under constant assault from the north and northeast.[32]

The Safavid Dynasty, which was founded in 1501, had a few strong rulers, such as Shah Abbas I. In its later years, however, it suffered a significant decline, due especially to incompetent leadership that was bred into its heirs by being raised almost exclusively in the harem that spawned them. After a revolt of the Afghan military auxiliaries in 1722, the capital, Isfahan, was occupied and the central government collapsed. The shah was taken prisoner by his erstwhile armed forces, and both the Ottoman Empire and Russia seized the chance to readjust the borders of Iran in ways that benefitted their territorial designs. The son the shah, Tahmasp II, declared himself ruler and prepared to make a last stand in the central mountains of the country. Iran looked as doomed as an independent entity as it had been at the start of the Mongol conquests.[33]

It was into this dire situation that the last great Asiatic conqueror arose. A boy named Nader ("prodigy") was born around 1698 in northern Khorasan on the northeastern Iranian frontier with humble if not downright impoverished origins among the seminomadic tribes that the Safavid government often employed to protect its frontiers. These tribes had a culture that was a combination of Persian settled attitudes and the Central Asian Turko-Mongolian tradition. These were inauspicious origins, indeed, from the perspective of Iranian attitudes of the time, but as Nader's official biography claimed in regards to his birth, "The sword takes its merit from the natural strength of its temper, not from the mine from which the iron was taken."

It was on this frontier, defending against a raid by enemy tribes as a young mounted musketeer, that Nader started a meteoric rise through the military hierarchy of the Safavid state. By the time the Afghan warlord Malik Mahmud had seized Isfahan and the shah of Iran, Nader was of sufficiently high rank to become the leading military figure in the resistance against the dissolution of the Iranian state.[34]

Claiming his loyalty to Tahmasp II, Nader set out to stabilize the military situation. His forces—modified along his own tactical lines emphasizing the mobility of cavalry and the accurate use of the heavy-caliber flintlock musket (which was far more accurate and long-ranged than the more famous European models)[35] as well as light artillery carried and used from camelback—reflected both the increasing technological sophistication of the settled areas outside of Inner Eurasia and the classic models of a nomadic or seminomadic steppe army. Using this new force, Nader struck at defecting or disloyal nobles in the west before marching on the Afghans in Isfahan. After a rout and brief siege, Malek Mahmud was captured and executed.[36]

Nader did, however, respect the fighting abilities and potential of the Afghans. So he pursued them east after their flight, not only to make sure they could no longer be a legitimate threat to Iran but also to create supplicants and vassal states out of many of the tribes, which gave him access to new recruits for his army.[37]

Ottoman attempts to ally with the remaining Afghan powers opposed to this newly resurgent Iran had to be dealt with as well before Nader could turn and oust the two predatory great powers that had staked new claims in Persia. He marched west and put the Ottomans to flight in a series of lopsided victories. By 1730, there was a de facto truce and reestablishment of the border to its precrisis extent. Hoping to encourage Nader to launch more attacks on their common Turkish foe, the Russians evacuated Dagestan in the northern Caucasus as an act of goodwill and opened up direct diplomatic channels with the Iranians.[38] This enabled the Iranians to set up yet more proxy allies in their northwestern frontier. The Armenians were co-opted by the granting of financial and domestic privileges in order to establish a loyal border column between Iran and the Ottomans. Georgia seemed secure, or at least under nominal Russian hegemony, and thus Nader turned south in an attempt to take Iraq and break Turkish hegemony in the Middle East for good.[39]

Despite the success of Nader's other actions on this front, the Iraq campaign turned out to be a disaster because of the incompetent military intervention of the shah, Tahmasp II. Tahmasp led an army against the Ottomans in an attempt to achieve some battlefield glory for himself, in all likelihood to check Nader's dominance of the military, but was decisively defeated. Nader had to campaign for a few extra years to return to the status quo he had worked so hard to build, including a disastrous invasion of Iraq that required a successive campaign to stabilize the initial gains made there. Meanwhile, using the shah's incompetence as an excuse, Nader imprisoned him and his son and acted as regent. He finally declared himself shah in 1735, and thus was able to enter directly into foreign negotiations as the head of state.[40] Nader the tribal chief and general had become Nader Shah, which is how he was known for the rest of his career and posterity.

Nader Shah's domestic policy had lower priority than his wars and diplomacy. Despite this, his approach to the pressing internal issues of Iran at the time showed the traditional flexibility of nomadic and seminomadic peoples and the kinds of influences they could have over the more-traditional states they often ruled. Nader Shah's religious policy was highly motivated from his practical and often even antireligious outlook.[41] He tried to end the diplomatic and cultural isolation to which Iran had been subjected by revising the militantly anti-Sunni

practices of the Shi'a majority. Nader instituted a ban on the traditional cursing of the first three caliphs and various other religious practices
that made the Shi'a creed so vile to the majority of the world's Sunni
Muslim populace. He also attempted to make the state religion neither
explicitly Sunni nor Shi'a, and thus could claim to his majority Iranian
populace that he was Shi'a but to foreign dignitaries claim that he was
Sunni. Given that Sunnis were also a significant portion of his armed
forces, this policy made sense for his more central goals as well.

With his position now secure, Nader Shah decided it was time to
launch a purely offensive strategy regarding his neighbors. His objectives were to achieve some kind of financial and territorial gain for the
Iranian homeland, which had been so devastated by the decline and
fall of the Safavid Dynasty. He also probably knew that his large polyglot army thrived on loot and conquest, and that the ravaged lands of
Persia would not suffice for this. Nader marched into Afghanistan to
seize Kandahar, not only to secure a troublesome imperial flank but
also to prepare for a drive onto Mughal India.[42]

The Mughal Empire that Nader Shah was planning on paying a call
to was not the mighty and flexible behemoth we saw the creation and
establishment of in the last chapter. Rotting from within owing to
decentralization and the power of regional governors, the empire also
had to deal with the rise of the Marathas and resurgent militant
Hinduism that came with it. With the Maratha leader Shivaji riding
roughshod over the now increasingly outdated Mughal army, the
empire had contracted to its northern core territories.[43]

Nader Shah's army invaded India from Afghanistan in 1737 and
drove toward the Mughal capital of Delhi. Having a small force and no
heavy cannons, his plan was to use the old nomadic trick of luring the
opponent out with a feint and drawing him into a trapped field engagement. After threatening the Mughal army's supply lines, Nader was
able to get his foes to leave their fortifications and attack him directly.
Here, on the open battlefield of Karnal, Nader was able to use his light
field guns and mobile cavalry wings to maximum effect. Though the
Mughals brought forth war elephants, they were easy targets for the
artillery, and the large, lumbering Mughal cannons fell into the hands
of Nader's light cavalry. The rest of the trapped Mughal army was

mowed down by the concentration of musketry brought to bear on the center by Nader's superior firearms. In the aftermath, the Mughal emperor was captured and Delhi was sacked by Nader's army.[44]

Nader did not try direct rule on the Indian subcontinent. He left the current ruler in charge (though substantially less wealthy and more humiliated) and settled for the annexation of everything west of the Indus, not a colossal area considering that he had crushed the armies and taken the capital of his enemies. What he instead demanded was loot and trade monopoly on the Afghan-Central Asian routes. This he achieved to such an extent that he could rescind even his exorbitant taxes on the people of Iran for three years. Economic recovery was strong enough because of this temporary tax remittance that even devastated Iran started to see an improvement in the general economy of the farmers and rural residents.[45]

The Mughals, on the other hand, were no longer a credible threat to Iran, and their weakness was exposed for all to see. A once-grand empire had become a de facto Delhi-based city-state. Most relevantly for the future, the British East India Company, which had been kept in check by Mughal power, now took stock of the totally changed political situation in India.[46]

After this success, arguably the pinnacle of his career, Nader Shah drove into Central Asia proper. Once he had received the submission of many of the post-Timurid princes in the region, made the right vassals, and ensured access to the regional trade routes, he was content to leave.[47] Again, Nader was showing that even as lord of a settled state in a time of rapidly changing technological and economic balances, the legacy of the Formless Empires of the past, while altered, was still very much in existence.

Nader suffered from malaria contracted on campaign and increasing mental illness. With the tax holiday over and his interest in securing Dagestan against any future Russian incursions, he increased taxes exorbitantly to pay for his increasingly bogged-down campaign to pacify the Caucasus tribes of that region. These harsh taxes provoked rebellion, which in turn provoked massive retaliation by the government. Finally, after Nader blinded his son and heir in a fit of rage over his unilateral execution of the deposed former shah and built pyramids of human skulls in rebellious areas, his own army elites assassinated him in 1747.

With the chaos caused by his death and the destabilized social and political situation his later reign had contributed to, Nader's multinational and seminomadic army began to break up. Karim Khan took the reins of government in Iran, and Agha Muhammad took his Afghan contingent east to take control of Afghanistan. Agha Muhammad would eventually clash in battle with the Marathas, bringing Nader's original style of warfare with him and fighting for the withering rump of the Mughal state. Other protégés of Nader took power in places such as Georgia and the Caucuses.[48] In his own way, Nader had left a legacy, even if it was overwhelmingly in the realm of warfare. It was, however, the last gasp of a dying way of geopolitics; the nomadic-centered army as major regional power was dead and buried. Or so it seemed.

Gunpowder, more efficient farming, and the rise of mercantilism had all done their parts to break the nomadic stranglehold on mobility and qualitative military power. Even so, while the balance of power shifted decisively in favor of the large agrarian states, the methods they used to facilitate that shift were often wholly or partially derived from the strategies most often used by the nomadic powers they sought to displace. As it was, many of the ruling classes of the new settled societies were in fact partially nomadic or at least frontier in origin. Nurhaci came from the Manchus, the descendants of the Jurchens, and a people who were largely nomadic but with a small amount of agriculture supporting them. Nader Shah came from a seminomadic Turkic tribe on the Persian periphery that guarded the borders of the state from other nomadic bands. The Russians, while not having a nomadic origin, carried over many of the policy ideas formulated during the reign of the Kipchak Khanate, especially in their desire to rule key trade routes and their utilization of the nomadic Kalmyks as proxies and the seminomadic Cossacks in pursuing actions on their southern and eastern frontiers.

All three—the Manchus, Nader Shah, and Russia—waged war against nomadic foes who, on the whole, were the last practitioners of the medieval type of formless geopolitics, and thus were, in a way, their inheritors as well as their displacers. They also waged war on settled states using lessons learned from their nomadic foes. In terms of military power and the combination of nomad-like mobility with settled technology, the Cossacks, Manchus, and Nader Shah all showed innovation, adaptation, and a merger of geopolitical worlds. Now, with the rise of Russia and China (and temporarily of Iran), it was time for a new kind of formless policy to arise. The settled state was about to increase its new role as the purveyor of this doctrine in Inner Eurasia. Indeed, it was the culmination of Sun Tzu's thinking in a way, since he originally wrote *The Art of War* for the agrarian settled states of pre-unification China. More than two thousand years after the supposed date of its publication, the strategies of the kind of sedentary states it was meant to advise had finally evolved to reflect its advice.

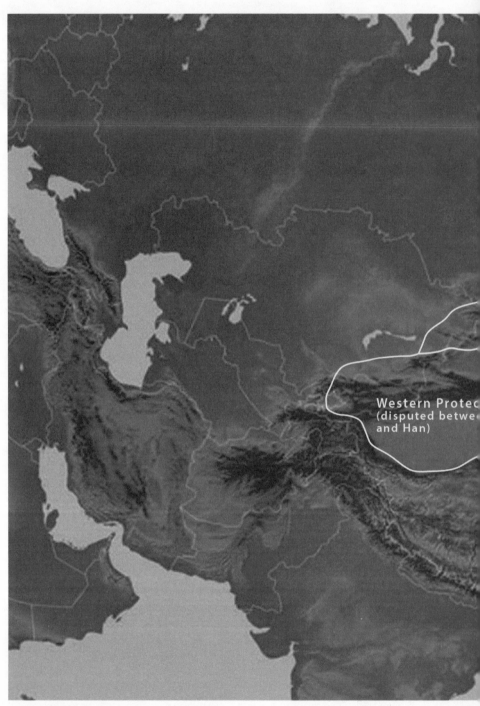

Map 1. Xiongnu and Han Bipolar Rivalry.

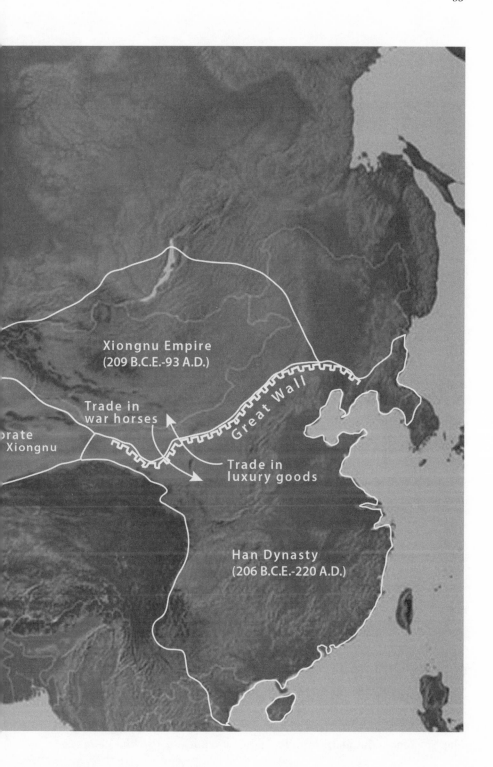

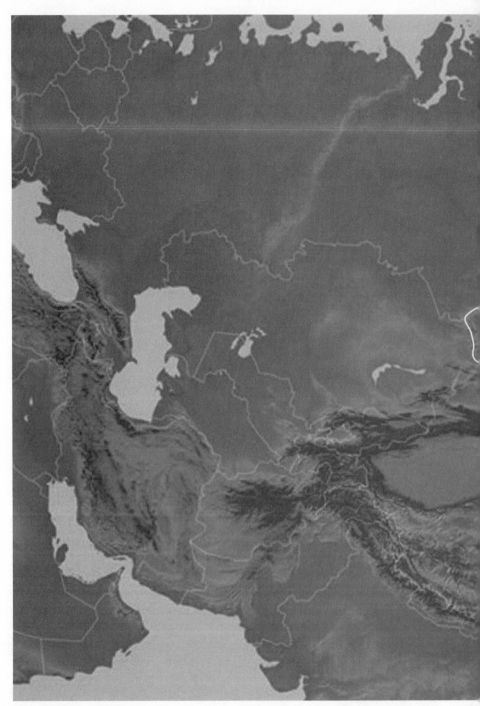

Map 2: China's Multipolar Frontier in the Eleventh and Twelfth Centuries.

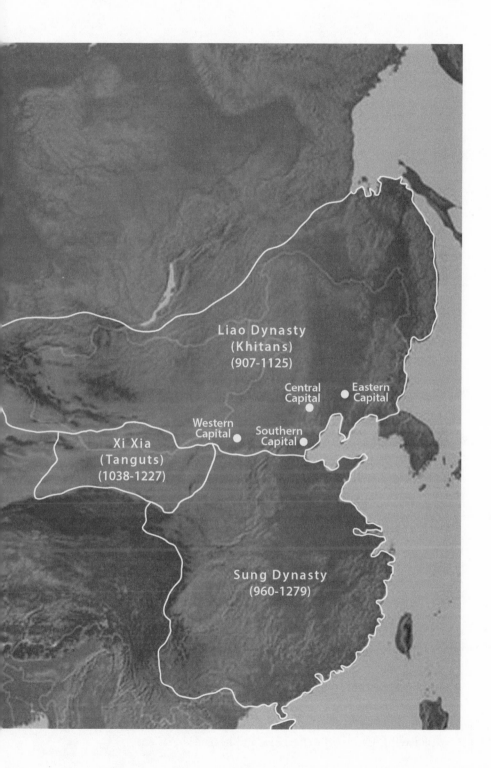

Map 3. Twelfth-Century Jurchen Rise and Khitan Migration.

Khitans Migration
under
Yelu Daishi

Jin Dynasty
(Jurchens)
(1115-1234)

Xhanate
s)
18)

Xi Xia
(1038-1227)

Sung Dynasty
(960-1279)

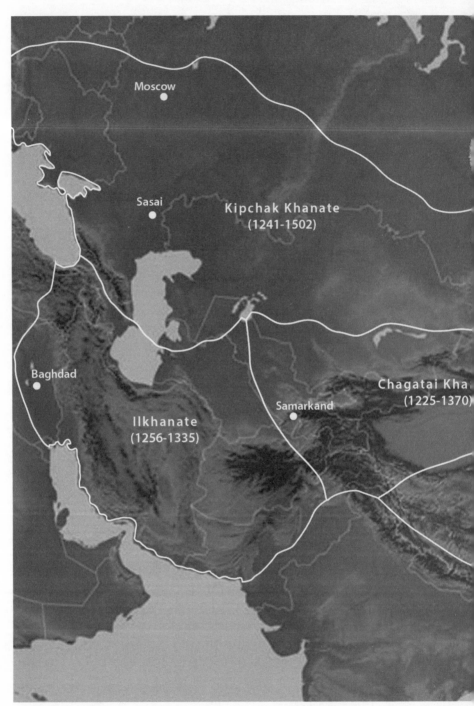

Map 4. Mongol Empire and Subdivisions in the Late Thirteenth Century.

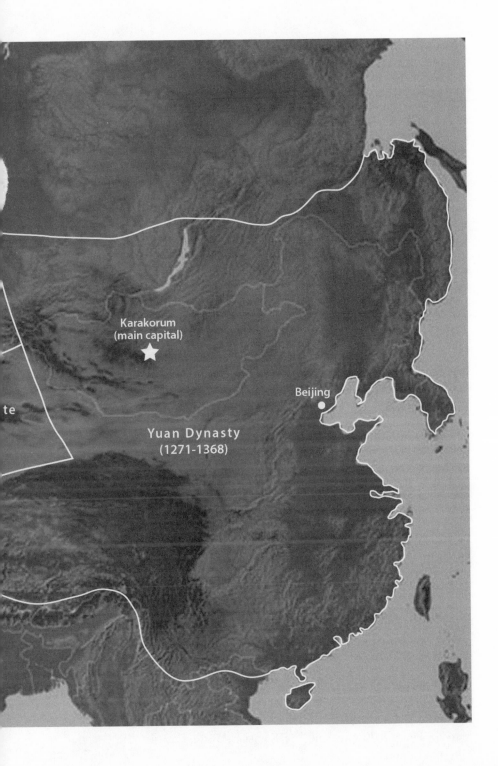

Map 5. Timurid Empire and the Eurasian World near the Turn of the
Fifteenth Century.

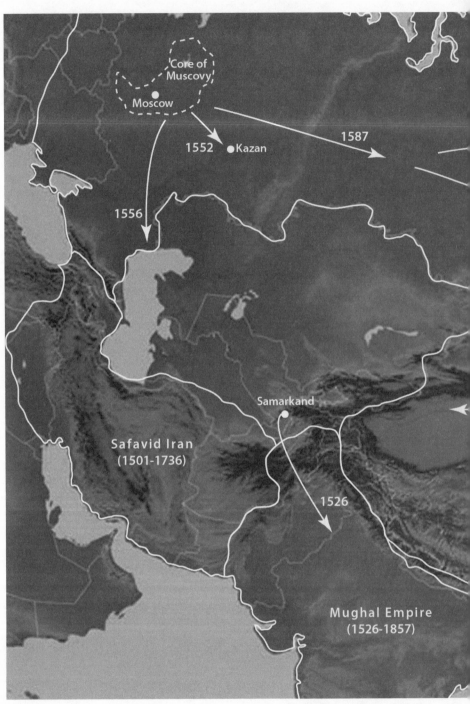

Map 6. Growth of the Sedentary Powers in the Sixteenth to Eighteenth Centuries.

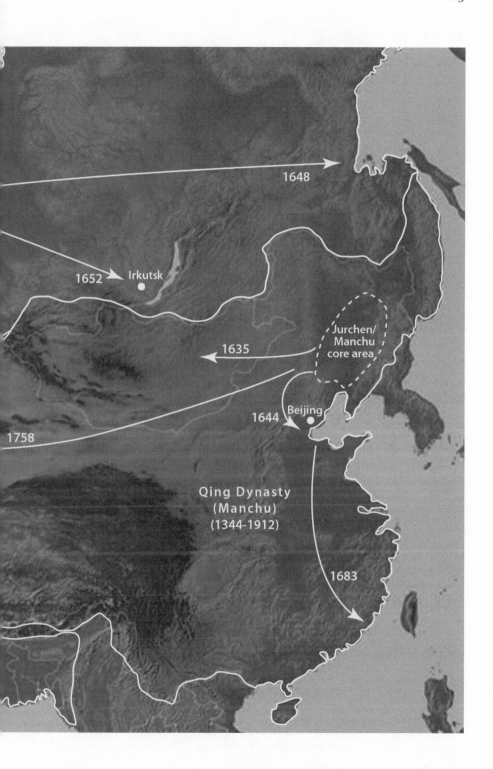

1648

1652 Irkutsk

Jurchen/
Manchu
core area

1635

1758

1644 Beijing

Qing Dynasty
(Manchu)
(1344-1912)

1683

Map 7. Littoral Intrusion on the Eve of the Second World War.

Map 8. Contemporary Eurasia.

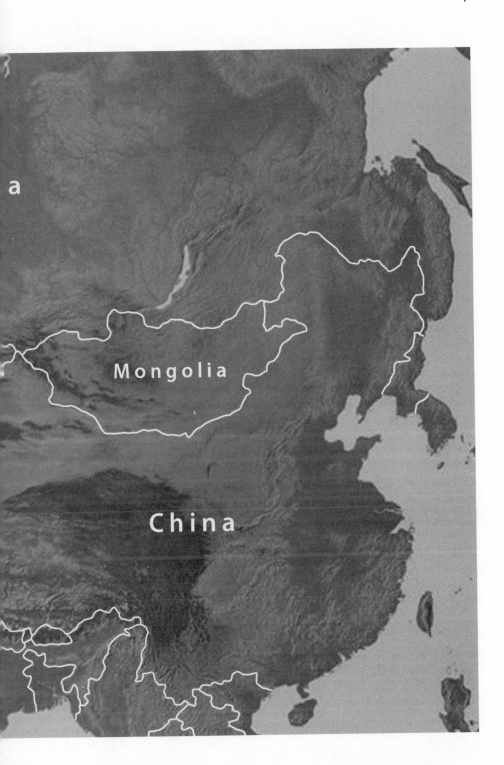

FIVE

THE INVASION
OF THE LITTORALS

The situation of Russia in Central Asia is similar to that of any civilized state that enters into contact with savage nomadic tribes that lack any form of social organization. . . . Consequently, the state must decide: to put an end to its efforts and leave its borders under constant threat, which means prosperity, security, and cultural progress all become impossible; or push further into the wild territories, whereby the increasing distances increase the difficulties and trials.

—Prince Gorchakov, Russian Foreign Affairs Minister, 1864

In the puppet regime they sought a form of colonial state that represented a new kind of collaboration between imperialist and subject, a formula for a colonial ruler neither formal nor informal that would accommodate nationalist demands for sovereignty and self-determination.

—Louise Young on the creation of Manchukuo

THE IMMENSE IRONY OF THE HISTORY OF EURASIAN GEOPOLITICS IN general, and the continuing evolution of the Formless Empire in particular, was that by the time the large and powerful settled states finally achieved hegemony over the troublesome interior peoples of the continent, they faced an equally large threat from a new phenomenon in the region: invasion by littoral naval powers.

The same technological change that had enabled China and Russia to finally establish military security and dominance on the frontier was being taken even further by the maritime nations in northern and western Europe, North America, and eventually Japan. Much as the cavalry-borne nomads once harried, subjugated, and broke into the internal affairs of the large Eurasian land powers using their superior mobility and strategic flexibility, so too were the naval powers able to achieve this feat using the powers granted by modern navies and industrialized economies. The same tactical advantages of speed, control of space, and concentrated firepower that brought the nomadic and seminomadic peoples of Eurasia so much success for so long, despite relatively small numbers, worked just as much in favor of the advanced maritime societies. The difference was that these powers were more alien, and they adapted to increasing contact with the Eurasian heartland with differing levels of success. All of which proved temporary once the land powers of China and Russia, which were more thoroughly adapted to formless geopolitics, recovered from the initial shock of their displacement by the new upstarts.

The littoral invasion's most lasting impact was on the societies that often barely survived its coming, and that had devastating consequences for people's freedom of movement and autonomy in the wake of their expulsion. But before the end of this period of invasion, the once-central but now-peripheral people of Eurasia (Turks, Mongols, and others) again played important roles, both in fighting and collaborating with the various great powers, indigenous and foreign alike. Through the interplay of espionage, war, and diplomacy, the effect of such titanic struggles for hegemony inside Eurasia have global consequences. Perhaps the most relevant aspect of this was in the evolution of modern warfare and the return of rampant mobility to the battlefield, as is illustrated in the evolution of Soviet combat doctrine. Many of these events also temporarily restored Manchuria and Mongolia, once the vital lynchpins of peoples and power under the influence of the Xiongnu, Khitan, Mongols, and early Manchus, to center stage, even if now all the most potent actors were strangers to the region using them as proxies.

First however, we must begin where we last ended, at the height of dominance by the agrarian powers. In their quest for secure borders, they set the frontiers of the next stage of Eurasian drama and developed a certain level of overconfidence in their own abilities that left them wide open from an unexpected flank. This is also where Russia and China, whose experiences if anything seemed to be moving toward convergence in the eighteenth century, began to radically diverge from each other in terms of relative success and power and the methods they used toward their vast borderlands.

The Qing Dynasty's campaigns in the west had secured Uighuristan, increasingly known in this era by its contemporary moniker of Xinjiang ("New Frontier"), which was obviously not very new nor much of a frontier to its Turkic inhabitants. Yet it was not just another province of China but rather an administrative zone managed using many of the adapted techniques that the Qing, and Chinese policy-making in general, had picked up in their long experience with nomadic allies and adversaries.

A gradualist approach to colonization that emphasized almost imperceptibly increasing levels of Manchurian control was employed toward the western and northern regions after the expensive failure of replacing regional warlords with Manchurian and Han governors in the mid-eighteenth century. The banner system discussed in chapter 4 was much more effective at slowly integrating certain useful and usually warlike peoples into the ruling elite. This was an embracement of the dynasty's Inner Asian heritage in policy–making. As C. Patterson Giersch puts it, "Due in large part to unique ideas and approaches, the Qing conquered and ruled a vast domain that was two times greater and significantly more diverse than their predecessor, the Ming."[1]

The emperor Qianlong saw regime security in this arrangement. The immediate frontier was always the threat to the Han, so he could provide security to his Chinese subjects while simultaneously giving him a large non-Han recruitment pool to shore up his alien dynasty.[2] Not being as fully nomadic as the Mongols and Khitans had been meant easier integration with the locals, but it came at the price of being more dependent on pleasing the native subjects—and, of course, lacking the ability to flee as easily if things turned sour.

The economic changes resulting from the strengthening of the settled powers in Eurasia led to the nomadic people reducing their ranges. No longer able to raid or migrate at will, they switched to trading, often at great disadvantage, with the Chinese and the Russians. The overland trade stimulated by the Qing campaigns and garrison towns created an exploitable niche for Russia to turn south. Having made it to the Bering and Okhotsk seas in the seventeenth and eighteenth centuries, Russian settlement had still not confronted their old foes out on the open steppe. But with the professional military and massive firepower of the army after Tsar Peter I's reforms and the chance of access to new Chinese markets, the Russians soon annexed Kazakhstan and were on the border of Transoxiana by the dawn of the nineteenth century.[3]

Meanwhile, the ever-troublesome Mongols had finally been reduced to nothing but an exploitable border population. The banner system had offered great opportunity to the best warriors of the Mongol tribes. This, of course, left the tribes weak and the state strong. The people who remained in both Inner and Outer Mongolia continued to live through pastoralism, though with increasing powers from Buddhist monasteries and missionaries from Tibet siphoning off yet more young adults. The success of these missions was facilitated by the economic devastation that resulted in the two-fold reduction of pastureland with the arrival of Chinese merchants and attendant loan sharks who made money off the fiscally naive Mongol herders. Inner Mongolia was better integrated and did a bit better, but Outer Mongolia became in effect a land in captivity, where the Mongols themselves became a type of criminal underclass in their own country.[4]

Barely half a century after the wrapping up of Qianlong's successful pacification of Xinjiang, and not much more than a century after the Manchu conquest of Mongolia, this carefully built house of cards received its first shaking. The coming of European navies, led by Britain, was the rude awakening that, after thousands of years of pursuing security to the north and west, the succession of states cumulatively called China had ignored the vast and most open frontier of all: their coast. The brief but far-ranging explorations of Zheng He in the Ming Dynasty had never established a Chinese blue water naval tradition, despite great promise and technical capacity, and this, combined with the previously impenetrable and hostile space of Inner Eurasia, had left China cut off from the rampant industrialization going on else-where.[5]

The giant, seemingly powerful Qing state now looked like a tottering paper tiger to foreign powers.

The British Empire and the East India Company had reached a point where their ballooning trade deficit with the Qing Empire threatened the profit margin of the company. Increasing the selling of opiates from India was a way to offset this balance. Meanwhile in China, the New World silver trade that the state had become financially tied to was starting to break down. Seeing a general decline in financial stability across the nation, the Qing used the burgeoning opium trade as a scapegoat for the nation's woes and initiated a crackdown. This increased the costs to British traders, but the real blow came with the confiscation of British ships and the destruction of twenty thousand chests of opium seized from their cargo.

The Qing military thought itself adequate for any response from faraway Britain, but it had fallen behind the times. In a quick succession of conflicts, the British navy, with its steam-powered warships firing explosive shells, decimated the Chinese fleet and enabled troops to land at various points on the coast of China. The Qing response, despite obvious numerical superiority, was constrained by having to retain the deployment of so many troops inland because of the commitments of the massive empire.

The intrusion of Britain, and then France, followed not long after by a less-militant but equally economic incursion by the United States, sparked a number of reactions throughout East Asia. Korea shut itself off from the world. Japan tried to become a modern state, but its government was toppled by a coalition of southern clans who then pursued a radical and ultimately successful course of modernization. But it was the massive market of China that the maritime powers really wanted access to, and for all the power the Qing state had acquired, it simply could not keep them out. This is not to say that the Qing state had been wrong in its priorities, for despite the spectacle of burning sailing junks blown apart by the modern guns of the steam-powered Royal Navy, the main threat was another Eurasian land power still lurking on the landward side—and it was noticing the delicate state of its rival's fortunes.[6]

While China had been growing complacent in its frontier victory, Russia had kept growing stronger. If the mid-nineteenth century was a time of perpetual decline in Chinese regional hegemony, it was also one of the constant rising of Russia—and Russia's region was a large percentage of Eurasia proper. Successfully retaining its Eurasian land power and unique access to frontier space from which to expand, Russia had also joined the European nations. Straddling the heartland and the littoral, in geopolitical terms, it was both established internationally as well as integrated regionally and thus had many advantages over increasingly lackluster China.[7]

Given the loose hold the Qing had on the outer regions of their homeland, Manchuria, as well as the poor showing of Qing armed forces against modern arms and the unequal treaties that Beijing was being obliged to abide by, the time seemed ripe for Russia to attempt to gain the Amur River valley. And this time would be no repeat of the failed Cossack invasion in the seventeenth century. Thus when Nickolai Muraviev became governor general of Eastern Siberia, he sensed an opportunity. The foreign incursions had touched off the largest war of the nineteenth century, the Taiping Rebellion. That civil war, started by an apocalyptic religious movement and fed off of disaffection with the ruling dynasty, raged from 1850 to 1864. Eastern China was a sea of destruction and despair, and the government of the Qing court was so desperate it had even taken to using the hated foreigners to train and even command some of its armies. The Qing state was still capable of crushing this colossal rebellion, and its hold on Xinjiang remained strong through this period of sudden and seemingly irredeemable weakness. But while it had focused on the immediate threats of foreign navies and internal rebellions, it had left its northeastern flank wide open.[8]

Muraviev plunged right into the gap. Throughout the 1850s, exploratory missions and even shallow-water naval gunboats worked their way through Outer Manchuria, charting and claiming as they went. Even Russia's qualified loss in the Crimean War (1856), which entailed it scrapping its Black Sea fleet and halting its southward expansion against the Ottoman Empire in the west, did not stop Muraviev from continuing operations in maritime Manchuria. Perhaps it even added further impetus to do so. Though the main theater of the Crimean War was the Black Sea region, a joint Anglo-French force cobbled together from various Pacific deployments attempted to take Petropavlovsk. After the unexpected suicide of the commanding officer and repulse from a small militia, the farcical assault withdrew to its ships and fled back south. The war henceforth was confined to the western half of Eurasia, ending only when Russia was removed as an immediate threat to British and French interests in the Ottoman Empire. [9]

Despite that, Muraviev's work was a success. Two years after the conclusion of that conflict, Russia was the beneficiary of the Treaty of Aighun. This treaty with China made Russia the protector of the Qing regime from British and French designs (on paper at least) in exchange for its annexing all of Outer Manchuria, some one hundred eighty-five thousand square miles. This became modern-day Primorye as well as parts of other modern Russian oblasts and the site of Russia's first major Pacific port, Vladivostok ("Ruler of the East"). [10]

As China contracted in territory, Russia continued to grow across the board. Transoxiana, that centerpiece of Inner Eurasian empire and the former seat of Emir Timur's vast domains, had entered rough times and no longer held anything near its former power or wealth. After Shaybani Khan ejected the Timurids, he redistributed much of their confiscated wealth among his own family and allies, creating a vastly powerful nobility that then plotted and schemed. This caused the various regions to divide along the lines of independent city-states with vast territories of pastureland between them. Bukhara, Khiva, and Kokand were the main statelets to form from the increasingly fractured Uzbek realms, and they were possessed of longevity if not dynamism, lasting from the fifteenth to the nineteenth centuries. [11] As was discussed in chapter 3, over the course of this large timeframe, more and more of their populations became settled agrarian farmers, and thus the states benefited from the taming of the nomads occurring because of Russian and Chinese expansion for security. But without the freedom of movement of the nomadic states, their already declining trade routes dried up into nothing, and the cities that were once at the heart of cosmopolitan commerce became impoverished and isolated backwaters. Now, despite Bukhara, Khiva, and Kokand having crops such as cotton to export, most Eurasian trade was conducted by sea.[12]

But the Russian state, concerned about British involvement in the region in the aftermath of the Crimean War and coveting the cotton plantations to its relatively open southern border, decided to make the mid- and late-nineteenth century the time of its biggest pushes of expansionism to date. This would represent the left wing of the giant pincer movement enveloping China, which had begun in Manchuria. The disastrous and ethnocentric policies of the Uzbek ruling class over their diverse subjects as well as the relative taming of the nomads had opened the way somewhat, but Russia's undeniable power at this time was the most important factor as its forces moved ever southward. As Seymour Becker put it, "Beginning in the 1820s, the advance of Russian troops southward from Siberia in search of secure boundaries and reliable neighbors ceased only when Russia's frontiers and her sphere of influence were finally anchored in the Central Asian oases, including those of Bukhara and Khiva."

By this time the populations of the rump khanates were majority sedentary, with rough estimates for Khiva being 72 percent sedentary farmers. There were, however, still enough nomads interested in raiding to create perpetual border insecurity issues. Regarded by the government in Saint Petersburg as a mere nuisance at first, these became a vital concern for the state—much like the acquisition of Outer Manchuria—after the qualified loss of the Crimean War and with the increasing fear of British agents operating northward from India. This inspired the first major advance on the khanates themselves in 1864, against Khiva and Kokand, and then a few years later a new advance, with Bukhara, the strongest, as the main target.[13]

The campaigns went well, as Russian rifles and logistics closed the gap of speed usually held by the defenders in Inner Eurasia, and the cities were occupied. Rebellions were put down rapidly, and the Russians could dictate the terms of peace as they willed. Interestingly, they did not go to outright annexation, instead making vassals and clients of their newly conquered lands. This had the effect of stalling British complaints in the region as well as reducing administrative costs.[14]

The legitimization of this postwar expansion was given by Prince Gorchakov: "To put a stop to raids, the tribes on the frontier have to be reduced to a state of more or less perfect submission. This result once obtained, these tribes take more to peaceful habits, but in their turn they are exposed to attacks of the more distant tribes."

This seemed to be an acceptable way to frame policy to the British, already contemplating doing much the same to Afghanistan even after their humiliating repulse there some decades before. The haughtily named ambassador to Russia, Lord Augustus Loftus, remarked in 1872:

> I believe the Emperor and the Imperial Government are anxious to abstain from extending Russian territory in Central Asia, whilst at the same time they are desirous of obtaining a complete control over the small states of which Central Asia is comprised . . . by avoiding collision to obtain entire influence over Turkestan by conciliatory means through the existing rulers of the several states.[15]

Anglo-Russian tensions still simmered, but imperial Russia's kind of expansion seemed easier to swallow at this juncture than a typical kind of annexation. This type of understanding did not, however, allay the threat each side felt from the other, as we shall soon see.

Despite this push from the Kazakh steppe into realms more settled with cities and agrarian economies, the methods of indirect rule changed little at first. The Russians were content to leave the local elites (or more-obedient relatives of the former elites) in power and in charge of domestic affairs as long as they controlled the foreign policy of the states, could settle within the territories of the former khanates, and build railroads connecting their new domains with Russia proper. Tashkent became a city that the Russians ruled directly in an enclave style and was the main military headquarters of operations in the region, but the newly conquered khanates were treated with relative laxity despite their now-prostrate status. However, Russia looked toward the crumbling Qing frontier with a sense of both alarm and opportunity.

A bizarre three-way competition now began in the mountainous southern regions of Inner Eurasia. This conflict did not end in a fiery

conclusion but rather through the offset of a new power intruding elsewhere from an unexpected direction.

It started, as so many things in the greater region of inland Eurasia
did, with the actions of a seminomadic warlord with imperial ambitions. This was Ya'qub Beg, a tribal leader from Turkestan. In the mid-
nineteenth century, when Qing rule was still strong in Central Asia,
Ya'qub seized the oasis towns of the Uighurs in Xinjiang by outmaneu-
vering the garrisons and expelling them into the sparse western sands.
Cut off from immediate resupply, the Qing had to withdraw from the
westernmost extremity of their empire. This allowed the feisty warlord
to set up his own ministate.[16]

Perhaps it was the nature of the times, with modernism and nationalism on the rise, or the small space he had to work with between the
now-dominant established powers, but Ya'qub Beg lacked the instinct
for flexibility that was the hallmark of all previously successful
Eurasian conquerors. His rule of the Uighurs was strict and religiously fanatical. It drove off many of the traders the oasis town needed to
prosper. While feelings toward the Qing remained highly negative, the
local attitude towards Ya'qub Beg became ever more negative as the
economy began to wither because of his actions. Even the devoutly
Muslim guardian of Sartuq Bughra Khan's shrine wrote, "Of the
Khitay, I hate them. But they were not bad rulers. We had everything
then. There is nothing now."[17]

It is interesting to note that despite the omnipresent European
threat to the coastline and the growing potential for a Japanese threat,
the Qing marshaled a huge number of forces to deal with Ya'qub Beg's
rebellion. The justification given by the government for this set of priorities shows clearly the Eurasian geopolitical focus that the state
retained even after fifty years of humiliation at the hands of the maritime powers. It is also possible that the same geostrategy developed
on the steppe, which was used far less successfully against the
European powers, was still working to keep the western frontier secure
even as the situation changed elsewhere. "As goes Xinjiang, so goes
Mongolia; as goes Mongolia so goes Beijing."[18] This succinct maxim,
spread throughout the Qing court as a pithy way to describe frontier
policy, was undoubtedly meant to cajole a domestic audience into

retaining military deployment in the northern and western reaches of the empire, and it turned out to be a fair approximation of the near future for the dynasty.

With an upgraded and reinvigorated army, and with the Taiping Rebellion long since crushed, the Qing troops moved west in 1878 and in seventy days crossed the desert and destroyed Ya'qub's forces with devastating firepower. The warlord died soon after in mysterious circumstances, and the Qing forces were back in control to a much greater degree than they had been. The Qing had finally succeeded in the realm of military modernization.[19]

For all their failures on other fronts, the Manchu rulers were dead set on controlling the western frontier, rightly seeing it as a potential nest for British and Russian spies if control of it was lost. With the 1878 expedition they were back on the scene as Central Asian powers. As *The Cambridge History of China* notes:

"Although Ch'ing [Qing] authority in Inner Asia was superficial, it was strong enough to guarantee the safety of increasing numbers of Han immigrants from China proper, who settled in Inner Mongolia, throughout Sinkiang, and on the eastern fringes of Tibet. Seen as a whole, despite rebellions and European encroachment and the sagging fortunes of the Manchus, the years from the 1790s to the 1860s were the great period of Ch'ing imperial power."[20]

One could make the case that with the crushing of Ya'qub Beg, the Qing restored and then retained that power of China in the western regions through to the next century.

The Qing also had suspected that Ya'qub Beg was sponsored by the British and that if they did not deal with him soon, either the British or the Russian Empire would take advantage of his presence to shave off parts of Chinese territory. This fear was proven valid when the uneasy détente between Britain and Russia was on the verge of breakdown because of the Russo-Turkish War of 1877. As Britain marshaled its navy to defend Constantinople from encroaching Russian armies that had already laid most of the Ottoman Empire's forces to waste in the Balkans, Russia responded by placing more armies in Central Asia for a three-pronged invasion of British India. Britain counteracted by preemptively invading Afghanistan (the traditional route of Central Asian conquerors into the subcontinent) and deploying forward units to control all of the choke points through the mountain ranges.

The cost of having to support Russia's troop deployments only seemed to exacerbate the potential of Muslim rebellion by effectively making the local Muslim subjects pay for their own occupation at a time when the newly unified nation of Germany was rising to world-power status on its western flank. Meanwhile, the initially successful British invasion of Afghanistan, known as the Second Anglo-Afghan War, had bogged down into an expensive debacle. The two powers began to negotiate and saw the Congress of Berlin as an opportunity to come to a settlement that guaranteed the neutrality of Afghanistan (though its foreign policy was to be controlled by Britain in great-power relations) and allowed Russia to construct massive rail networks through its vassal khanates. These railroad lines enabled Russia to exert much stronger control over its new dominions.

But that was a gradual process, and the occasionally rebellious khanates still largely controlled their own domestic policies. Bukhara in particular largely collaborated with the Russians and was rewarded with little internal interference. One ominous aspect for the khanates, however, were the Russian settlements—not just the military/depot system of Tashkent but cotton plantations (now a booming industry in Central Asia owing to the cutoff of American cotton because of the Civil War and subsequent blockade of Southern harbors) and factories owned and operated by Russians along the new rail lines. This in turn led to the expansion of Russian customs offices and legal councils. Not all natives were displeased. The native Jewish population, which was treated as less than second class before, welcomed the Russians, as did many merchants.[21]

In finally achieving control over its open southern flank, Russia succeeded in the dreams of tsars since Ivan the Terrible. The construction of railroads through the territory, as Halford Mackinder had noticed not long after it was done, was vital in rendering the vast spaces as (or even more) accessible for imperial designs as the Turkic and Mongol cavalry of old had. Rapid deployment without massive occupation, that perennial hallmark of the Formless Empire thought

quashed by earlier Qing and Russian victories, was now back, reintro-
duced by Russia using new technology for an old purpose. With the
increasingly apparent weakness of the Qing, it was now obvious that
the Russian Empire had achieved a state of hegemony over Inner
Eurasia of a kind not seen since the unified Mongol Empire of
Chinggis Khan through Mongke Khan.[22]

Russia did have a few setbacks. It was blocked in Afghanistan and
Xinjiang, but only just. After using proxy warlords to steal land from
China's western flank (if less than it originally wanted),[23] achieving all
that its expeditions had set out to gain, and earning a hefty profit from
the sale of cotton during and after the American Civil War, Russia was
on the rise. In its quest for an ice-free harbor on the Pacific, however,
the Russian state was not so fortunate, and the fate of two great
Eurasian empires strained to the breaking point because of a new
intruder into their deadly dance.

Because Japan did not control a primarily coastal land mass that
was still attached to Inner Eurasia (such as India), one might assume
that it would not be likely to compete with Russian or Chinese hegemony. And indeed, it did not have anywhere near the long-term success either of those powers did. But that had less to do with the nature
of its actions in the inland regions of the continent and more to do with
its hubris elsewhere. As it was, this new power rose and intruded at
just the time when the weaknesses of the big Eurasian giants were
beginning to show themselves. China was the first to feel the blow.

Ironically, it came at least partially because of China's comprehensive attempt to retain its Manchurian frontier from Russian aggression.
The introduction of industrial technology had shown just how economically valuable the resource-rich provinces of the Qing Dynasty
homeland could be. But it was not only the land that beckoned for
exploitation. The population had exploded as well.[24]

Using the Han as permanent migrants, which had worked so well
to harness Inner Mongolia to the Chinese base of the state, had been
rejected by Beijing as being unsuitable for the cultural preserve it
wanted Manchuria to be. The loss of Outer Manchuria, however,
seemed to jar the Qing into setting aside this concern. In 1860, they
had begun to allow Han settlement as far north as Harbin. Hoping to

create a large and permanent population that would make Russian influence hard to increase, the Qing found this newly opened territory an easy sell, with many impoverished farmers more than happy to escape the tight state controls of China proper for at least the opportunity that Manchuria represented. The first effect of this migration, aside from a regional population increase of somewhere in the millions, was a breakdown in the quality of the Manchu soldiers recruited under the banner system. The second was that despite the settlement, central authority seemed not to take.

This movement of population did scare Russia however. The newly constructed city of Vladivostok was vulnerable, and the population of this new eastern maritime branch of Siberia was far smaller than that of Manchuria. In what became a familiar refrain toward its easternmost flank, Russia responded to Chinese migration to Manchuria by beginning construction on the Trans-Siberian Railroad in the 1880s. The Pacific would be brought within Russia's sphere of mobility just as Central Asia was starting to be.[25]

The weakness and potential wealth of Manchuria was apparent to the resource-poor yet rapidly industrializing Japanese, but the expansion and hegemonic strength of Russia threatened to grab any concessions the faltering Qing state might give. Furthermore, the Qing still held delusions of their own primacy in East Asia, particularly their vassalage of Korea, where a new internal faction of nationalists that advocated breaking Qing control and allying with Japan was being persecuted by the pro-Qing government. The time to act had come. With its modernized army and navy, Japan would dislodge China from its increasingly obsolete privileged regional position.[26]

In 1894, a Japanese-backed coup overthrew the Korean regime. The Qing marched to war against Japan to restore their hegemony on the peninsula. In a quick series of engagements, the Chinese fleet was crippled at sea and its armies put to a succession of defeats on land by the smaller but tactically and technologically superior Japanese forces. Beijing and the only maritime part of Manchuria, Port Arthur, were captured, and the true weakness of the Qing state was exposed to a far greater extent than even the Opium Wars had shown. In the Treaty of Shimonoseki (1895), China renounced influence over Korea. It also ceded to Japan Taiwan, the Pescadores, and the southern part of the Liaotung Peninsula of Manchuria (named for the river valley that was the center of the Liao Dynasty), and it had to pay a large indemnity.[27]

This forced China open like never before, and all the European powers clambered for naval-base concessions. Japan was a bit too nearby for comfort, though, and France, Germany, and above all Russia forced Japan to relinquish its gains in Manchuria in the Triple Intervention. Now the Eurasian hegemon saw its chance to move into Inner Manchuria and complete its conquest of the central inland routes of the continent. The expert Russian diplomat Sergei Witte finagled many concessions from the Qing in exchange for getting the Japanese to back out of Liaotung.[28] Most important was the takeover of the Port Arthur concession and the right to build railways throughout Manchuria connecting that ice-free Pacific port directly to the Trans-Siberian Railroad.[29]

All these foreign concessions enraged the Chinese. Already nationalists like Sun Yat-sen were blaming the "alien tyranny" of the Manchus for China's inability to adapt to industrial civilization like Japan had. Attempts by Han bureaucrats to reform the system met with derision from the court, and the dowager empress Tzu-Hsi removed many of them from office and even tacitly supported the anti-foreign mob violence that broke out, which is known to posterity as the Boxer Rebellion. The rebellion was crushed by the multinational force assembled to relieve the besieged foreign garrisons. Most tellingly, the largest contingents of foreign forces were the Russians and the Japanese. The empress was forced to concede defeat, and China had to give out yet more crippling concessions. Most critically for the fate of the upcoming struggles for Eurasian hegemony was that using their new railways, one hundred fifty thousand Russian soldiers came to occupy Manchuria, all but officially detaching it from Qing rule. Meanwhile, Outer Mongolia was becoming a vacuum devoid of all but nominal Qing authority, and Russian traders and diplomatic personnel were penetrating this more-inland frontier, if in a less direct way than Manchuria.[30]

Finally, Russian armies achieved two notable objectives in the history of the Formless Empire. They started to infiltrate the homeland of their former Mongol conquerors, and they finally achieved what the Cossacks had failed to do in the seventeenth century in the occupation of Manchuria. But if Qing weakness had enabled this advance, Japanese strength now checked it. Japan saw how the power to gain most from its war with China had in fact been the Russian Empire, and now it sought to redress the balance. Britain, the other littoral intruder, felt much the same, and so in 1902, an Anglo-Japanese alliance was formed to break up the overwhelming land power of the Russian Empire. Now the two sea-based nations were balancing against the inland hegemon that kept much of Eurasia clamped down under its rule.[31]

Japan demanded that Russia cease interfering in Korea and withdraw from its massive deployment into Manchuria. Russia, confident in its position yet also insecure about its still relatively recent gains in maritime Siberia owing to Japan's rising power, refused in 1903. The reasons for this refusal, according to S. C. M. Paine, echo not just with the geostrategic thought of this era in Russian history but of the cumulative experience Russia had acquired since turning the tide on the Kipchak Khanate at the Battle of Kulikovo:

> Russia faced unique national security problems. Historically, its expansion had been the elusive quest for defensible borders largely absent on the great plains of Russia. But expansion created only very long and remote borders that proved extremely costly to defend. Enormous funds had to be funneled away from the civilian economy to defend the empire.

An empire approaching the size of Mongolia was much harder for even a semi-industrial society to keep hold of if it was a centralized and sedentary state. No matter the lessons learned from nomadic peoples and the success of the state in expansion, the cracks of the industrial era were starting to appear. Fear of the exposed frontiers of Primorye meant that even if Russia had wanted to evacuate Manchuria, it could not, at least in its way of geopolitical thinking. And so the stage was set. Japan began to plan to evict Russia before it added Manchuria to its ever-growing empire. In fact, over the course of the fifty years from the Treaty of Shimonoseki to Japanese surrender in the Second World War in 1945, a colossal proportion of Japanese foreign policy was aimed, directly or indirectly, at imperial and Soviet Russia. The first stage of this proxy war started with the Sino-Japanese War, and from 1904 on, it became a much more obvious battle for supremacy in eastern Eurasia. It was almost a precursor to US Cold War containment policy, and it was far more influential for the evolution of the Formless Empire.[32]

While Russia's navy was defeated in the Battle of the Yellow Sea and the decisive Battle of Tsushima (1905), its army received a series of defeats on land that crippled much of its offensive fighting power. Tellingly, all the land battles took place in Manchuria proper. The war ended with the 1905 Treaty of Portsmouth, in which Russia agreed to evacuate southern Manchuria, cease all interference with Korea, cede its lease on the Liaotung Peninsula to Japan, and cede its territory on the southern half of Sakhalin Island. Both sides became suspicious, however, that the arbitrating United States was playing them off of each other for its own interest. They suspected, rightly or wrongly, that the Americans wished to apply the Open Door policy they advocated for China proper to Manchuria via an American railroad magnate given permission to construct lines through the area by the Qing. So just a few years after their war, Russia and Japan began to collaborate on barring any influence from outside powers. Soon the private railroad scheme was blocked by both powers using legal methods, and Manchuria was regarded as a split venture, north and south. In exchange for Russia's many concessions in the war, Japan guaranteed that it would respect the de facto control Russia increasingly had over Mongolia.[33]

Both powers, having found a rough regional balance of power for the moment, now turned back to dividing their primary prey. The faltering Qing were no more popular in their traditional home-base frontier provinces than in China proper. As Japan's south Manchurian railway jurisdiction connected the resources of Manchuria to Korea (annexed to Japan in 1910), it began to create jobs and opportunity. Immigration from China proper increased, swelling the new cities of the region with Han workers. In a decade the population swelled from 9 million to 20 million, mostly Han, and traditional Manchu culture began to fade.[34]

Meanwhile, the Russians, left only with their northern toehold on Manchuria, refocused on the comparative backwater of Mongolia. After centuries of suffering at the hands of Chinese merchants, the Mongols welcomed the Russian merchants and diplomatic officers with open arms. There were very few Mongols, and even the tottering Qing state was still a behemoth oppressor, so the connections and potential assistance of the Russians were most welcome. These connections paid off in 1912, when—finally overwhelmed by internal rebellion and lack of legitimacy in the face of foreign concessions—the Qing state crumbled. The six-year-old emperor, Pu Yi, was dethroned as head of state and a republic proclaimed. Mongolia seized its chance by declaring its independence and driving the few Chinese troops stationed in the region out with weapons supplied by the Russians. No one recognized the independence of Mongolia, including Russia, and the authority of the spiritual leader (or bogd khan) was ineffectual outside the immediate area of that land's only city, Urga (present-day Ulaanbaatar). Russia was now compensated in former Qing space, if not in wealth and potential, for its losses in Manchuria.[35]

In this period of complete loss, indeed, the very end of the Qing Dynasty, China had one qualified victory. British attempts to do much the same to Tibet as Russia had done to Mongolia met decidedly mixed success. While the British expedition was able to set up some amount of administrative control over Tibet, the push inward made the Tibetans at large turn closer to, rather than further from, China.[36]

The Republic of China was as fractious as a supposedly unified state could be without totally collapsing. It was rife with internal division based on ideology and located in the south of the country, while warlords controlled the northern and western areas, Han and frontier alike. The country became pregnant with Japanese spy rings and patronage networks centered on certain amenable warlords. Russians, too, infiltrated as advisers for various warlords, if to a lesser extent. The proxy war for hegemony of eastern Eurasia was revving up to start again. The most effective intrusion was the Japanese influence over Marshal Zhang Zuolin, who set up his power base in Manchuria. Seeing this as an opportunity to gain the rest of the province, the Japanese went about making themselves Zhang's patron power. His relative success in holding onto his Manchurian fiefdom was helped, rather than hindered, by the Japanese-controlled railroads (territorial concessions following the track line that were considered the sovereign property of Japan) crisscrossing the land.[37]

Russia had little time to gloat over the collapse of its huge and long-term epic rival. Nor could it properly prepare for the coming storm of conflict over the carcass of the former Qing Empire when crisis brewed on other fronts. The doom of imperial Russia did not come from the east or Central Asia, but rather from its supposedly more fixed and stable western borders. This, of course, was the First World War. While Japan and Russia participated on the same side, it was a total war for the latter and light naval operation for the former. While Japan took the German concession port of Qingdao and some Pacific Islands, Russia fought desperately for its very survival against the armies of the Ottomans, Austro-Hungarians, and above all, Germans, sustaining massive losses. The epic collapse of 1917 was as much a shock to the regions of Inner Eurasia as had been the fall of the Qing, except that the echoes of this fall, being that of a great power rather than one that had been in terminal decline for almost a century, resounded over a much larger territory. Revolts had broken out in Russian Central Asia because of the burdens of taxation and conscription caused by the war. Russia had therefore taken direct control over its vassal khanates in Transoxiana. However, this occurred just twenty-nine days before the fall of the ruling government in Saint Petersburg.[38]

With the October Revolution and the subsequent Bolshevik coup, many parts of the Russian Empire sheared off into de facto independence, either under warlords or regional movements. Just as Russia had once aspired to be as powerful as China and ended up surpassing it in size and influence, so now did Russia follow China's political disintegration by surpassing the chaos and destruction that the latter's revolution had caused the state. Because of the massive size of the empire, we need not concern ourselves with every front between anticommunist White Russia and Bolshevik Red Russia; what matters most are the two fronts most directly connected to the geographic scope of this strategic overview, Siberia and Central Asia.

Both Siberia and Central Asia were remote from the core of the old state, and the new Soviet state controlled only the central urban belt of its predecessor, and at first that was tenuous too. Siberia had been politically free, by Russian standards, under the tsars; now, in a time of Bolshevik domination of the center of Russia's economic and cultural regions, this sparsely populated and resource-rich region was the largest bastion of the White movement. Cossacks (who fought overwhelmingly for the Whites on the Ukrainian steppes as well) and Czech forces (who had fought for the Russians against the Austro-Hungarians and become stranded in Russia because of the civil war) held the area in relative independence by controlling the only reliable route of ingress and egress, the Trans-Siberian Railroad. Equipped with heavy-artillery-toting armored trains backed up by cavalry forces, Siberia had the chance, however briefly, to go its own way.

White anti-Bolshevik forces gathered loosely in Siberia under the banner of Admiral Alexander Kolchak, and the Allies of the still-raging First World War came to assist them under the pretense of rescuing the stranded Czech soldiers and securing weapons from the Reds. It is telling that the Allied power that contributed the most time, money, troops, and effort to this enterprise was none other than the Japanese Empire.[39]

It was the Allied supreme commander, Marshal Ferdinand Foch who thought of the idea of using Japanese troops to effectively reopen the eastern front against Germany. Seeing the daunting task of sending entire armies across the thickest east-west axis of Eurasia amid the chaos of the enfolding Russian civil war, Japanese leaders asked for a high price for such an action—in effect total domination of Manchuria and de facto influence over far eastern Siberia, including the demilitarization of Vladivostok. After evaluating the various logistical and political difficulties, the Allies decided on a more scaled-down intervention. As Richard Ullman summarizes, "There was no greater possibility of 'open conflict' between the Japanese and the Germans than there was that Germany would ship dismantled submarines from the Baltic to Vladivostok."[40]

Despite the scaled-back objectives from the dreams of Allied board rooms, however, Japan had ambitions of its own in the region.

What was originally supposed to be a joint occupation of Vladivostok with the Americans rapidly escalated into an opportunistic—if poorly planned—attempt to wring as many concessions from Siberia as possible. The pretext for this rampant increase of involvement from Japan was the Bolshevik government in the west renouncing the agreements that the state had previously made with various powers, including Japan. Contemporary international law professor Ninakawa Arata put it bluntly: "Now that China is helpless and Russia on the verge of disintegration, Japan has no formidable rival."

The objectives of Japan in this intervention were familiar to the traditional geopolitics of the region and bore some similarity to how nomadic peoples once oriented their policies. Officially, no territory was directly annexed to the Japanese state; rather, the military provided a bulwark for administrators and above all local proxies to reorient the eastern region of Siberia toward Japan's economic needs while retaining a large degree of domestic autonomy under local rulers. Even with the conclusion of the First World War and the ebbing of the threat of German occupation and resource acquisition in Russia, the number of Japanese troops in Siberia was only barely scaled down, and they still ranged as far west as Irkutsk to secure the flank of Admiral Kolchak's regime and were in solid control of the Trans-Siberian Railroad (with reluctant American assistance). From Vladivostok, weapons and advisers flowed west, and from Irkutsk and through Primorye, plans were made to have resources and markets flow east.[41]

The problem was that Japan had little experience in this type of policy. Manchurian railways aside, all its territorial acquisitions had been through annexation and direct control. Most lacking in its strategy was the instinct for choosing reliable allies who could deliver more than short-term results. This was most telling in the particular warlords Japan found itself in bed with east of Kolchak's direct control.

General Grigori Semenov was a product of Siberia if ever there was one. Half native Buryat and half Cossack in ancestry, he had been active in the prewar operations to funnel weapons and support to the Mongolian independence movement in 1912. He had distinguished himself as a cavalry raider behind German lines on the Baltic front of the war and later had served successfully in the Caucasus against the

Ottoman Empire. Now he was effectively a Cossack chieftain in eastern Siberia, along with a "court" of advisers, many Japanese.[42]

Unlike Kolchak, based in Omsk, and then, when that fell to the Bolsheviks, Irkutsk, Semenov was not interested in setting up much of an official government and preferred raiding and looting no matter people's political inclinations. Receiving a generous paycheck from the Japanese, he and his followers established themselves as wealthy and violent raiders, though not much else. It is worth noting, however, that this mobile raiding band did keep the Soviets at bay longer than might be expected, and it was made up of a relatively diverse group of peoples. Waves of migration, mobile cavalry columns, and logistics backed up by armed and armored trains returned the fluid geopolitics of nomadic and Cossack-style power to the region, if at least temporarily and with gross abuses by an unloved despot. In addition, taking over Semenov and putting him directly in the Japanese pocket took him away from the potential of being influenced by the other allies, making him a reliable proxy. Among the people of Siberia, a new term arose that became all too familiar: *atamanschchina*—the rule of terror by Japanese-backed warlords.[43]

Despite these positive echoes of traditional Inner Eurasian strategy, the edifice crumbled almost immediately when the Japanese withdrew their support and Semenov fled to Manchuria. They had failed to maintain long-lasting networks of cooperation or wield influence indirectly. Admiral Kolchak himself commented to his British advisers in 1919 that it was Japanese policy to support a number of weak Russian forces rather than back a single strong opposition leader—like himself, one presumes. The White movement was effectively undermined by its largest outside backer. British support for Kolchak was effectively undermined by this Japanese backing of rogue warlords through armaments and paying the salaries of their Mongol troops.[44]

By the early 1920s, support was flagging for what became known in Japan as the Siberian Intervention. Kolchak's attempts to hold off the Soviets collapsed, and he was executed as Bolsheviks marched on Irkutsk. No overt advance occurred into the Pacific maritime area owing to Japanese occupation, for the Bolsheviks figured leaving it as a buffer for the time being would encourage Japan to depart rather than engage in further escalation. They were correct. Burdened by the cost and the meager returns, Japan began a phased withdrawal from the region of Primorye. The Far Eastern Republic, a detached autonomous entity based around Vladivostok and the eastern part of the Trans-Siberian Railroad that had grown under their protection, did, in fact, develop a regional economy oriented toward the Japanese, but it knew the writing was on the wall and hoped to negotiate a phased integration into the Soviet Union in 1922. Therefore, it asked the United States to pressure Japan to complete its scheduled withdrawal as fast as possible.[45]

Japan was only happy to comply at this point, after four years of fruitless guerrilla war and an obvious lack of gaining any foothold that could survive its inevitable pullout. In exchange for speeding up its timetable, it did manage to wring out a few concessions, such as Allied willingness to look the other way as it shifted its Eurasian arms and spying rings south to Manchuria and received acknowledgment of freedom of action from the other powers with its much more potentially lucrative Manchurian proxy, Zhang Zuolin.[46] The Whites who had demanded the withdrawal were taken aback by how suddenly the pullout came once these guarantees were assured and absorption by the Soviets became a given.[47] But before this withdrawal was completed, Japan used Siberia to stage one more operation, this time directed not toward the Bolsheviks but the Chinese.

The Russian Revolution had opened the way for China to finally strike back against all the concessions of the previous century. With the recall of Russian troops from Mongolia, Chinese soldiers soon entered the country and proclaimed it to be back under the control of their state. Soon, republican troops of the Kuomintang, or Nationalist Party, were making Mongols kowtow to them publicly in the traditional imperial act of submission.[48]

A protégé of Semenov's (who was himself now preparing a retreat for exile in Manchuria), Roman von Ungern-Sternberg, was organizing an attack on the Chinese in Mongolia. He was a Baltic German-Russian nobleman who had seen service in the First World War, where he had met Semenov. Violently unstable, virulently anti-Semitic and anticommunist, and with delusions of restoring the Mongol Empire with himself as khan while riding to Moscow in a sea of blood across

Eurasia, he was probably not the most ideal proxy for the Japanese to use. Nonetheless, many Japanese officers and soldiers covertly joined the multiethnic force of this seemingly up-and-coming "Mad Baron," as his enemies dubbed him. This force included mercenaries of all types, White Russians, a few Chinese, and at its core Mongolians. All his Russian officers were required to learn Mongolian to communicate with their troops. This force set out south of eastern Siberia for Mongolia in 1921.[49]

After a few failures at dislodging the Chinese from Urga, Ungern-Sternberg finally took the city by storm, perpetrating a truly Mongol-style sack and pillage to the only city in Outer Mongolia. The bogd khan was freed of his house arrest and made the spiritual head of a once-again independent Mongolia. The remaining Chinese broke and were ruthlessly captured and killed out on the steppe by the Mongol cavalry. Now the reign of terror began as Ungern-Sternberg publicly executed and tortured anyone perceived to be plotting against him, while he seized the livestock of the locals.[50] The liberator of the Mongols had become their tormentor in a short time, and many Mongols fled northwest to Bolshevik lines to join up with Soviet allied partisans under Damdin Sukhbaatar, a Mongolian independence fighter trained by the Russians before the First World War.[51]

The central government of the Republic of China ordered the warlord Zhang Zuolin to march west and remove the baron before the Bolsheviks did. But Zhang was a Japanese proxy, so he was content to take the money the government set aside for the cost of the expedition and open diplomatic channels with Ungern-Sternberg. To his credit, Zhang did try to bribe the baron to leave Mongolia, but this offer was refused.

Ungern-Sternberg decided he could not wait for the Soviet counterattack and drove northwest to meet his enemies in a preemptive campaign. In a series of cavalry battles, the baron found himself outmaneuvered by Sukhbaatar's Red Mongols and Bolshevik allies, who used traditional false retreat and ambush tactics against him in ways reminiscent of the thirteenth-century behavior of Mongol armies.[52]

The baron was driven back once, returned to initial success the second time, but was finally defeated in detail by Soviet reinforcements using aircraft. While the Mad Baron was trapped fighting against the inevitable in Siberia, Sukhbaatar's Red Mongols drove into Mongolia proper, taking over the regime and setting up the Mongolian People's Republic, the second country in the world to become officially communist.[53]

Abandoned and wounded by his men after they failed to kill him by raking his tent with machine-gun fire, and wearing nothing but a jacket and multiple shamanic talismans, Ungern-Sternberg escaped into the steppe, only to be captured and bound by Mongol herders seeking revenge. He was left tied up with his face in an ant hill until found by a Soviet patrol. Taken to Novosibirsk, he was tried for counterrevolutionary activities, denied none of the charges, and was summarily executed.[54]

Mongolia had now been detached from China (even if China would not admit it until after the Second World War), though clearly not in a way that favored Japan, as was intended by Ungern-Sternberg's financial backers in Tokyo. As a price for its assistance, the Soviet Union annexed the Tuva Republic from Mongolia's northern borders, and few in Mongolia proper questioned that they had traded one neighbor's domination for another's, even if they were now officially independent. After the death of Sukhbaatar, his successor, Choibalsan, working closely with Soviet leader Joseph Stalin (the successor of Vladimir Lenin), was an infamous lapdog for Moscow. The bogd khan ceased to have any relevance, and he died soon after these events with no proclaimed heir to the office. Furthermore, the assets of the extremely powerful Buddhist monastic system set up by the Qing to tame the Mongols were seized by the state, and it lost its influence in society.[55]

Japan had managed to squeeze concessions in northern Manchuria and mineral rights on northern Sakhalin from its Siberian ordeal and finally pulled troops out of its last Russian bastion on that island in 1925. But it had failed to gain a foothold in either Siberia or Mongolia. Manchuria was always the richest prize by far, however, and so by the standards of a new littoral power entering the hinterland of Eurasia, this was a qualified success made possible by the temporary collapse of both traditional regional hegemons. It was enough to make Japan begin to plan a bid for the whole region. But before we get ahead of ourselves, it is time to examine the other front of Russian collapse and revival, Central Asia.

Russia and China lost immense influence and relative power to Japan in the eastern extremities of Eurasia, but both countries, and in particular Russia, tenaciously held onto their hard-won gains in Central Asia.

The Russian Revolution and the Bolshevik takeover left a vacuum in Central Asia, where the local khanates carefully plotted either a return to independence or a way to gain back more of their former autonomy. Nearby Bolshevik takeovers seemed to show how little they were willing to accommodate former imperial Russian clients on the basis of ethnicity or culture. Thus the revolutionary forces seemed even more a threat to domestic autonomy than the old government had. In response, Bukhara declared that it would mobilize its army and refuse to nationalize property or banks within its jurisdiction. Bolshevik attacks south to dislodge the troublesome emir initially failed.[56]

The Soviets, reeling from the loss of so much territory to the Germans and embattled on every front even when the First World War ended, needed desperately to shore up their southern flank, especially because British involvement had become more noticeable since the collapse of the former government. The British entered in 1918 under the pretext of keeping Germans out of the region but stayed to support various anti-Bolshevik fighters and to flood the emirates with spies.

A fascinating example of spying in the fractured situation was the experience of British colonel John Bailey, who infiltrated Soviet-occupied cities in Central Asia and sent back (often intercepted) dispatches of troop movements and political changes to British intelligence agents in Afghanistan and India. Captured by the Cheka secret police, he was placed in prison, where he adopted the customs and dress of the Austro-Hungarian prisoners there and managed eventually to pass himself off as one of them. When the Bolshevik armistice was declared with the Central Powers of Germany, Austria-Hungary, and the Ottoman Empire, Bailey was released. He then realized that Britain would not intervene directly in the region and so resolved to flee. Still masquerading as a released Austro-Hungarian prisoner, he presented himself to the Cheka as willing to help it infiltrate British spy networks along the Afghan-Soviet border. Having been reported missing and presumed escaped from prison, he even said he would hunt himself down. He was given papers to pass the checkpoint and money, and he managed to escape back to British India. Thus we see that in such a crisis-laden situation, Britain, too, could produce its own agents of Formless Empire in Central Asia. [57]

The Soviets needed a local base in the region to overcome the logistical disadvantages of operating there and the potential of British troops crossing the border, so they turned to the old imperial stronghold in the region, Tashkent. It was reinforced, secured, and set up as the regional base for all Soviet operations in Central Asia. Because the original Soviet governor had attempted to defect to the Whites and set himself up as a regional warlord, the government was adamant that the city be well garrisoned and secure. This fortress city would pay back dividends on the investment placed into making it Red Russia's forward base in the region. Control of Central Asia was going to become far more direct than ever.

Soon the emirates were cowed and dismantled. The Communist Party coordinated rebellions in Bukhara and Khiva that then invited in Soviet troops as liberators. By the early 1920s, the base at Tashkent had sent forth a variety of campaigns that brought all former Russian territory and clients in Central Asia under Soviet control. With its newfound direct power, the government issued collectivization orders, which sparked guerrilla-style rebellions in the rural hinterland. This type of war was more challenging to the regime than the reconquest of the region's cities were, so it turned for help to Enver Pasha, the former de facto ruler of the now-defunct Ottoman Empire who was living in exile in the Soviet Union. Enver gained the loyalty of coethnic Turkic peoples for the Soviets in exchange for them backing him to return to power in what was now the Republic of Turkey.

Once he was in the field, however, Enver double-crossed his patrons and became the leader of what was known as the Basmachi Rebellion. He led raids of Soviet supply lines and received the endorsement of the deposed former emir of Bukhara. Under Enver's leadership, the rebellion was soon able to take towns and small cities and occupy them. Equipped with an entourage of veteran Ottoman officers, weapons imported from Afghanistan, and a German-style staff system, he represented the most dangerous threat the Soviets had yet faced in the region. Only in 1922, when all fronts except Siberia had died down for the Bolsheviks, did the state scrounge up the massive force it needed to defeat Enver in a decisive campaign. His armies disintegrating after a series of engagements with this new Soviet army, Enver and his few remaining followers launched a suicidal cavalry attack on the enemy line. They died in a hail of bullets near the Afghan border.[58]

The new state of the Soviets had triumphed. It had retained Central Asia and increased the power of central state authority there. Though it took a much more direct form of control over the region than imperial Russia had, which led to such problems as the Basmachi Rebellion, it had learned how to use the railways and the value of rapid mobility and deployment. It was the inheritor of imperial Russia in more ways than one. It even kept the language of local autonomy, if not the practice, by declaring that it would create nation-states in Central Asia that reflected the indigenous character of the places. This was a show for an audience abroad, however, as the states were well integrated into the party system based in Moscow. The national states themselves, being based on ethnicity, were nothing at all akin to the multiethnic and fluid norm of indigenous Central Asian states. And so it seemed that by 1924, the last echoes of the indigenous formless geopolitics of the region had died.[59]

Soviet rule, with its ultramodernist tendencies, was far more akin to Western European-style direct colonialism than was the rule of imperial Russia or any regional predecessor. For example, Soviet rule included travel restrictions and forced education in the colonizer's tongue. All other changes in Eurasian geopolitics before this point were far more gradual; this new era was quite an abrupt change of course.[60]

If the fluid ambiguity that characterized Inner Eurasia had gone into remission in Central Asia, it now resurfaced in a place where it first had been extinguished: Xinjiang. The death of Chinese revolutionary leader Sun Yat-sen opened the way for his successor, Chiang Kai-shek, under whom the government took a far right turn. The republic, known for its corruption, was becoming increasingly unpopular in the frontier provinces, and soon a young warlord known as Ma Zhongying, or "Young Ma," seized the area of Xinjiang for his own control and made moves toward turning it back into a pre-Qing Turkistan. The whole area of northwest China and Xinjiang was run by a series of warlords with the title *ma* (shorthand for *Muhammad*), and all were Muslim Hui people sharpened by struggle with both communist and Tibetan tribal foes. Young Ma, however, was not interested in loyalty to the republic and sought his own Muslim kingdom.[61]

At the time of Ma's usurping of the region, the central government was busy with its Northern Expedition, a giant military advance from the republic's base in the south into the domains of the northern warlords. Though it took his eye off of Central Asia, Chiang's bold move abolished the independence of the northern warlords during its two years of operation (1926–28). The Soviet Union, seeking allies for any future conflict with Japan, backed Chiang and his wobbly coalition with Chinese communists, and began to support the Chinese republic with weapons. The most powerful warlord, Zhang Zuolin (whose astute governance had actually paid off all regional debts and created an economic boom in Manchuria), was expected by the Japanese to stop the Nationalist advance with their support.

Owing to his numerous wars of conquest however, the once strong regional economy was beginning to falter, as was his military machine. When he was defeated outside Beijing by Nationalists, he had outlived his usefulness and was assassinated by Japanese agents who bombed his personal train. Thinking his eldest son, an opium addict, would be a more pliable replacement, Japan moved to install Zhang Xueliang as leader of Manchuria. This backfired because the son took an even more independent path from his father, executing several Japanese advisers publicly and trying to gain close ties to foreign powers such as the United States. Xueliang soon after publicly declared his support for unification under the Kuomintang government of Chiang Kai-shek. Altogether, the Northern Expedition was a resounding success that shored up Chiang's base. Brimming with confidence, he broke with his communist allies and initiated a general purge of great violence within the party and throughout the country. The Soviet Union balked at the display of treachery and withdrew its support. Chiang prepared to turn west and finally bring Xinjiang under full government control.[62]

The Soviet Union needed its own warlord in Xinjiang. Large numbers of nomadic peoples had migrated from Soviet Central Asia to Xinjiang to escape forced collectivization and were seen as potential threats by the paranoid Stalin. Young Ma was rejected as a fanatic likely to whip up sectarian strife throughout Turkestan if allowed to become too powerful. More dangerous, from the Soviet perspective, than the specter of Muslim revolts were Ma's increasingly apparent contacts with Japanese intelligence. If Ma became an ally or proxy of the Japanese, that would effectively put the critically important Baku oil fields within range of Japanese bombers. Thus the Soviets decided to collaborate with Sheng Shicai, the Kuomintang general sent west by Chiang Kai-shek to restore control of the province. They could remove Young Ma and turn the Kuomintang victory against the Republic of China in one go.[63]

What happened next showed that the Soviet Union was indeed developing its tactical doctrine in line with the new technology of the times as well as the tried-and-true methods of formless geopolitics, even if they no longer practiced those doctrines in Soviet Central Asia proper. Governor Sheng's army (made up of almost as many White Russian Cossacks in exile as Chinese) advanced west into Xinjiang, while a Soviet force wearing no insignia or national emblems crossed the border from the west heading east. Between these armies, Young Ma's horsemen were massacred. Soviet armored cars and strafing planes, having taken up the role of the mounted archers in the twentieth century, decimated the Muslim horsemen. Ma disappeared, likely into Soviet captivity. Sheng seized control of Xinjiang in 1933, ostensibly for the Kuomintang, but in effect he had signed a secret treaty with the Soviets in exchange for their support. This treaty made him clear all his policies with the Soviets first and turned Xinjiang into a puppet protectorate for the Soviet Union, not unlike what Manchuria had officially become for Japan two years earlier (*see map 7*).[64]

The already quite extensive sway held by the Japanese over Manchuria was under threat by the unexpectedly independent posture of the new warlord, Zhang Xueliang. In addition, the stock market crash of 1929 had placed great pressures on resource-poor Japan, which lacked the space and materials for an expansion of heavy industry. The railway concessions were no longer enough; a more absolute hegemony needed to be established.[65]

Though a settled, littoral, and agrarian power, Japan took a page from the book of Eurasian migrations in its plans to harness the eastern edge of Inner Eurasia to its empire. It would be a frontier space for disgruntled and impoverished farmers coming from Japan. Mass migration would tie the region absolutely to the empire. Already, Manchuria contained many foreign migrants who would likely support the construction of a new non-Chinese state—the virulently anticommunist White Russian émigré community being the most politically significant. In addition to immigrants, the dwindling numbers of Manchurians still lived in what once was their exclusive domain.[66]

On September 19, 1931, after staging a bombing of the Mantetsu railway, the Kwantung army (the division of the Imperial Japanese Army responsible for operations north of Korea) began an invasion of Manchuria. This was done without orders from the civilian government, but the nation soon capitalized on the opportunity the semi-rogue army had given them. Within a few months the entire region was under Japanese control, save a few pockets of bandits and communist guerrillas out on the frontiers. A lightning campaign by a quick-moving foe (the Japanese army had armored cars, light tanks, and cavalry of its own) had overcome larger enemy forces to establish control in Eurasia. This was a familiar story, except this time the aggressor was an alien naval power. The regime set up in Manchuria showed that the Japanese had learned from their earlier experiences of qualified failures in Siberia and Mongolia.[67]

Cooperation with locals, especially elites, became a key factor in the making of what was passed off as a new state, a homeland for the Manchus named Manchukuo. The new state was officially proclaimed in 1932, and local merchants and affluent settlers were brought into the government as well as White Russian exiles. The exiled former emperor, Pu Yi, was invited to become monarch of the new state and was installed as emperor of Manchukuo.

Immediately, massive investments were transferred to the country from Japan. Heavy and general industrial output soon reached parity with homeland, investments were returned two or three-fold, and the Manchukuo yuan reached parity with the Japanese yen by 1937. Most of the world did not recognize the Manchukuo yuan, just as the state itself was not recognized. Indeed, Japan had left the League of Nations in protest of the condemnation of the world powers to its invasion of Manchuria in the first place. Investment in Manchukuo was opened up to powers that did recognize the state, and companies used their profits to pursue diversification. Profits from various industrial projects often were reinvested in the massive soybean and fishing sectors. To shore up the still-ambiguous borders with the Soviet Union, these job opportunities were often used to get Japanese farmers to settle near the borders of the state to provide a bulwark as well as frontier economic integration with the now-booming cities of Harbin and Mukden.[68]

Meanwhile, in addition to its disproportionate wealth growth through trade compared to China proper, this puppet state's cultural development began to bear certain similarities to its geographic forebear, the Liao Dynasty. Though it didn't have a rotating capital system, and the government was not based in tents, it did straddle the lines between ethnicities, state building, imperialism, and consciously trying to retain a separate identity from China despite the largest single group of people being Han Chinese. Most interesting in the context of the past of Manchuria was the attempt to preserve the way of life of what hunter-gatherers and nomads the state had left. Connections were drawn up between Siberian shamanism and Manchurian folklore and the traditional Japanese religion of Shintoism. The forests of Manchuria were protected by an extensive conservation program, and Pu Yi was declared to have been reborn through the Japanese goddess Amaterasu. Shintoism became one of the state religions of Manchukuo, even though it had no followers outside the Kwantung army and the Japanese settler community.[69]

The most striking example of the formless identity of this state was Kawashima Yoshiko, born into the royal family of the Qing and

Nurhaci as Aisin Gioro Xianyu. An extended relative of Pu Yi, Kawashima had been brought up in Japan and used by that nation's intelligence service as a valuable spy in the region. She had briefly married the leader of the Inner Mongolian independence movement, who was also a pawn in Japanese plots to carve apart China into vassal states. After the invasion of Manchuria, she moved to the new region that her extended family was ostensibly now the head of state of. She was a spy and, once she became famous enough to have her cover blown, an outright antiguerrilla leader in the less secure parts of the kingdom. In a fitting last gasp for the Manchurian Qing royal family, she led a force of cavalry recruits made up of Manchus, Chinese, and Mongolians in operations against both communist bands and bandits. Once the pacification of the countryside was largely complete, she became a public personality in the state, recording radio broadcasts and even her own songs.[70]

With the outbreak of full-scale war in China proper in 1937, however, the Kwantung army was put in charge of raising funds for operations. It did this by becoming a patron of the opium market, which was aggressively aimed at the Chinese population. Events like this and many others caused a local backlash, as the booming economy of Manchukuo was harnessed more and more to Japan's ever outwardly spiraling wars. These changes drove the former intelligence, military, and propaganda asset Kawashima Yoshiko to become sharply critical of the direction of the regime. As a result of these criticisms, she was soon sidelined by her erstwhile patrons.[71] With her effective silencing, the last flame of Qing pride and defiance was snuffed out, and any pretense that Manchukuo was an independent nation and partner with the Japanese Empire was gone.

Still, the state was remarkably good at keeping most of the populace loyal and productive, using—in the social sphere at least—a relatively hands-off approach. Japan had learned much about dealing with the geopolitics of Inner Eurasia. These lessons were soon repeated with the creation of Mengjiang, effectively a Manchukuo for Inner Mongolia also containing its own royal family, military units, and the like. It is likely that had Japan been a victorious power in the Second World War, many regions of China, if not all of it, would have been organized in this fashion. A model of indirect control was exported to Southeast Asia after Japan's massive maritime conquests in 1942, though its execution was often haphazardly carried out.[72]

While Japan was honing its political acumen to deal with the region, its long string of military victories had made it complacent. In comparison, various struggles to survive and military setbacks had made the Soviet Union the new regional vanguard of military innovation. Indirect administration is a core value to running a Formless Empire successfully, but it is only half of the equation; the other half is a rapid mobile military that emphasizes speed and firepower. Though Japan's conquest of Manchuria may have fit this description, it was nothing compared to the evolution of the Soviet Union's military doctrine since the end of the Russian civil war, but this disparity would not become clear to either power until both had tested themselves against each other.

A shockingly overlooked battle, from a historical perspective, occurred in the very birthplace of the Formless Empire that sounded the end of the infantry armies that had come to dominate Inner Eurasia and give the large settled states that now controlled it the one weapon that made them as flexible and potent a force as the Mongols had been in the thirteenth century: the wholly mechanized army. It came as the long and cold indirect struggle for hegemony between Russia and Japan flashed hot in 1939, and it was one of the most important battles in the history of the evolution of Eurasian battle tactics.[73]

The Soviet Union had begun to clamp down on the notoriously porous Siberian frontier and seemed willing to placate Japan on most issues for some time. This led the Japanese to assume it was weak, so they adopted a belligerent posture. As the British ambassador to Moscow quipped in 1934, "Soviet-Japanese relations are good, but Japanese-Soviet relations are not so good."

Stalin's current army purge did not help the perception that the giant nation was a paper tiger. Sensing imminent liquidation, General Genrikh Lyushkov, a high-level commander of the Soviet secret police known as the NKVD, defected across the Primorye-Manchukuo border to the Japanese in 1937. The information he gave them on parts of the disputed border led a Japanese force to launch a night attack into Siberia that killed or captured all Soviet units on a disputed hill.

The Soviet army in the region, owing to inept handling, as its upper ranks had been purged, launched a series of clumsy counterattacks to retake the hill. For days the armies battled, and despite having much larger numbers and more artillery, the Soviets failed to dislodge the Japanese. Finally, the Japanese government, not wanting to divert troops from the massive military operations in mainland China, put the brakes on the operation and withdrew from the disputed heights. The territory may have been ceded to the Soviets, but the Russian military performance had only seemed to confirm the sense of superiority of the Japanese army, which had held its position and suffered significantly fewer casualties than the Russians.

Farther west there was another section of disputed territory, between the puppet states of Manchukuo and Mongolia. This Khalkan Gol region was a hot spot for the migrations of Khalkha Mongols seeking pasturage. Not used to modern states or fixed borders, they traveled along the border with their herds. Russia and Japan realized they did not quite agree on where exactly the borders of their clients were located in the region. Nomonhan was the only permanent town in the region and soon became the focal point for the two sides. Once again, Japan took the more belligerent position, sending a detachment of Manchukuo native cavalry to occupy the town. Mongolian cavalry then engaged them in battle along the frontier. It seemed like a reenactment of early Qing expansion into Mongolia in the seventeenth century, but for the massive modern build up taking place behind both sides of the line.[74]

The reenactment ended with a massive Japanese offensive that overran Soviet headquarters, killing many of the commanding officers and appearing to be on the verge of crushing their forces there. The Soviets withdrew but, using their superior mobility, were able to check the Japanese advance. As in Siberia, both sides backed down from further fighting, leaving the Soviets in control of the disputed territory. Not willing to trust that the Japanese would stay put, Stalin called for Grigori Zhukov, a decorated cavalry commander and proponent of tank warfare, to take charge of the forces in Mongolia. Upon arrival he immediately ordered air raids on the Kwantung army's forward positions, which threw the Japanese, used to air superiority as they were, off balance. They responded a few days later with a crippling mass fighter bomber attack on Soviet air bases throughout Mongolia, destroying upward of a hundred Soviet planes. It was a prelude to another attack that began a few days later, once again meeting initial success.[75]

The battle raged for days, and Zhukov lobbied for armored reinforcements. He was going to use massed columns of tanks to swing around and envelop the advancing (if slowly) Japanese army using the speed and firepower mobile armor could achieve out on the steppe. At this point, just before the outbreak of the Second World War, this was a new tactic: the concentrated and decisive push for a primarily tank-based offensive. This contrasted with the more common using of armor as infantry support, as the Japanese did.[76]

A coordinated counterattack hit both Japanese flanks as intended. Mongolian cavalry drove off the Manchukuoan cavalry scouts, and Soviet tanks nearly enveloped the Japanese army. What little was left broke out and retreated back to Manchukuo. It was one of the decisive victories in Inner Eurasian history and finally checked the landward advance of Japanese arms, which had begun in 1894. The high tide of Japanese power in Eurasia had been met, but with war in Europe only (as it turned out) two days away, Stalin was as anxious to come to peace over the border as were the Japanese. The first example of large-scale limited war between industrial powers had been fought, but anyone familiar with the history of empires in Inner Eurasia knew that decisive battles and campaigns in the service of limited objectives was really more of a return to the norm that existed before unchecked Sino-Russian hegemony.[77]

The nonaggression pact that Japan and Russia signed dramatically altered the war. Had Japan joined Germany's 1941 assault on the Soviet Union, that state likely would have been crushed. It was only Japan's turning south and striking the maritime powers in 1941 (a move based in no small part on what it called "the Nomonhan incident") that allowed Zhukov's army to rapidly redeploy, using railways, and speed across virtually all of Eurasia, becoming the critical reinforcements that stopped the German advance on Moscow that very year and saved the Soviet Union from calamity. Zhukov learned from his bold experiments on the Manchu-Mongol border and became the engineer of many of the Soviet Union's most impressive victories against the Germans, using the firepower and mobility that became his trademarks. Of all the powers in the Second World War, only the United States successfully fought simultaneously on two fronts. The Soviet Union was in a much more dangerous geostrategic position, and so was able to fight Japan, Germany, and then Japan again at separate times. This was made possible by the combination of railroads and armed forces mechanization.[78]

Russia's position as hegemon was about to return, and it had mastered space like never before. It went on to play the single largest part in the Allied victory against Germany, just as Japan's decision to bring the United States into the war made that country the single largest contributor to Japanese defeat. Even though no large-scale land war broke out in Eastern Eurasia, Nomonhan had affected the entire course of the war's Pacific and European fronts.[79]

With the Red Army victorious over archfoe Germany in 1945, and Japan's navy effectively sunk and all its best army units and equipment stripped from the China front and Kwantung armies to fight disastrous battles in the South Pacific, Japanese influence on the Eurasian landmass was about to expire. Hours after the second atomic bomb was detonated over Nagasaki, a massive Soviet army, once again shipped in speedy fashion over most of Eurasia, crashed into Manchukuo. The sad remnants of the once mighty Kwantung army were utterly destroyed, and other assaults hit the Japanese in their previous gains at Russia's expense, the Kuril Islands and South Sakhalin. The battle-hardened and thoroughly mechanized Soviet armies, with the state-of-the-art IS-2 heavy tanks and T-34/85 main battle tanks that emphasized speed and maneuverability, crossed Manchuria and into Korea within weeks.[80] Japanese settlers either killed themselves or were repatriated to Japan after the war, while prisoners became fodder for the labor gulags of Siberia. Pu Yi was captured and turned over to the Chinese communists, while Kawashima Yoshiko was eventually apprehended by the Nationalist forces and executed in 1948. The White Russian community and its pro-Japanese spy network also met grisly fates, with the old Cossack Ataman Semenov entertaining his NKVD guests for a dinner party before they arrested him and sent him off to execution in the country he had exiled himself from. The most successful attempt by a littoral power to create an empire in Inner Eurasia had lasted all of fourteen years and ended in a matter of weeks. Japan once again became an island-only nation with no mainland holdings, while the Soviet Union gained influence in Manchuria and North Korea, and won back its old maritime territories.[81]

Stalin had apparently learned a thing or two over the decades, and rather than retain an empire in Manchuria as the tsars had wanted, he dismantled some of the heavy industry there as war booty and left some, along with all the Japanese war materiel captured, to communist leader Mao Zedong. Soon after gaining control over former Manchukuo, the Chinese communists rushed south, much as the Manchus had once done, and defeated the Nationalists in a series of victories utilizing both lent Soviet armor and partisans and guerrillas. By 1949, the republic was in exile on the former Japanese colony of Taiwan, and the communists were in near total control of the mainland, with partisan operations continuing in Tibet. After sweeping through the Gansu corridor in western China to remove the Kuomintang warlords from Xinjiang (Governor Sheng had been removed after turning on his Russian masters at the time the Nationalists and Russians became allies in the war), the Communist Party began to adopt the same outlook on the importance of frontier securitization its Qing forebears had had.[82]

At the height of power in Eurasia, when Russia and China had established hegemony and security over their border regions, after centuries for one and more than two millennia for the other, their system came wildly crashing down on their heads. It was not because their former enemies who had become subject peoples had counterattacked successfully, but rather that outside maritime powers had broken in and reoriented the system to suit their own ends. Chief among them for the regions this book looks at were the British and the Japanese, particularly the latter.

Firearms and changing economic systems moved the technological edge to the maritime states of Western Europe and North America, and then later Japan. The forces that once tamed Eurasia could not be used to fight these new alien intruders, who moved and deployed faster than any steppe nomad because of their steam-powered navies. Only in resistance to these powers did these old continental hegemons learn how to innovate, but the collapse of their own regimes when trying to do so only increased the unraveling of the system they had worked so hard to create. Japan even became good at the game after initial reverses, creating in Manchukuo a multiethnic and commodity-driven state that resembled, at least superficially, a modern exhumation of the Liao Dynasty, its geographic forebear.

What Japan learned politically, Russia learned militarily, which, in this era of the early to mid-twentieth century, seems to have been the more decisive strategy for the Formless Empire. Once the powers had recovered from initial intrusion and had some time for regime consolidation, war in other realms of the world initiated the decline of, above all, Britain and Japan. When the Eurasian powers began to recover, they did so with a vengeance, particularly the Soviet Union, whose experiences in the Russian civil war, with armor experiments, and at Nomonhan led it to develop a robust mobile military more than capable of dealing with the challenges of pan-Eurasian hegemony and warfare on distant fronts in a mostly landlocked country. Zhukov in particular showed a flair for nationwide grand military movements and battles that was truly Mongolian in scope. A single nation being able to wage large-scale wars in Europe and Asia in close temporal proximity by shifting forces rapidly across the continent was an achievement thought lost to the height of the Mongol Empire, when Batu and Kublai waged their separate yet connected wars of conquest in Russia and China. The settled societies, now modern states, first won with technology and economics alone. Now they could emulate and even surpass the abilities of the nomads in maintaining military hegemony.

The long era of chaos unleashed by the nearly simultaneous fall of the Qing and imperial Russia was over, and Russia and China were once again the undisputed powers over the region, with the former being the stronger by far. But if the Soviets thought they had finally achieved total Eurasian hegemony, with a pliant Chinese vassal thoroughly in their sway and permanent borders of stability, they were about to be disappointed. A region accustomed to rapid changes in hegemony and fluctuations of frontiers was not yet out of the game.

SIX

REBIRTH
THROUGH SMOTHERING

Men and nations have from time to time concluded that some
single faith is destined to prevail throughout the world and that
institutions professing and applying that faith are fated to
become universally regnant.

—Adolph A. Berle

Comrade Stalin showed us how to build socialism in a backward country: it is painful to begin with, but afterwards everything turns out just fine.

—Haffizullah Amin, president of the
Democratic Republic of Afghanistan

Ethnic, regional, and local conflicts and aggressive separatism
in states cause the main threat to universal security since the
end of the Cold War, especially if this kind of confrontation
turns out to be a powerful influence in the hands of some states,
which seek to maintain and protect their own interests and
zones of influence or to change the strategic balance of power in
their favor.

—Uzbek president Islam Karimov

THE TRIUMPH OF STATE POWER IN ITS MOST AUTHORITARIAN, IDEO-
logical, and hypermodernist form inside the two giant Eurasian
states that most dominated the inland reaches of the world's largest

continent exterminated the flexibility that so symbolizes the nature of the Formless Empire's politics. The Cold War became a dark age for the dynamic, indigenous geopolitics of the region—but also a period of relative stability. It was, however, the most temporary of respites when taken in the grand scheme of things.

The unity of the two former rivals, Russia and China, was short lived despite a newfound commitment toward ideological unity through Marxist doctrine. As countless other practitioners of various messianic religions and revolutionary doctrines had already found out, ideas are a poor substitute for the realities of competing interests between states. Once it was apparent that China's interests no longer lay with being a de facto vassal to the Soviet Union and that it would no longer willingly do so, the divide was swift and absolute. This often led to direct clashes on the borders or indirect clashes through proxies in such places as Afghanistan, which once again became the troublesome border zone of Inner Eurasia.

But even this cataclysmic rupture in the communist world was nothing compared to the epic calamity that awaited the Soviet state, which had put so much effort into shoring up its borders and centralized method of rule. When that state collapsed in the early 1990s, it shed territory at an astounding rate. Central Asia was independent, but it inherited artificial ethnic identities, rampant environmental destruction, and mutilated borders drawn up generations before by an out-of-touch political class during the Soviet era. Despite these handicaps, Central Asia had been injected with many benefits from the Soviet period, some of which mirrored older forms of governance under the various Turko-Mongolian ruling houses: relatively secular governance, an openness to regional cooperation and regional trade, and in some cases recognition of ethnic plurality. Now Central Asia had a new beginning.

So did Russia. Acknowledging the independence of its former colonies, Russia adapted (or, one might say, readapted) to wielding its power indirectly over its former territories. Massive security interests were still invested in the region, and in a variety of situations it became more economical and realistic to return to a time when hegemons needed only speed and striking power, rather than occupation and assimilation, to wield their influence.

China went another way, retaining its position in Central Asia while opening up relations with the now-independent states of the region. Clamping down, it followed the old Han Dynasty policy of having western lands under direct rule and a further western protectorate to secure those gains beyond traditional core territories. In effect, the present contemporary situation, with which we will end this chapter, mirrors a return to the beginning of this book: the bipolar system of the loosely, lightly populated, but immensely mobile and powerful Xiongnu Empire in the north sharing an intermittent rivalry with Han Dynasty China. The Xiongnu has been replaced by Russia and the dynastic system with the People's Republic of China, but the technologies of the modern world have given the Formless Empire new relevance and a rebirth from its twentieth-century remission.

The process of turning Central Eurasia from the center of the continental military and economic system into a peripheral province began centuries earlier, but it was only now that the reversal seemed entirely complete.

In the era after the Second World War and before the collapse of the Soviet Union, the heartland of Inner Eurasia reached its greatest levels of colonization and control by outside powers. The dreams of the Han Dynasty and Ivan the Terrible had finally been realized, and the rancorous tribes and flexible statelets that had once been the engines of economic growth and large-scale security were defeated. But to add even to the ephemeral victory won by late imperial Russia and the Qing Dynasty, it was not only the tribes that had been defeated but the space itself, and the weakness of authority with which even those previous conquering powers had wielded over their more-distant possessions. There was no question now that state power in the most modern definition of the term was here to stay, and the freedom of movement that had so defined the steppes of Eurasia was confined only to the militaries of the two powers that had finally triumphed—or so they thought at first.

The Second World War had finally locked down the troublesome far east of Siberia. Once so open that Lenin had to in effect purchase security from other powers by offering the United States and Japan competing concessions, the area now was rebuilt by the labor of

Japanese prisoners of war, and Vladivostok became a restricted naval base allowing no foreign entry. Eventually, economic normalization with Japan commenced, restoring the tenuous trade links of the prewar era while leaving behind their unequal legacy.[1]

Siberians, who had never been treated well under the imperial system, actually gained rights under the Soviets as opposed to the now-quiet Central Asians.[2] Such improvements to local political power and living standards came at a cost, however, as the confiscation of shamans' drums by commissars of the party came to be seen as a direct replay of the actions of orthodox missionaries. Mining, particularly of gold, became a massive boom industry in the region, and the central government began to work on massive damming projects in the rivers of Siberia.[3]

During the early delineation of the Central Asian republics, the mullahs and local potentates lost out. In the prewar era, the Soviet Union had carried out many reforms, such as mandatory education for children, the political emancipation of women, and the encouragement of university attendance. But massive agricultural expansion, particularly of cotton and other irrigation-thirsty crops, and certain heavy-metal industries and the Soviet space program led to cesspools of toxic waste and environmental devastation, particularly to the Azov Sea. There were both benefits and drawbacks to Soviet rule, and its policies served to tie Central Asia closer to Russia proper as never before. Considering that there were certain benefits, the region acquiesced with uncharacteristic yet understandable cooperation.[4]

The Soviet Union was recovering from the massive losses and efforts of the Second World War, and economic and technological innovation seemed to be moving the nation toward the future promised by the revolution. This era began with the ascension of Nikita Khrushchev to power as the first secretary of the Communist Party and saw the first man-made satellite to orbit the Earth, the first man in space, the denunciation of Stalin and his political legacy, and a relative relaxation of the state's rigid security network. Things seemed solid in the Soviet heartland.[5]

In Mongolia, the attempts to find an urban proletariat (and in light of not finding one, making one) under the Stalinist strategies of

Choibalsan had failed because of an economy still dominated by pastoralism. A more gradual approach was adopted, and the world's second communist state became one of the most stable, albeit under the tutelage of its northern neighbor and while still fearing the machinations of its southern neighbor. Across the border, in Chinese-ruled Inner Mongolia, where even more Mongols lived, the Chinese sought to quell any nationalist yearnings to join with Outer Mongolia. They did this by reintroducing the Ming Dynasty history of the Inner Mongols as the more civilized of the tribal branches that stood as China's gatekeeper to potentially turbulent northern realms. Whether it worked or not as propaganda is questionable, but the Inner Mongolian frontier seemed stable for the time being.[6]

In the inland frontiers of the newborn People's Republic of China outside of Mongolia, however, things were not so stable in the immediate postwar era. The Qing and the Kuomintang had both kept a loose hold on the region, and as we have seen, this allowed the Soviet Union to also infiltrate the region of Xinjiang and gain some indirect influence there as well. Mao Zedong, who was chairman of the Central Committee of the Communist Party and held the reins of power in the new Chinese state, was not pleased with this immediately apparent unequal relationship between these two supposedly equal states in an era when the Soviet Union had supposedly renounced the special concessions enjoyed by its tsarist forebears. This meant that one of the first geopolitical projects of the Chinese regime was the same as many other new dynasties: bring order to the western frontier. Tibet also still had an ambiguous relationship with the government, which had existed since the British opened relations with the Dalai Lama on a somewhat separate basis from the rest of the government in 1905.

China struck back against these slights to its sovereignty on its officially recognized borders. The first target was Tibet. The catalyst for decisive action was the outbreak of the Korean War. Before committing its troops directly to stem the tide of allied counterattack that followed the botched North Korean invasion of the South, China reasserted its hegemony over Tibet and shored up a flank with the potential rival of the newly independent India. The fighting was brief. In a matter of weeks, and despite some of the most forbidding terrain in the world, a

rapid advance convinced the Tibetan government to surrender. Little
was done, however, except to assert hegemony, until after the Korean
War ended in 1953. Then, in 1955, collectivization was enforced on
the territory, leading to widespread revolt, full military occupation,
involvement of the US Central Intelligence Agency in the form of sup-
plying weapons to the rebels, and the flight of the Dalai Lama to
India.[7]

China was back on the march into the frontier. Now it was time for
the already controlled yet potentially trickier problem of Xinjiang.
Initially, the region was loosely governed (as previous regimes had
done) by General Wang Zhen. After the Korean War, the government
changed course and instituted a purge of all Turkic party leaders in the
local administration. This was followed by unsuccessful attempts to
collectivize much of the nomadic economy outside of the cities, which
nonetheless increased party control over the actions of the mobile and
restive nomadic population. These mobile people, who understood
little of Marxist conceptions of economics or property management,
had been awkwardly classified as "proletariats" by the central government.[8] Eventually the nomads, who had little concept of class warfare,
were combined with cooperative farms to make joint herding-farming
units, which encouraged the nomads to adopt more-defined and less-
expansive ranges for grazing.

This was soon followed by a massive influx of Han Chinese immigration and economic development programs. Considering the rapidly strengthening position of the republic in what was acknowledged to
be its sovereign territory, Mao felt strong enough that in 1954, he
ordered the Soviet Union's advisers out of the region and accused
them of treating the frontier like semicolonies and negotiated the selling off of their public stocks in the region's industries.[9]

It was in this most unlikely of eras, when the past was disregarded
for dreams of the future and the power of centralized state control was
on an inexorable upswing, that the Chinese communists turned to a
certain historical figure to legitimize their rule over such a diverse population. Once the outlying regions had been brought largely under
control, the government of China began to extol the virtues of a great
foe of the Chinese nation: Chinggis Khan. For bringing unity to differ-

ent lands and peoples as well as encouraging intercultural cooperation and establishing the first international postal service, he became almost a role model of the state that was at that very moment destroying the ways of life of pastoralists and ignoring the principles of freedom of movement that the Mongol Empire had propagated in its social and economic administration so thoroughly.[10]

Despite having cooperated in the Korean War and solved some of their border disputes, the two former rivals turned allies—the Soviet Union and the People's Republic of China—could no longer deny that ideology had not smoothed over the bridges of the geopolitical rivalries that still lie between them. The alliance that held the Eurasian heartland together was showing its first cracks, and soon they would widen into canyons.

Despite the catastrophic results of many of the policies of the economic and social campaign called the Great Leap Forward in 1958–1961, China was growing in assertion and power. The leaders of China, feeling let down by Khrushchev's denunciation of Stalin's radical development method and personality cult (in other words, what Mao was doing at the time) and horrified by Soviet attempts to downplay confrontation and seek more-amenable relations with the United States and other powers, began to assert their nation's independent power more overtly. If the Soviet Union would no longer be a stalwart ally on issues such as reunification with Taiwan while China had borne the brunt of the Korean War, then perhaps the problem was not just differences of doctrine and hierarchy that lie between the nations but the fact that the centuries-long geopolitical rivalry between them could no longer be contained.[11]

The first big split occurred in the wake of increased militarization in Tibet to put down another rebellion. Because of border disputes in the region, India took the opportunity to assert its sovereignty over areas of nebulous ownership, in part as a precautionary measure in reaction to increased troop presence on the Chinese side of the border. India had friendly relations with the Soviet Union, and perhaps the objective of the government in taking such an action was to exploit a breach between the two communist countries. China did not allow this deployment to go unopposed and launched a full-scale assault on the Indian positions, driving them out and claiming the disputed mountain passes for China. The Soviet Union was outraged that it had not been consulted or even told about the forthcoming operation. It was time to reassert hegemony over the socialist camp as far as Moscow was concerned. In 1963, Khrushchev initiated a campaign that railed against "splittists" in the communist movement.[12]

The danger of nebulous borders was thus made clear to all, even China. This last remaining vestige of formless geopolitics had to be thrown out in the era of radicalized nation states, and so Beijing made every effort to resolve as many of its remaining border issues as it could with compromises. By 1963, it had signed fair border deals with Mongolia, Burma, Nepal, Afghanistan, and Pakistan. Notoriously absent from this list was the biggest neighbor of all, the Soviet Union.[13]

Mao realized he could gain much from no longer being assumed to be a de facto vassal of the Soviets. Many of the various leftist factions ignored by the Soviets in Africa and Asia could be picked up as useful contacts and proxies. More importantly, with North Vietnam closer to the Soviet Union than to the People's Republic and the new enemy India still maintaining good relations with Moscow, Chinese leaders feared encirclement, something the Americans could never accomplish but the Soviets clearly could.[14]

Mao acted decisively, fearing a Soviet-sponsored coup. His first targets were Soviet citizens, students, and diplomatic personnel within China. Those living in Xinjiang were especially targeted for deportation and intimidation. Incensed, the Soviets retaliated by evicting all Chinese students from their places at Russian and Eastern bloc universities and sending them home.

But picking on each other's students was just the beginning. In 1964, Mao decided to up the stakes by reopening the debate on Mongolia's independent status, accusing the Soviet Union of vassalizing a state wrongfully snatched from Chinese clutches in the era of imperialism. Even more worrying to Moscow, Mao made much the same point about Outer Manchuria (that which had since become Primorye and the base of the Soviet Pacific Fleet at Vladivostok). This was likely a ploy to get a better treaty for the disputed Sino-Soviet border that was a leftover of the territorial ambiguities from the era of

Manchukuo. Simultaneous with this aggressive assertion was the outbreak of China's Cultural Revolution, one objective of which was to
root out Soviet sympathizers from the government as well as increase
Mao's personal power. In this time of fragility and upheaval in China,
it was necessary to rally support with a foreign power as scapegoat,
and the one that most threatened Chinese borders would do—even if
it wasn't a capitalist power.[15] Many temporarily buried issues had risen
to the top:

> Soviet accusations [against China] focused on chauvinism,
> racism, leadership cult and the like, charges virtually indistin-
> guishable from the period of struggle against Nazism during
> World War II, and against Western imperialism. At times they
> even exceeded accusations against the latter. The Chinese accu-
> sation in turn centered on Soviet hegemonism and great power
> ambitions. . . . Not only were the forces of communism weak-
> ened and split by the Sino-Soviet rift, but the two communist
> giants were at sword's point, ready to give battle along all but
> military lines.[16]

There was to be no turning back now. The Eurasian Cold War had
begun, and Inner Asia was its largest new front.

North Korea saw the brewing tensions and started to tilt toward
China, denying the Soviet Union the right to station nuclear weapons
on its territory.[17] Mongolia, unsurprisingly, took the opposite path, and
then-leader Yumjaagiin Tsedenbal requested Soviet reinforcements to
protect his sparsely populated country from a hypothetical invasion of
the giant to the south. The new Soviet premier, Leonid Brezhnev, used
the phrase coined for operations in Eastern Europe, limited sovereignty, to uphold the Soviet claim of preeminence in the communist
world—with an obvious eye toward China and the Cultural
Revolution that held so much of the socialist world aghast. In 1968,
Mao massively reinforced Chinese military divisions in Manchuria,
while six Soviet divisions arrived in Mongolia and more in Siberia.
Two considerations played into this escalation of tensions: the Soviet
Union's crushing reform attempts in Czechoslovakia, showing blatant
disregard for the domestic autonomy of its allies, and the increasing
likelihood of American withdrawal from South Vietnam. The govern-

ment of China increasingly saw all alliances with the Soviet Union, not just its own, as unequal relationships set up by an increasingly imperialistic power. The Chinese even began to build bunkers and fallout shelters in anticipation for a Soviet invasion.[18]

The slow-burning fuse had finally lit the bomb, and in only a few years, the two former allies became die-hard foes. At Zhenbao/Damanskii Island, which was one of the disputed territories on the badly demarcated Ussuri River, artillery fire was exchanged, and Chinese military units began crossing into the areas of contention. All bets were off now as the situation had gone from rivalry to outright physical danger.[19]

Despite the apparently huge disparity of technology, economy, and stability between the powers that decisively favored the Soviets, the situation was more dangerous for them than might be assumed. The same vast spaces with very small populations (compared to China) and barely enough infrastructure to support massive and prolonged military deployments put immense strain on both Siberia and the central government. Most military forces had to stay in the primary theater of potential conflict in Eastern Europe, and so the Soviet Union effectively put together something it had learned from long periods of conflict in Inner Eurasia: a rapid-reaction mobile strike force for punishing expeditions rather than broad-front warfare.[20]

A pattern emerged: first the Chinese would cross the disputed boundaries, then the Soviets would try to drive them off. At first there were fistfights, then the Chinese soldiers would open fire, Soviet tanks would run over Chinese infantry, and artillery fire would be exchanged. The first combat deployment of the T-62 tank occurred in this engagement, and the armor-led Soviet counterattack finally swept the Chinese from their encroachments and returned the frontier to what it had been before the escalation.[21]

It was now that Mao, remembering that even Stalin made pragmatic alliances with capitalist countries, decided to become receptive to a more friendly relationship with the United States. Mao reportedly reminded his advisers of an ancient Chinese proverb advocating the position that it was more secure to make alliances with faraway countries and to have the state's enemies nearby.[22] Sun Tzu would have been pleased with such an application of geopolitical logic.

On the other side of the Pacific Ocean, the United States was also probing for a closer relationship with the Chinese. Henry Kissinger, national security adviser to President Richard Nixon (and later secretary of state), saw in the breakdown of the Sino-Russian relationship a golden opportunity to counter growing Soviet power. Wishing to move past an era of ideological dogmatism in foreign policy, he wanted to create and maintain a beneficial balance of power against the Soviet behemoth. The Chinese had reached similar conclusions from their own perspective. It was decided to recognize Communist Party domination of China in exchange for establishing a new balance of power. This way the United States could offset the growing strength of the Soviet Union by playing the role of offshore balancer, with China as the land-based leverage to check Soviet ambitions in the east. This maneuver would ensure that the United States retained the decisive position in world affairs.[23]

Given that this international rearrangement came in the wake of the Vietnam War debacle, when the influence of the United States was at a low ebb and the Soviet Union was riding comparatively high as far as defense spending and internal stability was concerned, this kind of a change could rob the Soviets of their momentum. With the official visit of Nixon to China and opening of formal relations in 1972, the two countries signed the Shanghai Communiqué, which stipulated that neither country was to negotiate with third parties in the region without consulting the other and that both China and the United States would seek to prevent the domination of any one power over the Asia-Pacific region. The following year the diplomatic ties grew even closer, culminating in what was effectively a defensive pact. The Soviet Union was caught off guard and now had not only the Iron Curtain in Europe to worry about defending but also a vast border with China in East Asia. As Kissinger explains:

> The United States was not about to back the stronger against the weaker in any balance-of-power situation. As the country with the physical capacity to disturb the peace, the Soviet Union would be given an incentive to moderate existing crises and to avoid stirring up new ones while faced with resistance on two fronts. And China, which had its own capacity to upset the

Asian equilibrium, would be restrained by the need for American goodwill on setting limits to Soviet adventurism. Through all of this, the Nixon Administration would try to solve practical issues with the Soviet Union while maintaining a dialogue on global concepts with the Chinese.[24]

Although it was feared that this game was dangerous and would greatly upset the relations of the two superpowers by introducing China as the wild card, the reverse happened. With the Soviets realizing the danger of the situation, their foreign policy became more conciliatory, and Nixon was invited to Moscow the following year. From the Chinese perspective, Manchuria (or Northeast Province, as it became known), that eternal and dangerous frontier, was finally secure. It was not so farther west.[25]

Eurasia had approached the closest it had ever been to being united since the Mongol Empire. Yet it had not quite made it. The Cold War now had three fronts, as became manifestly apparent in the coming decade.

The death of Mao and the rise of Deng Xiaoping to power over the People's Republic of China ushered in a reining in of extreme government policies, and this was felt in the hinterlands.

If inequality of alliance was one cause of friction between two powers claiming absolute truth, it could also be a problem for the different groups of citizens in a single country. With China and the Soviet Union having turned (with differing degrees of success) to their main adversary as an ally in a potential war with the other, much of the ideology in the communist world became bankrupt as cohesive policy.[26] China, being the more extremely doctrinaire of the two powers, was the first to begin domestic reforms to its economic system and its political apparatus. Though limited in scope, many of these reforms ameliorated the situation of Xinjiang to a considerable degree. Deng condemned policies of "Han chauvinism" in the frontier provinces and gave the Uighurs and others more local control over their party apparatus, though he did nothing to stem the floodgates of ethnic Han migration to the region. After all, it was still a sparsely populated, turbulent, and border-disputed place with the Soviet Union.

But now, with the region open to investment from abroad and with an increasingly market-based economy, its fate slowly began to change. As Millward states:

> Xinjiang had been relegated to a status of strategic buffer zone and economic cul-de-sac since the rise of Sino-Soviet tensions in the late 1950s and 1960s. In the new international context Chinese leaders moved simultaneously both to open the region as the conduit for the rest of Eurasia and to integrate it more firmly with the rest of China.[27]

This mixed policy, reminiscent in geopolitical terms of the old Han and Tang policies of keeping solid bases in the west surrounded by a "protectorate," reaped solid benefits in the decades to come. It was to be a different story across the border in the Soviet Union.

After several decades of direct rule by the Soviet Union, certain benefits were manifest in Central Asia during and immediately after the Sino-Soviet split. Soviet health programs had led to a population explosion throughout the region that was followed by an economic expansion in line with increasing industrialization. Unfortunately, this also increased the environmental damage, particularly from the massive irrigation works of the growing cotton fields. This strengthening of regional positioning in the importance of the various constituent parts of the Soviet Union often took form in resistance to cultural integration, despite welcoming the economic ties of the state. This in turn increased Moscow's fears of infiltration of the region by Islamic radicals, particularly in light of the recent Islamic revolution in Iran. It quickly became apparent to the originally gleeful Soviets that the Iranians' ouster of the pro-American government there was of no benefit to them.[28]

As the Soviets turned a paranoid gaze to their south, events unraveled in the perennial borderlands of Afghanistan. It had been a stable buffer ever since the wars of disputes of the nineteenth century, but in the late 1970s, just as it was starting to develop, calamity struck. The Daud dictatorship, which had seized power from the monarchy not long before, had good relations with the Soviet Union. So the Soviets were surprised and dismayed when it was toppled by a cadre of radi-

cal leftist revolutionaries with an extensive and potentially destabiliz-
ing package of sweeping reforms for a country with little state infrastructure outside of the major cities. This sudden shock of regime
change and the heavy-handed tactics of the new government caused
widespread rebellion to break out across the country. Fearing an opening for US, Pakistani, or even Iranian involvement in the rebellion, or
even worse, a rebellion that might leak into the Turkic realms of the
Soviet Union, the Soviets decided to support the new Taraki government by dispatching advisers and army trainers (usually of Central
Asian extraction), as well as special forces to bolster the new regime.

The situation further deteriorated when the Democratic Republic
of Afghanistan's government split after Hafizullah Amin, the former
ally of Taraki, staged his own coup. This was one step too far for the
Soviets, who saw Amin behave like his self-proclaimed mentor Stalin
and drive the government deeper into a crisis by attempting to conduct
massive purges. Moscow now found itself in the awkward position of
having to shore up a faltering allied government by invading that allied
country and decapitating its leadership. The special forces sent to protect the government in Kabul were ordered to storm the presidential
palace and assassinate Amin, and a two-pronged invasion of Soviet
mechanized units made a massive pincer movement around the ring
road of the country and occupied the majority of the urban areas,
largely without a fight. The normal conventional doctrine of deep battle strategy was of no use against a sparse and tribal foe, so the lines of
advance for armored columns were secured by paratroopers landing
on the mountains near the roads.[29]

Though the initial invasion was unquestionably a success, many in
the Soviet Politburo had deep reservations about an open-ended commitment. Anatoli Adamishini, a foreign ministry official, remarked,
"The action in Afghanistan is the quintessence of our internal affairs.
The economic disorganization, the fear of the Central Asian
Republics, the approaching Congress, the habit of deciding problems
by force, the ideological dogmatism—what sort of a socialist revolution
is that [Afghanistan's], what sort of revolutionaries are these?"[30]

As the years dragged on, the system that had tried to bring unity to
modern Central Asia was taxed to its limit.[31]

Full-scale combat operations lasted a decade. The Afghan forces bore the brunt of it, and the Soviets had clearly learned from American experience in Vietnam by remaining largely in reserve until needed, then intervening with air power and armored columns once called on. Still, owing to the United States, China, and Pakistan lavishly arming the various insurgent forces, and the forbidding terrain, a stalemate continued until the Soviet Union withdrew in 1989. Left behind were SCUD missile operators and KGB agents, both of whom helped repel an attack on Kabul in 1991, but they were withdrawn that year when the Soviet Union fell. The communist government in Afghanistan actually outlived the Soviet Union by several years, even if it dwindled to a greater Kabul city-state before finally falling to the Pakistani-backed Taliban in 1996.[32]

Perestroika, Soviet leader Mikhail Gorbachev's attempt to save the faltering command economy of the Soviet Union, had been an encouraging sign to the peoples of Central Asia, even at a time when the Afghan war was burning right across their borders for a prolonged period. The Jadid School of Islamic learning (which sought to reconcile secular governance with Islamic principles) was a common intellectual strand of the region. It was born from the thinking of Crimean and Kazan Tatars (the descendants of various branches of the Golden Horde) and gradually spread south toward Central Asia. The general mood in Central Asia was one of optimism that Moscow would now respect local cultures, take a more hands-off approach, and maintain the economic relationship perhaps with a bit more concern for environmental issues.[33]

But these things were not to be. The Soviet Union was finished. Though the Afghan war had shown the limitations of its logistics systems, the true cause of the collapse came from an unsustainable economic model coupled with a bloated defense budget (which was increasingly a product of the rivalry with China adding to the already massive costs of occupying Eastern Europe). When a reactionary left-wing military coup was staged against the reforming Gorbachev in Moscow, the game was up, even though the uprising was quickly and nonviolently quelled. Estonia was the first republic to declare independence; the rest followed throughout 1991. Central Asia—in light

of its dependence on the central government, the threat of Islamic radicals from Afghanistan, China's rising power since the 1980s, and generally improving social and political conditions—was the last region to
break off from Russia. But even it took the path of independence to
begin a new era in the history of Eurasia's heartland (*see map 8*).[34]

In the latter stages of the Cold War, certain leaders rose to power in
the Central Asian republics. With the breakup of the Soviet system
and its total dissolution at the dawn of 1992, these men seized the
chance to declare their nations as independent and sovereign.[35] But
this was to be a very different kind of nationalism or independence
than existed in Eastern Europe or East Asia (though it was unquestionably touched by modernist notions of nationalism through the
Soviet experience). This nationalism acknowledged its history of a
region reliant on mutual dependence and the confluence of multiple
cultures. Despite the unprecedented and often arbitrary separation of
the region into various republics, the era of independence saw more
resurgence of regionalism than farther drifting apart:

> The artificial Soviet division of Central Asia into five "ethnical-
> ly based" countries has not weakened regional ties. Among
> other factors, the existence of almost all the [Central Asian] eth-
> nic groups in every [Central Asian] country has provided a sit-
> uation that is conducive to the expansion of one country's insta-
> bility to other regional countries. As a result, no single [Central
> Asia] state can be stable so long as others are unstable; in par-
> ticular, a regional approach to their common security problems
> seems necessary for the five regional states.[36]

Because the region has always been a nexus of migration, each of
the five republics—Kazakhstan, Kyrgyzstan, Uzbekistan, Tajikistan,
and Turkmenistan—contains massive minority populations from
neighbors. Almost a quarter of Tajikistan is Uzbek, and Uzbeks make
up over 10 percent of Kyrgyzstan's population. A western chunk of
Uzbekistan's territory was the semiautonomous ethnic enclave of
Karakalpakstan. Russians make up just under 40 percent of the population of Kazakhstan, and they live in settlements throughout all of the
republics. Hooman Peimani elaborates:

> The history of the five [Central Asian] countries is the history of a region, not of five separate political entities. Over time Central Asia has been ruled either by foreign empires, which incorporated the region into their territories as a single political unit, or by a few regional multiethnic states. Rulers of these states never identified themselves with specific ethnic groups. As a result, for most of their history the indigenous ethnic groups of this region have seen themselves as members of a regional community sharing the same fate, rather than citizens of different states.[37]

This is not to imply that as independent states, these new nations would not pursue divergent paths, but in order to pursue their own paths they had to have a level of regional flexibility and adaptability that was relatively unique to their geopolitical circumstances.

A mere two years after official independence, with the ex-Soviet party leaders still firmly in power though divested of communist ideology, a Central Asian Union was created with the goal of furthering economic integration among Kazakhstan, Kyrgyzstan, and Uzbekistan. By this time, Turkmenistan had gone fully down the path of neutrality under a closed and retro-Stalinist political system, and Tajikistan was then descending into chaos. But among the three Turkic countries that wished to stay engaged in the region, there was an acknowledgment that issues such as limited water resources and pipelines for oil and gas required increasing levels of regional cooperation between the states.[38]

Uzbekistan took the lead. As president of the most populous state with the largest army, Islam Karimov saw his chance to play for top regional influence. It helped that now the region was open to investment from and political connections with other countries. Turkey, Iran, and the United States played the biggest roles in increasing foreign investment and establishing political ties with the new governments. Reaching out to Turkey as a culturally common counterpoint to Russia was a big part of Karimov's program for more independent action. Even so, in 1992, he hosted the official signing of the Tashkent Collective Security Agreement, a defensive alliance with provisions for mutual military cooperation, and he even called for continued Russian troop presence in the region to stem any potential tides of pan-Islamic ideology coming out of Afghanistan or Iran.[39]

According to Karimov's own book, Uzbekistan is pivotal as the center of Central Asia, the true axis between any competing power poles. Thus he advocates an equitable division of responsibilities among the nations of the Commonwealth of Independent States (CIS)—the association of Central Asian, Russian, and Belarusian interests formed during the breakup of the Soviet Union—as well as using the framework of that organization to explore new methods for interrelation and interdependence throughout the region. With such objectives and the capacity to be a regional power, it is no wonder Uzbekistan is leading the integrationist charge. Russia is often irked by Uzbekistan's pretensions to be the leader on such issues, but as we shall soon see, they have far too many common interests to openly compete for influence in the area and so are more often confederates.[40]

Kazakhstan, the second-strongest regional player by most reckonings, was also a country that immediately began to pursue the integrationist line for the region. Kazakhstan had and still has a valid reason for keeping regional integration and stability at a maximum: its massive Russian population. President Nursultan Nazarbaev made it a point to lead an officially multiethnic and religiously pluralist state. Fearing the rise of power of a right-wing government in Russia that might demand that places like the north of Kazakhstan (where a majority of the people are Russian) be incorporated into the Russian state, the Kazakh nation has welcomed its sizable Russian minority into the government and political structure. Furthermore, in 1998, it moved its capital from the far southeastern city of Almaty to Astana, near the center of the country and much closer to the areas of Russian settlement. Soon after, in 2000, a massive reserve of oil was discovered in the already resource-rich nation.[41]

Kyrgyzstan, poor and small compared to most of its neighbors, also has a significant Uzbek minority population. Therefore, it seems unlikely that Kyrgyzstan will take an independent line against Uzbek interests any time soon. Kyrgyzstan was the first Central Asian state to open its airspace to the United States after the 9/11 terrorist attacks, allowing the massive Manas Air Base to temporarily come under

American jurisdiction for the purpose of supporting operations in Afghanistan. Though Kyrgyzstan suffers from widespread political and ethnic turmoil, it still fits the regional rubric of being a "secular authoritarianism with some state capitalism."[42]

Turkmenistan, the most naturally well endowed with resources of the former republics and the only state sharing a border with Iran as well as its former corepublics, may have partially removed itself from the regional states' integration movement, but it has done so by becoming the most authoritarian state in the region. With all the rotating golden statues of the "founder" of the nation (now deceased) and heavy obstacles to foreign investment, it still lives behind a Soviet-style twentieth-century guise.[43]

Tajikistan was the other republic not interested in unity, for alone among the new states, it was of primarily Iranian rather than Turkic cultural identity. That had not stopped it from being a fully integrated part of the region before, but of all the nations in the region, it was to have the most tragic experience of the post-Soviet period. That experience, however, was also one of the most illuminating examples of the changing power politics of the region, which we will explore below.

Of course, the post-Soviet era in Inner Asia was not simply restricted to the now-independent republics that once were the southern bulwark of the imperial Russian and Soviet empires. Xinjiang, needless to say, was not among the new states born in the 1990s; however, it was still affected by the developments in Central Asia to a significant degree, even as the rest of the region took a significantly different course.

Decades of integrationist policies had flooded the region with Han migrants on a scale that dwarfed Russian settlement in Central Asia except in northern Kazakhstan. By 1990, the population of the region was half Han Chinese and half Uighur. Xinjiang, after thousands of years of struggle, was finally, firmly, and unquestionably under direct Chinese administration. But this did not mean that it was no longer relevant to the region—far from it. Xinjiang benefitted immensely from the large number of newly independent neighbors it found itself near, with their resource-rich markets opening to foreign investment. Seeking more regional connections, post-Cold War Xinjiang became what the Han Dynasty had originally tried to make it long term—a directly controlled Central Asian base from which to indirectly influence the western neighbors, who, like after the historical breakup of the Xiongnu, were ideally divided. Soon, Xinjiang became the de facto base for Chinese business dealings throughout Central Asia. Its regional trade (and consequently, its level of economic development) was growing at an astounding pace, showing it to be the biggest initial benefactor of Central Asian independence from an economic perspective.[44]

The Chinese government was able to extract certain promises from its new neighbors that showed just how important its influence now was. Its own ethnic situation in the region was (and remains) one of potential volatility, with occasional outbursts of strife. But since the 1980s, a gradual improvement in relations with the Uighurs and Kazakhs has calmed things down significantly. With the base secure, Chinese frontier diplomacy went on the offensive in the region for the first time since the eighteenth century. In 1996, China extracted promises from all the Central Asian countries to not harbor separatist Uighur groups and to turn over anyone who advocated the creation of such groups.[45]

One thing that did not change in the region was the nature of military deployment. Nuclear weapons testing and missile deployment had long been a local specialty in Xinjiang, and the "great wall of steel" defense network that had arisen during and after the Sino-Soviet split was based on a rapid-reaction force of highly mobile mechanized units meant to operate in sparsely populated areas with minimal logistical capabilities. It was something Ban Chao would have recognized from his campaign and occupations against the Xiongnu.[46]

Finally in our overview of the post–Cold War geopolitical situation we come to the one country that alone had once achieved total hegemonic status in Inner Eurasia, Mongolia. Much reduced from its once mighty position, the present nation could almost be described as a city-state with vast pastoral properties. The least densely populated independent country in the world, it is also the one that maintained its official status as its own nation despite that fact that it was an indirectly controlled puppet of the Soviet Union for all of the Cold War.[47]

Freed from domination and with the political monopoly held by the Communist Party broken, Mongolia became the most open and democratic of the former Soviet-sphere countries outside of the Baltics. However, as with the Central Asian republics, it was not necessarily in Mongolia's interests to pursue a wildly independent foreign policy that deviated from a Russian-dominated security network. With only two neighbors, both giant and powerful nations, Mongolia has tread lightly in the post-Cold War era.[48]

Mongolian liberalism (compared to that of the Central Asian states) is not so much a break with the past as it is a continuation of a premodern tradition—that of the protoconstitution that governed the Mongol Empire, the Yasa. Owing to its location, Mongolia is dependent on one or both of its neighbors for sea access, and Russia for overland access to Kazakhstan and the rest of Central Asia. This does not prevent Mongolian politicians from looking for other countries to have close relations with—particularly Japan and the United States—as Mongolian presidential adviser L. Galbagrakh stated: "Mongolia lies between two giants, therefore our cooperation with the United States is very important from the point of view of security as well as progress towards democracy."[49]

Mongolia views one of these giants as much more threatening than the other. Historically, as we have seen, the Russians have used Mongolia as an indirect buffer for the southern frontier of sparsely populated and often vulnerable Siberia, whereas the Chinese have sought to reclaim the region and have directly administered and integrated Inner Mongolia into their home realm. Combined with the perception after the Cold War of a Russia on the retreat and in decline and a rising China, Mongolia has been steadily pursuing policies that keep the close (if not as close as they once were) ties with Russia in matters of security and maintain a skeptical—though not unfriendly—position toward the Chinese. In the past, Russia has been quick to remind tiny Mongolia that it cannot pursue a path of independence toward China on its own or in conjunction with faraway states with which it shares no border.[50]

After the Soviet Union shed many territories, Russia became its de facto successor, taking over the nuclear arsenals deployed in the former empire and inheriting much of its diplomatic authority in the region. It no longer had the economic or military power to dictate events directly in its regional neighborhood or the will to behave as an interventionist policeman. And so, at first by necessity and later by intent, Russia adapted itself to the new geopolitical situation by rediscovering the virtues of a formless geopolitical strategy. As Deputy Prime Minister Yegor Gaidar stated as early as 1991, "We would be much better off on our own, for then Russia could be a great power again."[51] Given the calamitous state of Russia's internal and economic stability in the coming decade, this sentiment may have been premature, but Gaidar was right that Russia could and would adapt successfully in light of the circumstances. Both the history and the geographic realities of the region offered the guide, and the situation that arose in Tajikistan soon after the fall of the Soviet Union was the first case study.

In a fashion typical of post-Soviet Central Asia, Tajikistan had a local former party power broker who held on to power by reinventing himself as a nationalist president. Unlike in those other states, however, Rakhmon Nabiev was forced from power by massive protests early in his rule. A democratic opposition with Islamist tendencies grew into a regional movement in the south, and its Islamic character grew proportionally because of influence from nearby Taliban Afghanistan. Tajikistan had split into armed camps, and infiltration by the militant forces was feared.

Russian troops were deployed into the country to shore up the government, and Uzbekistan began to fund Uzbek warlords in the country, getting them to back the regime against the upswing of antigovernment momentum. These limited deployments and construction of Russian military bases checked the democratic and Islamist advances, and the war stalemated. In 1996, a tenuous peace deal was enacted that gave political concessions to the democratic side of the opposition while marginalizing the Islamist side.[52]

From an international perspective, the effect of the war on Tajikistan's standing was the most interesting outgrowth of the conflict. The war had been seen as an attempt by Iran to gain influence as Russian power waned; surely its results dashed the hope that Russia was on the retreat in the region after initial withdrawal.[53] The nominally independent country was now host to the largest joint CIS peacekeeping force of any part of the former Soviet Union. In effect, Tajikistan had become a joint Uzbek-Russian protectorate.[54] Russia effectively took over border control and policing in the region, regulating the Tajik border as it saw fit.[55] This was the run-up to a counterthrust into Afghanistan, though not one at all reminiscent of the previous decade's conventional occupation strategy. Another effect of the war, and one enhanced by the reassertion of Russian control over the country, was that now there was direct access to the anti-Taliban resistance in Afghanistan—the so-called Northern Alliance under Ahmed Shah Massoud—one of the greatest foes of Soviet forces in Afghanistan in the previous decade.[56]

Russia funneled money and guns to its erstwhile foe, picking up the pace whenever Massoud suffered a defeat or it looked like the Taliban were on the march. Massoud remained by far the largest thorn in the side of the Taliban until his assassination one day before the 9/11 terrorist attacks. Much of the organization for those attacks took place in Afghanistan, and its mastermind, Osama bin Laden, was living under the de facto protection of the Taliban regime. Suddenly, the situation had changed.[57]

President Vladimir Putin offered the United States use of Russian airspace for it to launch the initial military operations against the Taliban that became Operation Enduring Freedom. But he was soon taken aback by the enthusiasm that many CIS states showed for American entry into the region, and the large Manas Air Base in Kyrgyzstan being rented out to the United States was a particular sticking point. Fearing that perhaps the CIS area was being taken advantage of in ways that undermined Russia hegemony in the region, he took countermeasures. The Chinese government took a highly negative view of these developments as well, as US involvement in Central and South Asia increased continuously in the following years. Despite benefiting from the removal of the Taliban, it was time for the empires to strike back.[58]

The increased relevance of terrorism, particularly of the Islamic variety, in the plans of nations offered the opening for Putin to hold onto Central Asian influence. If the United States could infiltrate the region under such a pretense, then so could Russia use terrorism as a rationale for expansion (or reexpansion) of its own regional sway. Putin was quick to sign joint military and security deals with the CIS states in the aftermath of 9/11 and set up a rapid-reaction response force in Kyrgyzstan not far from the Manas base.[59]

But the Taliban remnants and other radicals were still considered the primary enemy, and even as a vigorous response to US regional expansion was pursued, cooperation between Russia and the United States in Afghanistan continued. The de facto goal was to have the United States neutralize the Afghan problem while simultaneously preventing it from spreading its influence into Central Asia proper. Uzbekistan was the country least dependent on Russia and therefore the one most welcoming to the American presence. But that relationship quickly fizzled when American, British, and French diplomats insisted on criticizing the Uzbek government's human rights record, and Russia and China more effectively reasserted themselves.[60]

By 2005, the threat of expanding US influence in Central Asia was effectively neutralized. Uzbekistan was back in the CIS fold. The Kyrgyz took back outer security operations for the Manas base (now referred to as a transit center and its status still under negotiation), as Ariel Cohen states: "While the US may maintain some presence in the area in the future, it will only be one of a much larger concert of powers, each with its own ties, clients and agendas. The US is not about to dominate Central Asia anytime soon."[61]

Even officially neutral Turkmenistan was still paying for the upkeep of Russian military bases on its borders, though the new leadership after the death of authoritarian president Saparmurat Niyazov maintained the structure of the closed-off state. Dilip Hiro summarizes the position of the Central Asian nations in the post-9/11 world perfectly:

> Such were the compulsions of history, geography, and economics that none of these presidents could set themselves completely free from the embrace of Mother Russia. True, every now and then, a Central Asian leader struck a defiant pose only to realize that he could not sustain it for long. Indeed, as Russian President Vladimir Putin started transforming Russia's political

system into a "managed democracy" during his second term in office (from 2004 to 2008)—marginalizing the opposition, gaining almost full control over the electronic media, virtually renationalizing energy and other important industries—the authoritarian and proto-authoritarian rulers of Central Asia began to feel at home once more in the Kremlin.[62]

This rebuilding of strategic ties between Russia and the new Central Asian states came with a new and evolving framework for regional integration, something we must now turn to in order to understand the current evolution of the Formless Empire.

As Russia and China began a coordinated pushback against the United States and its growing influence in the region, the benefits of cooperation and the potential conflicts became more apparent. In 2001, the Shanghai Cooperation Organization, a regional network of military cooperation among China, Russia, and all the Central Asian countries excepting Turkmenistan, was born. Eventually it included India, Iran, Afghanistan, Pakistan, and Mongolia as observers. The primary goal of this international network as stated in a 2002 press release was to "combat the three evils: terrorism, religious extremism, and ethnic separatism."[63]

Not as explicitly stated but just as real is its purpose to keep outside powers at bay from the heart of Eurasia. Too weak on their own to do this, Russia and China must act in conjunction and in collaboration with, rather than with dominance over, the Central Asian states. The effect of such traditional indirect methods with modern means was aptly stated when President Dmitri Medvedev of Russia wrote off $180 million of Kyrgyzstan's debt and promised $300 million in loans to the country in exchange for upping the rent and making life more difficult for the US base at Manas.[64]

But such loose alliances usually do not outlast the containment of a common foe. Under the surface of this alliance, many potential tensions still simmer between the two main powers in Inner Eurasia. Though they may be quiet now, two nations of such size and power competing for influence in many of the same places does present potential danger. To keep the CIS together and remain its guarantor, Russia may need a new common enemy when the United States is no longer a major regional player. This is, perhaps, somewhat intention-al. As Jennifer Anderson states, "Russia and China's strategic partner-ship is unwieldy and imprecise. Weighed down by contradictory com-mitments, hyperbolic rhetoric and a wide variety of intersecting inter-ests, their relationship is inherently and deliberately vague."[65]

In addition to actual policy moves toward cooperation, joint mili-tary exercises through the Shanghai Cooperation Organization have become common. Russian and Chinese forces have participated with each other in mock military operations and continue to cooperate in counterinsurgency training. China and Kyrgyzstan have also conduct-ed joint military exercises along their common border. China's fear of instability or encirclement seems to have been allayed for the time being, as mutual economic interests and the need to access Russian raw materials to fuel the rapid pace of Chinese industrialization pro-vide great incentive for cooperation between the two states. Oil pipelines constructed through eastern Siberia also offer lucrative incentives to maintain this stable relationship. Meanwhile, Russian arms and other equipment are sold at steady rates to the Chinese mil-itary and the CIS states.[66]

Perhaps even more relevant, Russia has learned how to use proxies in the form of nonstate actors to a large degree, being able to stoke frozen conflicts in many parts of its frontier by funneling equipment and indirect support to rebels in eastern Ukraine and the breakaway regions of Georgia. More traditionally, Russia does what it can to sup-port an embattled Syrian regime. As of this writing, the effectiveness of these efforts is still in question, but in a world riddled with electronic communications and often-disingenuous proclamations of support for international law, it seems likely these tactics are an updated use of older strategies that were variously useful to large but not necessarily dense political entities, such as Russia has become.

This type of loose confederation against a common foe is hardly new in the region, but such coalitions also tend not to be permanent. This relationship is fraught with potential difficulty, as it always has been since two countries with different ways of adapting diplomacy and military policy toward the security concerns of the Inner Eurasian steppe have shared massive, sometimes ambiguous frontiers. Russian policy-makers tend to view the situation as an unequal alliance and fear nationalist Chinese designs on what was once called Outer Manchuria. Furthermore, the sparsely populated and resource-rich areas of eastern Siberia are often considered to be vulnerable to a country with a teeming population just across the border. Chinese designs for expansion of influence in Central Asia are feared as well, by both Russian and Central Asian policy-makers.[67]

The system is in flux, as it ever has been. In an era of satellites, armored columns, air power, special forces, electronic financial trans-actions, and at least token respect for national sovereignty, the Formless Empire is back and stronger than ever. It is likely that the countries best adapted through long (and often hard) experience, with centuries of conflicts and moving borders in Inner Eurasia, will retain a decisive advantage in the geopolitics of this region.

From their height of domination, the Soviet Union and the People's Republic of China had finally achieved the full-scale pacification of Inner Eurasia. Their unity was temporary, however, and divisions between the two poles of communism became more extreme with time. But even the division of the two powers could not bring back the famous fluidity of the steppes, for while their militaries and borders continued to shift to meet changing circumstances, their internal poli-cies became more rigid. As the once-open steppes were brought under both countries' central control and were integrated into their economies, the era of multicultural fluidity that had defined the region seemed to come to a close. But it was the seemingly stronger Russia that had feet of clay in the end, and the apparently weaker China that endured the tumult of the 1990s unscathed—even strengthened.

Present-day China holds a favorable geopolitical position com-pared to past dynasties. It meets all the territorial requirements neces-sary for border security (as the Chinese have come to understand it), having pacified the western regions through direct settlement and sta-bilized Mongolia through border demarcation. Manchuria, the other region of danger, has been thoroughly sinicized and now can be viewed as a province of China (with the identity-stripping name of Northeast China no less). Russia is the weaker power (though it still has the most nuclear weapons in the world), and it remains a proper regional military power with secure borders for the time being. It is easy to say that the poles have reversed from the last several centuries and returned to when Cossacks first met the Qing Manchus in the Amur River valley back in the seventeenth century. There is a sparsely populated Russian frontier, a strong state in China, and many smaller powers in between. But in the conclusion, we will examine how this Chinese victory—much like that past one—might hide the true amorphousness of the situation.

While there is little to no room for the indirect and informal political arrangements of past days, the dynamism of technology, a globalized economy, and regional independence in Central Asia mean that, as tactical doctrine, the Formless Empire has the potential to return. Not as it once lingered in frontier states, but as foreign policy strategy toward the frontier of the most established states in the region as they seek to rebuild relationships with former rivals and neighbors while bypassing more-official channels. Already, proxy wars shake regions on the Russian periphery. So while the core realm of Eurasian states may now host various versions of a modern state, frontier breakdowns in the Caucasus, Ukraine, or even as far away as the Syria-Iraq border create vacuums where less-conventional actors (by our era's definitions anyway) can thrive. Whether such breakdowns will become the norm for our era remains to be seen. No matter what happens, it is as good a time as any to remember the nature of the advice given to the world by Ibn Khaldun on the disproportionate importance of actors on state peripheries, where a greater level of group cohesiveness, or *assibiya*, often means major political events can be born in the people of the frontier. It is in those places outside the centers of power where many innovations in strategy or governance can arise and, in so doing, change the fortunes of nations.

After all, the Formless Empire is just back in full swing now—and it often thrives with many players in the game.

CONCLUSION

A S NOTED IN THE INTRODUCTION, WE HAVE BEEN SELECTIVE IN THE case studies chosen to represent what the Formless Empire in Central Asia is all about: speed, mobility, indirect action, unconventional strategy, and geographic and circumstantial adaptation to vast and often sparsely populated land spaces. Scythians, Sarmatians, and Hepthalites, to name but a few, have been excluded. A greater focus on the eastern edge of the region has kept us nearer Sun Tzu's homeland and the modern nation-states and empires that have been more directly influenced in their policy-making by being exposed to both the benefits and calamities of contact with various Inner Eurasian societies. In a few cases where the influence spread west or south, we have tracked that as well to show the overall applicability of formless geopolitics.

The Xiongnu and their unified empire showed the adaptive nature of formless geopolitics. One of the earliest powerful confederations of steppe people, they not only demonstrated the remarkable speed and utility of the Eurasian cavalryman over vast spaces despite their often-small numbers, but they also executed the indirect methods of politics and diplomacy that often arise from such a situation. The destruction of the Xiongnu Empire by the Chinese was an early example of a settled state adapting to the superior mobility of its steppe neighbors and training and recruiting its own all-cavalry armies. After Ban Chao's truly epic victory over the Xiongnu and the establishment of the Han Dynasty in Inner Asia, it was not administered as a Chinese province but rather in a more indirect method. Certain critical geographic points were occupied, and the spaces in between were left to be ruled indirectly and through local elites. The western half of the Xiongnu domains was left almost entirely untouched and largely served as a buffer state between the new Chinese realms farther east and any new unruly tribe migrating through Central Asia. If the largely independent realm of western Xiongnu turned against the Chinese, there was still eastern Xiongnu to absorb the shock before any core Chinese territories were affected.

The creative and clever use of large spaces occupied by small numbers of mobile forces remained and in some ways was even strengthened by the successor Tang Dynasty, its founder part Turkic in origin. Spreading east from northwesterly origins, the Tang was renowned for its military power and Central Asian influence. Controlling the Silk Road trade routes gave it unprecedented wealth as well.

After a ruinous civil war, the Tang gave way, and migratory nomads broke into China once again. While the Chinese carried on as before in the south under the Sung Dynasty, the nomadic Khitan people drove out from Mongolia to seize Manchuria and parts of northern China. Being outnumbered by their settled subjects, the Khitans adopted an indirect method of rule, a pattern that would be common to all nomadic people for centuries. The Khitans were the first to codify this into law in the Liao Dynasty, and their governance was largely based on the idea of several permanent Chinese-style cities holding the reins of power, but with a nomadic aristocracy riding between them in a mobile tent city. Civil law was applied differently to nomads, forest dwellers, and agrarian Chinese, and a true multicultural state of remarkable legal diversity was born from this nomadic minority.

But even this startling innovation could not hold back the turbulent tides of other mobile people. The Jurchens rebelled and stormed out of Manchuria, soon taking over the former territory of the Khitans. Yet it was in this moment of ultimate crisis that the Khitan political system, which allowed the nomadic population to retain its mobility despite ruling over a predominantly settled state, showed its greatest degree of flexibility. Prince Yelu Daishi, many of his courtiers, and a substantial segment of his cavalry rode out west and built a new kingdom among the oases and rivers of Transoxiana. Despite the new and alien settings, this second gasp of Khitan power, that of the Kara-Khitai, lasted for another century and was one of the dominant nations of Central Asia. It was largely able to do this by retaining the decentralized, flexible system of governance it had formed through experience in Manchuria. When it fell because of its own attempts to subvert this tried and true system by imposing Buddhism on its primarily Muslim subjects, it was at the hands of another rising power, the Mongols, who were learning the lessons the Khitans had apparently unlearned. They went on to consume Khitan and Jurchen alike and went farther afield than either of those had dreamed.

The Mongols were the apogee of nomadic power in Eurasian history, and the last gasp of the near-total military dominance of entirely nomadic people over settled people in warfare. After the unification of the various previously marginal tribes by Temujin, who was proclaimed Chinggis Khan in 1206, they became the most successful land-based conquerors in history. At first lacking the sophistication and nuance of the Khitans, they proved remarkably adaptable to foreign ideas, and they recruited heavily from new subject populations to staff their bureaucracy and governing classes. Especially popular were Khitans and Jurchens, who were from similar nomadic backgrounds as the Mongols but also were somewhat integrated into the civilization of the Chinese.

Once the Jurchens and Khitans were absorbed, the Mongols began to expand elsewhere. A war started by the Turkic rulers of Persia brought them west through the rest of Central Asia and into the Middle East. From there the door lay open to a country that so far had been removed from integration into the Inner Eurasian system, Russia. After Batu and Subotai's campaigns in Russia and Europe, which struck into unfamiliar forest terrain by invading along the frozen rivers during winter, both Russia and China were harnessed to a single empire and a single pancontinental trade system. The small Mongol armies, supplementing their ranks with local recruits, took advantage of their ability to live on horseback and their unprecedented mastery of strategic deception and mobility. From Russia to Korea and Siberia to Persia, a small group of people dominated Eurasia through local proxies enforced by speed, flexibility, and an efficient international postal service. Even this massive success could only hold for a few generations, as regions began to split into successor states that in turn adapted to more-immediate local concerns, but the trade network lasted for centuries. But the Mongols' success brought about the end of the nomadic dominance of the region by connecting the future nations of continental dominance to each other as well as to the Mongolian methods of empire and strategy.

The farther from the political center a successor kingdom was, the more true it had to remain to its formless nomadic roots in order to remain in power. Of the successor states, it was the Kipchak Khanate, or Golden Horde, that retained the greatest degree of formless principles, despite its distance from the core regions of the Mongol Empire, and the forested terrain many of its vassals were shrouded in. The Kipchak Khanate became most skilled at manipulating its vassals, deflecting expansionist wars launched from the west with buffers, and acquiring tribute and security with minimal military cost to itself. Even with the periodic civil wars for succession that began to occur a few generations into its hegemony, it was usually not too difficult for the victorious party of the internal struggles to reassert the power hierarchy of the region with a campaign or two. The method was effective enough on the Russian principalities that the Grand Duchy of Lithuania ended up growing immensely to the east using similar methods in the aftermath of the Mongol conquest. This system, which the Russians in later years called "the Mongol Yoke," was only overthrown from the outside by the next stage in the evolution of the Formless Empire: the Timurids.

The Timurids represented the start of the transformation of the Formless Empire from a purely nomadic model to a coalition of artisan agrarian cities led by a seminomadic ruling class in charge of nomadic armies. Rather than merely enrich the nomadic tribes, the purpose of their often seemingly apocalyptic campaigns was to enrich their patron cities at the expense of others. This was accomplished not merely by looting but by destroying the economic viability of certain trade routes (particularly the northern ones of the fantastically wealthy Kipchak Khanate) in order to redirect wealth back to the increasingly marginalized Central Asian oasis area. In this mission, the Timurids were somewhat successful, gaining an additional century for Inner Eurasian states to stay the dominant and most dynamic of military and economic powers. But their political project, founded as it was on large-scale economic calamity, was not successful, and the empire shrunk to a rump state almost immediately after the death of its founder.

The Timurids, finally reduced to nothing but a city-state, were finally driven even from that rump territory a century later by the migrating Uzbeks, who were descended from a branch of the Kipchak Khanates. It was then that the Timurids, like the Khitans before them, performed the feat of state migration and became, under Prince Babur, the Mughal Empire in northern India. Babur retained the cavalry focus of the army but added large cannons and matchlock guns to its repertoire. At the Battle of Panipat, he showcased the technological adaptation of the seminomadic army and defeated a much larger—and slower—enemy force. The Mughals flourished, adapting to the new circumstances and forging a bridge between Central Asia and India. Eventually, they became so invested in India that their Central Asian segment of the empire shriveled to an afterthought, and their armies became more infantry and artillery based, similar to what happened to the Ottoman Empire out west. Once the governing elite dropped its more-tolerant social policies and the state became more overtly bureaucratic and centralized, it—like the Kara-Khitai—began to lose ground to competitors. Interestingly, the biggest foe of the Mughals at the start of their decline was the cavalry-dominated military of the Hindu Marathas. Soon after this check on their power in the south, the seminomadic Afghans and the sea-controlling British entered the scene, all using superior mobility to force the increasingly conservative and rigid Mughal state to its knees.

No longer a continent-spanning empire, the Mongols still managed to regain much wealth and security, even after their total collapse in China, through the machinations of Queen Manduhai. She wrestled the Mongol tribes back into a unified entity, kept the resurgent Chinese at bay largely through guile, and placed Mongol horsepower in the center of a trade axis from East Asia to Central Asia. She returned prosperity to her people at minimal cost in administration of military operations. It was a small snippet of the history of the region, but one of the most telling examples of the Formless Empire at work for a small state rather than a massive one.

The initial deathblow against parts of Central Asia and Mughal India was struck by another empire whose ruling elite originated in Central Asia but who had come to rule a long-established civilized land: Iran. Nader Shah was an archetype of an up-and-coming warlord in the old Turkic mold, but being a frontier dweller in the service of Persia, he sought his fortune as a Napoleonic figure there. His military innovations pushed the region further toward a synthesis of settled technology and nomadic mobility, not only by having the dominant weapon of his armies be guns (which the Ottomans had done by this point as well) but by retaining the cavalry as the dominant tactical branch (which the Ottomans did not do). His speedier army put a larger Mughal force to flight outside of Delhi in the Battle of Karnai in 1739.

Then, for the first time in Eurasian history, the strategic pendulum swung to the civilized countries in a decisive and irrevocable manner. Naval technology and logistics had reached the point where naval power was more effective at spreading commerce and military power than land power, and the increasing levels of British, French, and Portuguese influence on the outskirts of littoral Eurasia boded ill for the nomadic, seminomadic, and caravan-based entities dwelling within the Eurasian heartland. The ability of naval power to harness the wealth of two entire new continents (North and South America) to Europe jump started this previously tenuous process.[1]

But this was a gradual change overall, and the new up-and-coming powers that shared frontiers with the nomadic people had learned about frontier strategy at the hands of their unruly neighbors, like the Han Dynasty before them had. With the addition of military technologies that put the initiative back in the hands of the agrarian powers, their own take on the Formless Empire began, now heading in the opposite direction.

If the reign of Nader Shah and the rise of the Mughals showed the total merger of nomad and settled, the expansions of the Manchus and the Russians showed the total displacement of nomadic peoples as the settled people finally took the long-term, sustained offensive. The increasing sophistication of gunpowder weapons, the greater economic might of cities and farms, and the lessons learned from the nomads in the military sphere proved an unbeatable combination when harnessed to the larger populations and resources of Russia and China. Each of those two nations had been provinces of the Mongol Empire, and each now wreaked its vengeance in overlapping yet differing ways.

In terms of amount of territory conquered, Russia was the big winner. Using Cossacks, themselves seminomadic bands of societal outcasts who had developed their own horse-borne culture, the Russian state drove into the Caucuses and Siberia largely in pursuit of security from raiders in the case of the former and profits from the fur trade in the case of the latter. Along the way they dismantled many successor fragment states from the Kipchak Khanate and even gave some of their ruling elite titles of nobility for defecting peacefully. Despite its authoritarian latter-day reputation, in terms of expansion, the Russian Empire was almost as ethnically and religiously tolerant as that of the Mongols. In Siberia in particular, it was entirely driven by economic goals. Initially very sparse settlements and Cossack bases cropped up only at strategic locations, and the native people were largely worked into more of a tribute system than one of direct rule. Eventually, a turn south into Central Asia proper was greatly facilitated by the deployment of railroads, sealing forever the fact that it was now the settled societies that had the truly decisive strategic mobility over the nomadic and seminomadic peoples.

When the Manchus took over China, they governed different populations using a variety of methods, much as the Khitans had. The Chinese were subjected to their usual bureaucratic system of governance—and perhaps even a particularly conservative variety of it as the dynasty aged—while the Mongols, Manchus, and Tibetans were placed under their more-traditional kinship-based systems.

Though the new Qing Dynasty did not expand as far or as fast as the Russian state, it faced much more difficult opposition to its westward drive, and its gains in territory and vassals were thus just as impressive. Galdan Khan's attempt to forge an independent Mongol state gave the Qing many a smarting blow in battle. As Russia and China, the two traditional sufferers of nomadic power, grew toward each other, they replaced their original enemies as the driving strategic forces of Inner Eurasia. In so doing, they became each other's largest rival.

At first it was the Qing who came off for the better in the skirmishes on the new Manchurian/Siberian frontier. Not much more than a century later, however, the tables began to turn in favor of Russia. After a long drive, it finally managed to wring so many concessions from a weakened and tottering Qing, which was besieged by Britain and France, that by the dawn of the twentieth century, Russian ports opened in the south of Manchuria, and the interior of the province was crisscrossed by Russian-controlled railroads. This threatened Britain, inspiring limited British intervention in the southern reaches of Eurasia, showing just how powerful naval powers could be even inland—and even if their gains were marginal at best.

But this only helped bring a new rising power into the fray. Maritime dominance was in full swing in the geopolitics of the era, and even upstart Japan burst its way into the Eurasian scene after humiliating China and driving into Manchuria to defeat Russia in 1905. Despite the epic land battles, with Manchuria being the contested ground, the most decisive victory earned by Japan in its war against Russia was the Battle of Tsushima, at sea. Nonetheless, the results of the Treaty of Portsmouth brought a new actor into Inner Asian affairs with the Japanese takeover of many of the Russian concessions in Manchuria. In the coming decades, both the Qing Dynasty and imperial Russia collapsed under revolutionary pressures, and Japan seized the initiative at both of the current Eurasian hegemons' expense. Soon both countries were engulfed by instability and civil war, with Japanese agents and proxies infiltrating deeply into their various conflicts. Many of the warlords they supported also had brief reigns of indirect rule before being swallowed up by other parties.

In many ways, Japan was an astute learner. Using spies and criminal connections, it wrung concessions from warlords in Russia and China. This paved the way for the eventual wholesale seizure of

Manchuria and the creation of a puppet regime there that in some ways echoed the old indirect Eurasian method of rule (and in many other ways was quite wanting by such standards). Massive intervention in the Russian civil war by the allies of the First World War was relatively fruitless, aside from a few temporary economic gains and control over several White Russian community leaders, but China eventually ended up divided and torn asunder by Japanese policies. Despite this apparent adaptation, Japan, like Britain, did not meet with total success as it forayed farther from the waves. Its military adapted to the new circumstances far less effectively than its policies did, and attempts to further push the Soviet Union and test its capabilities ran into the jaws of Grigori Zhukov's more-mobile, armored army and was crushed on the frontier between Manchuria and Mongolia.

Even as the Soviets did away with the various indirect and decentralized methods of rule of their predecessors, their army resuscitated the combination of speed and firepower that nomadic armies had once deployed. And in an era of industrialization and state power, it was the military that was the most decisive arm. The Soviets' tactics played the primary role in the defeat of Germany in the Second World War, from Kursk onward, and their armies crushed a weakened and almost-already defeated Japan in a campaign of Manchurian conquest of nearly textbook success. A few years later, China was reunified under communist leadership, and it appeared that the traditional antinomadic hegemons had been restored to the Eurasian throne, this time under a red banner instead of dynastic ones.

But sometimes, the more things change, the more they stay the same. Communist solidarity did little to stop interstate rivalry between the two countries. China looked for more-distant (and thus less-threatening) allies elsewhere and found one in the unlikely yet sensible choice of the United States. Russia floundered diplomatically, and border skirmishes rocked the old troublesome Siberia-Manchuria frontier. Conflict also stirred in Afghanistan, and while Soviet forces conducted themselves well, showing off their army and its rapid-deployment and campaigning ability, it was used for direct, rather than indirect, control, and so its battlefield successes could not translate into any kind of political results.

This was a symptom of the greater modernist-style communist project in Russia and China. Both empires were built using mixed methods that took the indirect and formless style of their nomadic opponents and adapted them to settled agrarian states. In an age of ideology and party rule, however, rampant centralization of culturally and geographically diverse people was an unsustainable dead end, at least in the Soviet Union, whose peaceful implosion implied resigned acceptance of even those committed to the core state. In China, the state remains intact, in fact stronger than ever since the dawn of the People's Republic. But it is still rocked by ethnic upset in its various frontier regions, and it guards its borders carefully. When dealing with peoples outside of its borders, however, it has shown a remarkable level of subtlety that the Soviet Union never did. Despite its much larger share of regional power compared to the new Central Asian states, the Chinese foreign policy establishment signed treaties on borders that divided contested territory equitably between the nations. With new economic dynamism, the Chinese state began to set up investment and resource extraction around the region while pursuing friendly relations with the local elites. Perhaps it is fitting that the nation in which Sun Tzu was born adapted better to the changing realities of the post-Cold War era.

The scaling back of Russian power meant its reappraisal, from indirect involvement in the Tajik civil war to shoring up its alliances with former Soviet states in Central Asia, particularly against Taliban influence and later against an encroaching United States. There was nothing quite like an absolute crash to start a full reappraisal of foreign policy. So the deployment of Russian power and the nature of the country's geopolitics changed to those of small army bases, checkpoint control, helicopters, special forces, and personal relationships between elites. Gone was the Soviet juggernaut of massive troop deployments and direct occupation, replaced by a streamlined machine in an era when the Russian state plays trendsetter and arbitrator among a cluster of de facto junior allies.

What will happen in the future to the people of Inner Eurasia is unknown, but by looking at the grand trends of geopolitics in the region, as we have done, we can discuss a few possibilities. Already we see in places like Ukraine and Syria how even a Russia attempting a comeback as a military power is far more likely to use proxies and special operations than it is to deploy massive conventional forces. By using its naval base in Syria to help coordinate an alliance with the government of President Bashar Hafez al-Assad against Islamist rebels and the Free Syrian Army, Russia wields influence without having to fully commit to a state of war or the mass deployment of its own forces. In Ukraine, conventional operations are coupled with proxy warfare (the outright Russian seizure of Crimea followed by the ambiguous situation of supporting pro-Russian rebels in various enclaves near the eastern border with Russia) in order to make clear the price of denying Russian regional hegemony. At the time of this writing, no conclusions regarding Russian actions in Ukraine could be made about that conflict, as its ultimate success or failure remained in question.

Despite the many mutations and occasional abrupt periods of waning of the Formless Empire, its key concepts survive and even thrive. Adaptability is, after all, the central one of those concepts, and changing winds of fortune for different nations and tribes hardly stop others from learning from cumulative regional experience. Mobility and speed trump size, and indirect control is a cost-effective method of power projection that also allows one to retain a large number of reserves to deploy decisively if it proves inadequate. Sun Tzu's formless doctrine would not only have been at home in the Inner Eurasia of the past had it been born there but also in the Inner Eurasia of the present.

The current priority of both Russia and China is superficially similar to that of the old nomadic powers, which is that the primary purpose of foreign policy is to secure favorable trade and economic enrichment through resource control. This is the obvious goal of the Chinese leadership, whereas Russia, resource rich as it already is, seems to focus on more tactical goals of securing space around it while it develops its domestic economy.[2]

The means of upholding a type of formless hegemony are not as ambiguous as the potential for their future use. When it comes to information gathering, the use of agents, highly mobile military units with great firepower, and the ability to deploy forces at the decisive moment, there is no better era for that than the present. The retention of many military bases, certain collective security agreements like the Commonwealth of Independent States to facilitate cooperation on crime investigations, customs, and diplomacy, as well as the Shanghai Cooperation Organization and other joint security initiatives and dialogue keep a vast area open to indirect methods of geopolitical strategy. Uzbekistan, long playing the role of team leader in Central Asia proper, works with Russian influence rather than against it in order to better secure political and economic stability, but now being independent, it also pushes its own agenda for further regional integration on the Turkic countries. In contemporary Uzbekistan, and to a lesser extent Kazakhstan, policies seem to reflect the former strategy of the once tiny and vulnerable city-state of Muscovy, which strengthened itself gradually by becoming the active collaborator and tax gatherer of the Kipchak Khanate.

The biggest issue in Central Asia today, given the reduced American influence there, will most likely remain the ongoing relationship of its two strongest countries. This could go in a variety of directions, with three primary branches: continued or even increasing cooperation, the retention of the present ambiguous relationship, and increasing division if not outright rivalry.

Continued cooperation seems the most likely in the immediate short term. The United States is still a more powerful country than either Russia or China, and the threat of Islamic radicals to both Eurasian powers is still palpable. Increased cooperation would be a victory of foreign-policy planning and regional stability and would most likely favor China more than Russia overall, as it has the stronger economy and larger population. For this reason, only two situations could likely bring this scenario about: a drastic weakening of the Russian world position or a weakening of the Chinese state to the extent that Russia would no longer be threatened by such an unequal alliance. But no matter which power was the dominant actor in such a hypothetical alliance, such a large and necessarily loose partnership would be a victory for the Formless Empire on a huge scale to whoever could pull it off and keep its hegemony as indirect as possible. For the long run, however, this should probably be considered a less-than-likely scenario.

The retention of the present ambiguous relationship is also worth examining. The advantages of maintaining a loose status quo are many, mainly because nations can adapt their policies to events as they occur. But the Central Asian states' acting against Russian interests, or seeking close ties to Japan, Turkey, or the United States, would cause a change in the status quo, with defensive reactions likely by the big regional powers. Even if this way forward might at first seem the most appealing for the smaller states of the area, it likely would simply lead to a backlash from their larger neighbors, which would put them into an even-more-unequal and precarious situation than they are in now. After all, their biggest neighbors are also their largest economic partners. As Uzbek president Islam Karimov states in his book, both interrelation and interdependence are the way forward for the new states of the region.[3] If there is one thing that the concept of the Formless Empire can teach us for certain it is that these concepts are not contradictory but rather complementary.

Increasing division and/or outright rivalry is the final and most dramatic option to consider. This has been the norm in relations between China and Russia since they came to be the dominant powers in the Eurasian heartland. They began their rivalry with skirmishes in the Amur basin, put it aside briefly to deal with the scourge of remaining nomadic people farther west, then returned to it nonstop until both regimes were under the control of communist parties in 1949. Their second period of cooperation was unprecedented in scope compared to anything prior but lasted barely two decades before tension reignited in the same Amur basin and led to a rivalry that lasted until the end of the Cold War. Now the rivalry has been set aside, but the situation between the two powers is reliably friendly in the short term only. Differences in their circumstances change their positions and priorities. China's economic growth is much larger, and mostly fed from industrializing, whereas Russia is largely dependent on resource exports. These economies seem compatible, and they are, but the situation leaves Russia in the weaker position. Most Russian gas is shipped to Europe, and the oil pipelines in the east are often looking for Japanese investment to avoid being entirely dependent on the Chinese.[4]

Russia's position in the region is largely carved from the former Soviet husk. It is more likely to degrade than improve, though neither eventuality is certain. China becomes a more-attractive trade partner every day, and India, Iran, Turkey, and Japan all have various economic connections in the region now. Were a falling out to occur between Russia and China, Russia would be on the defensive and China would likely hold the advantage in any conventional conflict owing to its much larger population and economy. Would a threatened Russia ramp up competition and rhetoric to hold onto the Moscow-centered order in Central Asia? Given fear of the immense population disparity of Siberia versus the bordering Chinese provinces that once were Manchuria, it is likely that whether the government wants it or not, a popular backlash against getting too close to the Chinese state is a possibility for Russian policy-makers. But in order to be able to rely on regional support, Russia must hold the reins loosely rather than tightly, just as the dictates of formless strategy in the region's history would imply. At the same time, the rise of an increasingly fascistic Eurasianism—a political philosophy that says Russia is uniquely destined for regional rule over many of its neighboring states as both an anti-Chinese and anti-Western authoritarian power bloc—has debatable levels of influence on Russian foreign policy. Russia has a central role to play in the region, but overt declarations of hegemonic intent could present dangers to Moscow's ability to keep a calculated grip on the region, denying as it does the large role that multicultural and open borders have had in the history of Inner Eurasia. So, too, must Chinese policy-makers occasionally deal with irredentist calls for lost territory now belonging to Russia and constantly strive for balance between building bridges abroad and appeasing a domestic audience stoked to nationalism by turbulent economic and political times.

What would a split look like between these two giants? Given the level of regional integration in Central Asia, it seems Russia would have the built-in home field advantage in case of another split between the Eurasian hegemons. But China has learned from its modern past; its foreign policy in Central Asia is often conducted with a humility and equality that Russia lacks. Were some kind of devastating rift to grow between the powers—because of competition over regional allies, general fear and suspicion, or something else—any conflict would most likely be indirect. Since both nations are nuclear powers, it seems unlikely either of their territories would be violated. The countries that lie between them, however, may not be so lucky. Drawing on their collective heritage, however, might increase regional solidarity against both current powers. Even so, the danger for the smaller countries in such a situation would be immense.

The best chance for the small states to prosper is not through nationalism or embracing neoliberalism with the same utopian gusto their ancestors once had for Bolshevism, but rather to take what is best from the regional historical experience of power politics in informal transnational networks and adapt it to contemporary contexts. The region has a remarkable legacy of geopolitical fluidity and dynamism, which could be a perfect fit with the integrated and fast-paced nature of the contemporary world. Whether unity or division lies in the future of Inner Eurasia, the best guide forward will be the one that recognizes that the region works best when geopolitics is formless and adaptable to the local circumstances on the ground. Wide spaces, mobility, multiculturalism, and a civic polity based on acceptance of divergence rather than enforced unity are key. If the Central Asian republics can look more to their history and less to the history of romantic nationalism, they can better form coalitions with each other to affirm their independence or increase their bargaining power in panregional alliances with larger states. If Russia and China could overcome their seemingly increasing flirtations with xenophobia and centralization, they too could guarantee greater success in building the links required to wield stable influence in a place like Central Asia.

But if the lessons of the past are ignored, political projects like the Shanghai Cooperation Organization and political philosophies like Eurasianism will bear bitter fruit, if any at all. Chinggis Khan's Yasa code of law, Khitan acceptance of differences, and traditional Turkic and Mongolian adaptability serve as stronger policy benchmarks than contemporary Han chauvinism or Russia's increasingly racist political culture. Empire is not an anachronism but a present reality in a new and adapted form, one with deep historical precedent and hardly relegated to specific periods of European history.

Despite having long been made militarily irrelevant, nomadic peoples still have much to teach us about how to govern diverse regions and plan for prosperity while keeping military forces at the peak of efficiency by being low in number but high on range and mobility. Above all is the knowledge and willingness to always adapt to changing circumstances. As Sun Tzu put it, "So it is said that if you know others and know yourself, you will not be imperiled in a hundred battles; if you do not know others but know yourself, you win one and lose one; if you do not know others and do not know yourself, you will be imperiled in every single battle."[5]

The Formless Empire is a unique, indigenous geopolitical development that shows the societal adaptation of cultures and states in the particular geographic context of the inland realms of Eurasia. Rather than an intentional process, it was the outgrowth of a confluence of terrain, population density, and the highly mobile lifestyle adapted to either live within those contexts or compete with those who did. As times changed, the logistical necessity of the nomadic lifestyle gave way to the material superiority of technologically advanced settled states, but even they took with them many of the influences of their waning foes. In an era now dominated by mechanized armed forces, electronic communication, and flexible international business models, much of the world has become more formless in its diplomacy and warfare, but the long-standing nature of Inner Eurasian geopolitics remains a peculiar and steadfast example of a region that has always been so.

NOTES

Introduction

1. Stuart Legg, *The Heartland* (New York: Farrar, Straus & Giroux, 1970), 31–39.
2. David Christian, *A History of Russia, Central Asia, and Mongolia*, vol. 1, *Inner Eurasia from Prehistory to the Mongol Empire* (Oxford: Blackwell, 1998), 5–6; Legg, *Heartland*, 37–39.
3. Jane Burbank and Frederick Cooper, *Empires in World History: Power and the Politics of Difference* (Princeton, NJ: Princeton University Press, 2010), 3.

Chapter One: Overview of Central Asian History

1. Rhoads Murphy, "An Ecological History of Central Asian Nomadism," in *Ecology and Empire: Nomads in the Cultural Evolution of the Old World*, ed. Gary Seaman (Los Angeles: University of Southern California, 1989), 45, 46–48.
2. Christopher I. Beckwith, *Empires of the Silk Road: A History of Central Eurasia from the Bronze Age to the Present* (Princeton, NJ: Princeton University Press, 2009), 11–23, 76.
3. Burbank and Cooper, *Empires*, 115.
4. Richard N. Frye, "Central Asian Concepts of Rule on the Steppe and Sown," in *Ecology and Empire: Nomads in the Cultural Evolution of the Old World*, ed. Gary Seaman (Los Angeles: University of Southern California, 1989), 135–37.
5. Halford J. Mackinder, "The Geographical Pivot of History," *Geographical Journal* 23, no. 4 (1904): 421–37, http://www.jstor.org/discover/10.2307/1775498?sid=21105999540243&uid=2&uid=3739864&uid=4&uid=70&uid=3739256&uid=2134.
6. Colin S. Gray, "In Defense of the Heartland: Sir Halford Mackinder and His Critics a Hundred Years On," in *Global Geostrategy: Mackinder and the Defense of the West*, ed. Brian W. Blouet (New York: Taylor & Francis, 2005), 19.
7. Ibid., 9–11.
8. Victor H. Mair, *The Art of War: Sun Zi's Military Methods* (New York: Columbia University Press, 2007), 27.
9. Ibid., 12–13.

10. Mark McNeilly, *Sun Tzu and the Art of Modern Warfare* (Oxford: Oxford University Press, 2001), 5–6, 68.

11. Sun Tzu, *The Art of War*, tr. Thomas Cleary (Boston: Shambhala, 1988), 66, 58, 43.

12. Mair, *Art of War*, 53–54.

13. Sun Tzu, *Art of War*, 9.

14. Fuad Baali, *Society, State, and Urbanism: Ibn Khaldun's Sociological Thought* (New York: State University of New York Press, 1988), 66, 73–74.

15. Ibn Khaldun, *The Muqaddimah: An Introduction to History*, tr. Franz Rosenthal (Princeton, NJ: Princeton University Press, 1958, first published 1377), 254, 265–82.

16. Ibid., 295, 347.

17. Basil Henry Liddel-Hart, *Strategy* (London: Faber & Faber, 1954), 324.

18. Ibid., 137–42.

19. John Gray, *Black Mass: Apocalyptic Religion and the Death of Utopia* (London: Penguin, 2007), 99.

20. Beckwith, *Empires*, 23.

21. Steven E. Lobell, Norrin M. Ripsman, and Jeffrey W. Taliaferro, eds., *Neoclassical Realism, The State and Foreign Policy* (Cambridge: Cambridge University Press, 2009), 22–26.

22. Jeffrey W. Taliaferro, "Neoclassical Realism: The Psychology of Great Power Intervention," in *Making Sense of International Relations Theory*, ed. Jennifer Sterling-Folker (Boulder, CO: Lynne Rienner, 2006), 109–16.

23. Stuart J. Kaufman, Richard Little, and William C. Wohlforth, eds., *The Balance of Power in World History* (New York: Palgrave Macmillan, 2007).

CHAPTER TWO: HISTORIC EXAMPLES OF THE PREMODERN FORMLESS LAND EMPIRE

1. Legg, *Heartland*, 37.

2. Murphy, "Ecological History," 46.

3. Desmond H. Martin, "The Mongol Army," *Journal of the Royal Asiatic Society of Great Britain and Ireland* 1 (Apr. 1943): 46–85, http://www.jstor.org/stable/25221891.

4. William Samolin, *East Turkestan in the Twelfth Century* (London: Mouton, 1964), 21.

5. Carter Vaughn Findley, *The Turks in World History* (Oxford: Oxford University Press, 2005), 32–33.

6. It was thought, probably correctly, that trading with nomadic barbarians would make the nomads stronger. Many Chinese governments in history, most notably the Ming Dynasty, effectively instituted economic blockades on nomadic neighbors. Usually, however, this just made warfare more frequent rather than less frequent, even if it often resulted in Chinese acquisition of superior horses from the northern

pasturelands. See Beckwith, *Empires*, 21–23 and 89 on trade, and Samolin, *East Turkestan*, 42.

7. Christian, *History of Russia*, 185–86, 187–90, 192.

8. Findley, *Turks*, 35.

9. Sun Tzu, *Art of War*, 49.

10. Christian Tyler, *Wild West China: The Taming of Xinjiang* (London: John Murray, 2003), 31–32.

11. Samolin, *East Turkestan*, 42.

12. Beckwith, *Empires*, 125–27.

13. Findley, *Turks*, 41.

14. Rene Grousset, *The Empire of the Steppes: A History of Central Asia* (New Brunswick, NJ: Rutgers University Press, 1970), 101.

15. Grousset, *Empire*, 116.

16. Legg, *Heartland*, 213.

17. Herbert Franke and Denis Twitchett, eds., *The Cambridge History of China*, vol. 6, *Alien Regimes and Border States, 907–1368* (Cambridge: Cambridge University Press, 1994), 47.

18. Thomas J. Barfield, "Inner Asia and Cycles of Power in China's Imperial Dynastic History," in *Rulers from the Steppe: State Formation on the Eurasian Periphery*, ed. Gary Seaman and Daniel Marks, Ethnographics Monograph Series, monograph no. 2 (Los Angeles: Ethnographic Press, 1991), 24, 43.

19. Franke and Twitchett, *Cambridge History*, 56–62, 78.

20. Beckwith, *Empires*, 173.

21. John Meskill, "History of China," in *An Introduction to Chinese Civilization*, ed. John Meskill and J. Mason Gentzler (New York: Columbia University Press, 1973), 144–46.

22. Franke and Twitchett, *Cambridge History*, 67.

23. John Keay, *China: A History* (London: HarperCollins, 2008), 305–6.

24. Franke and Twitchett, *Cambridge History*, 86, 95, 99, 105–10.

25. Meskill, "History of China," 142–43.

26. Naomi Standen, *Unbounded Loyalty: Frontier Crossing in Liao China* (Honolulu: University of Hawaii Press, 2007), 64, 131.

27. Legg, *Heartland*, 217–18.

28. Michael Biran, *The Empire of the Qara Khitai in Eurasian History*, Cambridge Studies in Islamic Civilization (Cambridge: Cambridge University Press, 2005), 22–32.

29. Ibid., 39–44.

30. The Kara-Khitan khan was known as khan or *gurkhan* in Central Asia but still had official Chinese imperial titles, and the empire was referred to as the Western Liao by both Jin and Sung courts. The Sung, of course, realized by this point what a mistake they had made in supporting the Jurchens against the Khitan and sought to build up the credit of the old Liao over the present Jin foe. Christian, *History of Russia*, 378.

31. Biran, *Empire of the Qara Khitai*, 135.

32. Ibid., 85–86.

33. Grousset, *Empire*, 165.

34. Biran, *Empire of the Qara Khitai*, 87–89.

35. Luc Kwanten, *Imperial Nomads: A History of Central Asia, 500–1500* (Leicester, UK: Leicester University Press, 1979), 145–50.

36. Rashid al-Din, *The Successors of Genghis Khan*, tr. J. A. Boyle (New York: Columbia University Press, 1971, first published 1317), 74, 77.

37. Igor de Rachewitz, tr., *The Secret History of the Mongols: A Mongolian Epic Chronicle of the Thirteenth Century* (Leiden, Netherlands: Koninklijike Brill NV, 2004), 124–25, 129, 254.

38. Biran, *Empire of the Qara Khitai*, 87–89.

39. David Sneath, *The Headless State: Aristocratic Orders, Kinship Society, and Misrepresentations of Nomadic Inner Asia* (New York: Columbia University Press, 2007), 167–74.

40. Ibid., 44.

41. Beckwith, *Empires*, 188.

42. Jack Weatherford, *Genghis Khan and the Making of the Modern World* (New York: Crown and Three River, 2004), 227–38.

43. Amy Chua, *Day of Empire: How Hyperpowers Rise to Global Dominance—and Why They Fall* (New York: Doubleday, 2007), xxi, 300–305.

44. F. W. Mote, *Imperial China 900–1800* (Cambridge, MA: Harvard University Press, 2000), 489.

45. Gary Seaman and Daniel Marks, eds., *Rulers from the Steppe: State Formation on the Eurasian Periphery*, Ethnographics Monograph Series, monograph no. 2 (Los Angeles: Ethnographic Press, 1991), 4.

46. Kwanten, *Imperial Nomads*, 223, 260.

47. Christian, *History of Russia*, 410–12; Leo de Hartog, *Russia and the Mongol Yoke: The History of the Russian Principalities and the Golden Horde, 1221–1502* (London: British Academic Press, an imprint of I. B. Tauris, 1996), 62.

48. The reason for selecting this particular realm of the Mongol Empire is largely because the vast empire behaved in very different ways after it began to fragment. Each of the regions of the empire can be looked at as a case study, but the best one to illustrate the nature of Formless Empire is almost certainly the Kipchak Khanate.

49. Viacheslav Shpakovsky and David Nicolle, *Kalka River 1223: Genghiz Khan's Mongols Invade Russia* (Oxford: Osprey, 2001), 83–86.

50. Peter B. Golden, "The Qipchaqs of Medieval Eurasia: An Example of Stateless Adaptation in the Steppes," in *Rulers from the Steppe: State Formation on the Eurasian Periphery*, ed. Gary Seaman and Daniel Marks, Ethnographics Monograph Series, monograph no. 2 (Los Angeles: Ethnographic Press, 1991), 135–37.

51. George Vernadsky, *The Mongols in Russia* (New Haven, CT: Yale University Press, 1953; repr., London: University Microfilms International, 1979), 110–15.

52. Beckwith, *Empires*, 189.

53. Vernadsky, *Mongols*, 117.

54. Ibid., 133.

55. De Hartog, *Russia*, 46.

56. Vernadsky, *Mongols*, 209.

57. Charles J. Halperin, *Russia and the Golden Horde: The Mongol Impact on Medieval Russian History* (Bloomington: Indiana University Press, 1987), 29.

58. Vernadsky, *Mongols*, 210–11.

59. Grousset, *Empire*, 596.

60. Janet Martin, *Medieval Russia 980–1584* (Cambridge: Cambridge University Press, 1995), 142.

61. Ibid., 148.

62. Halperin, *Russia*, 39–43.

63. Martin, *Medieval Russia*, 186, 188.

64. Vernadsky, *Mongols*, 127.

65. De Hartog, *Russia*, 50–51.

66. Martin, *Medieval Russia*, 161.

67. Halperin, *Russia*, 82.

68. De Hartog, *Russia*, 92.

69. Vernadsky, *Mongols*, 144–59.

70. Martin, *Medieval Russia*, 211–16.

71. Ibid., 204.

Chapter Three: Post-Pax Mongolica Through the Timurid Powers

1. Kwanten, *Imperial Nomads*, 167, 170, 173.

2. Hilda Hookham, *Tamburlaine the Conqueror* (London: Camelot Press, 1962), 43–44; Justin Marozzi, *Tamerlane: Sword of Islam, Conqueror of the World* (Cambridge, MA: Da Capo, 2006), 30–31.

3. Hookham, *Tamburlaine*, 48–50.

4. Kwanten, *Imperial Nomads*, 267.

5. Beatrice Forbes Manz, *The Rise and Rule of Tamerlane* (Cambridge: Cambridge University Press, 1989), 69–73.

6. John Darwin, *After Tamerlane: The Global History of Empire* (London: Allen Lane, 2007), 5.

7. Hookham, *Tamburlaine*, 65.

8. Marozzi, *Tamerlane*, 139.

9. Hookham, *Tamburlaine*, 92–94, 125–27.

10. Ibid., quoting Sharaf al-Din Yazdi, 131.

11. Ibid., 132.

12. David Nicolle and Richard Hook, *The Mongol Warlords* (Dorset, UK: Firebird, 1990), 178–79.

13. Halperin, *Russia*, 57.
14. Marozzi, *Tamerlane*, 214–15.
15. Hookham, *Tamburlaine*, 172–75.
16. Ibid., 162.
17. Marozzi, *Tamerlane*, 351.
18. Hookham, *Tamburlaine*, 251–54.
19. Manz, *Rise and Rule*, 128.
20. Beatrice Forbes Manz, *Power, Politics, and Religion in Timurid Iran* (Cambridge: Cambridge University Press, 2007), 20–21.
21. Manz, *Power, Politics*, 28, 126.
22. The preceding narrative about Babur is derived from Zahir ud-din Muhammad Babur, *The Baburnama: Memoirs of Babur, Prince and Emperor*, tr., ed., and annot. Wheeler M. Thackston (Oxford: Oxford University Press, Smithsonian Institution, 1996, originally completed 1530), 35–49, 89–93, 98, 136, 138, 162, 186.
23. Harold Lamb, *Babur the Tiger* (London: Robert Hale, 1962), 75–80.
24. Jon F. Richards, *The Mughal Empire* (Cambridge: Cambridge University Press, 1995), 8–9.
25. Babur, *Baburnama*, 323–24, 326–28; Catherine Asher, "India: The Mughals 1526–1858," in *Great Empires of Asia*, ed. Jim Masselos (London: Thames & Hudson, 2010), 169.
26. Babur, *Baburnama*, 369, 386, 421.
27. Asher, "India," 170–71.
28. Richards, *Mughal Empire*, 17, 20, 23–26, 33, 58, 60.
29. Prasad Tribathi, "The Turko-Mongol Theory of Kingship," in *The Mughal State, 1526-1750*, ed. Muzaffar Alan and Sanjay Subrahmanyam (Delhi: Oxford University Press, 1998), 115–16.
30. Richards, *Mughal Empire*, 63, 74, 110, 142–43, 133–35, 155, 175–76, 179.
31. Asher, *India*, 188–199.
32. J. F. Richards, "The Formation of Imperial Authority under Akbar and Jahangir," in *The Mughal State, 1526-1750*, ed. Muzaffar Alan and Sanjay Subrahmanyam (Delhi: Oxford University Press, 1998), 126–27.
33. R. G. Mukminova and A. Mukhtarov, "The Khanate of Bukhara," in *The History of Central Asia*, vol. 5, ed. Chahryar Adle and Irfran Habib (Paris: United Nations Educational, Scientific and Cultural Organization, 2003), 35–44, 60.
34. M. Annanepesov and H. N. Bababekov, "The Khanates of Khiva and Kokand," in *The History of Central Asia*, vol. 5, ed. Chahryar Adle and Irfran Habib (Paris: United Nations Educational, Scientific and Cultural Organization, 2003), 63.
35. John W. Dardess, "From Mongol Empire to Yuan Dynasty: Changing Forms of Imperial Rule in Mongolia and Central Asia," in *Monumenta Serica* 30 (1972–1973): 117–25, 143–49, 154.
36. Almost symbolically, the rebels posed as Chinese merchants and blew open the palace grounds with a disguised gunpowder bomb. It was a sneak attack using tech-

nology that later came to symbolize the eventual end of the era of nomadic military dominance.

37. Jack Weatherford, *The Secret History of the Mongol Queens: How the Daughters of Genghis Khan Rescued His Empire* (New York: Crown, 2010), 129–31, 125, 152, 171, 185–86, 196–204, 234–37, 248.

38. Ibid., 249; Hidehiro Okada, "Dayan Khan as Yuan Emperor: The Political Legitimacy in 15th Century Mongolia," *Bulletin de l'Ecole Francais d'Extreme-Orient* 81 (1994): 51–53.

39. Weatherford, *Secret History*, 256, 260–62.

40. Ibid., 227.

41. Darwin, *After Tamerlane*, 7.

42. Beckwith, *Empires*, 219.

43. Annanepesov and Bababekov, "Khanates of Khiva," 68.

CHAPTER FOUR: THE RISE OF STATES AND THE TRANSFERENCE OF A GEOPOLITCAL LEGACY

1. Peter A. Lorge, *The Asian Military Revolution: From Gunpowder to the Bomb* (New York: Cambridge University Press, 2008), 31; Dominic Lieven, *Empire: The Russian Empire and Its Rivals from the Sixteenth Century to the Present* (New York: Cambridge University Press, 2003), 207.

2. Gertraude Roth Li, "State Building before 1644," in *The Cambridge History of China*, vol. 9, pt. 1, *The Chi'ng Dynasty to 1800* (Cambridge: Cambridge University Press, 2002), 8–14, 18, 27–29, 31, 34–38.

3. Peter C. Perdue, *China Marches West: The Qing Conquest of Central Eurasia* (Cambridge, MA: Belknap Press of Harvard University Press, 2005), 111.

4. Kwanten, *Imperial Nomads*, 282–83.

5. Perdue, *China*, 127.

6. Ibid., 128.

7. Jerry Dennerline, "The Shun-Chih Reign," in *The Cambridge History of China*, vol. 9, pt. 1, *The Ch'ing Dynasty to 1800*, ed. Denis Twitchett and John K. Fairbank (Cambridge: Cambridge University Press, 2002), 83–84.

8. Perdue, *China*, 114, 137.

9. Darwin, *After Tamerlane*, 125–27.

10. Perdue, *China*, 5–10.

11. Darwin, *After Tamerlane*, 121.

12. Donald Ostrowski, "The Growth of Muscovy: 1462–1533," in *The Cambridge History of Russia*, vol. 1, *From Early Rus' to 1689*, ed. Maureen Perrie (Cambridge: Cambridge University Press, 2006), 218, 239.

13. Sergei Bogatyrev, "Ivan IV: 1533–1584," in *The Cambridge History of Russia*, vol. 1, *From Early Rus' to 1689*, ed. Maureen Perrie (Cambridge: Cambridge University Press, 2006), 256.

14. Ibid., 319; Taras Hunczak, ed., *Russian Imperialism from Ivan the Great to the Revolution* (New Brunswick, NJ: Rutgers University Press, 1974), 36.

15. Grousset, *Empire*, 471–72.

16. W. Bruce Lincoln, *The Conquest of a Continent: Siberia and the Russians* (Ithaca, NY: Cornell University Press, 1994), 43–46.

17. Perdue, *China*, 90.

18. Ibid., 69.

19. Ibid., 161.

20. Ibid., 108–11, 247; Kwanten, *Imperial Nomads*, 282.

21. Perdue, *China*, 144, 199–202, 272–77.

22. Beckwith, *Empires*, 240.

23. Perdue, *China*, 288–89.

24. Ibid., 161–63.

25. Beckwith, *Empires*, 240.

26. Michael Khodarkovsky, "Non-Russian Subjects," in *The Cambridge History of Russia*, vol. 1, *From Early Rus' to 1689*, ed. Maureen Perrie (Cambridge: Cambridge University Press, 2006), 525–27.

27. Perdue, *China*, 161.

28. Beckwith, *Empires*, 242–50.

29. A further examination into the extent of surviving nomadism will be undertaken later, but for now it is worth mentioning that this claim is not meant in any way to say that pastoralism went extinct in Eurasia at this time, or ever. It merely was phased from a primary activity to a secondary one in terms of economic priority.

30. Hunczak, *Russian Imperialism*, 241–44.

31. Khodarkovsky, "Non-Russian Subjects," 530.

32. Stephen F. Dale, *The Muslim Empires of the Ottomans, Safavids, and Mughals* (Cambridge: Cambridge University Press, 2010), 3–16.

33. David Morgan, *Medieval Persia: 1047–1797* (Harlow, UK: Longman Group, 1988), 145–49, 152–53.

34. Michael Axworthy, *The Sword of Persia: Nader Shah, from Tribal Warrior to Conquering Tyrant* (New York: I. B. Tauris, 2006), 17–19, 61–68.

35. Ibid., 84, 112.

36. Ibid., 70–72.

37. Ibid., 82; Morgan, *Medieval Persia*, 171.

38. Axworthy, *Sword of Persia*, 146.

39. Ibid., 112.

40. Ibid., 156.

41. Ibid.

42. Morgan, *Medieval Persia*, 154–55, 187.

43. Lorge, *Asian Military*, 147.

44. Morgan, *Medieval Persia*, 154–55.

45. Axworthy, *Sword of Persia*, 206.

46. Dale, *Muslim Empires*, 267.

47. Axworthy, *Sword of Persia*, 225.

48. Ibid., 281, 283–84.

CHAPTER FIVE: THE INVASION OF THE LITTORALS

1. C. Patterson Giersch, *Asian Borderlands: The Transformation of Qing China's Yunnan Frontier* (Cambridge, MA: Harvard University Press, 2006), 46–48, 64.

2. Ibid., 97.

3. Marcus Rossabi, *China and Inner Asia from 1368 to the Present Day* (London: Thames and Hudson, 1975), 139, 164, 179.

4. John K. Fairbank, ed., *The Cambridge History of China*, vol. 10, pt. 1, *Late Ch'ing, 1800–1911* (Cambridge: Cambridge University Press, 1978), 352–53.

5. Mote, *Imperial China*, 950–61.

6. Julia Lovell, *The Opium War: Drugs, Dreams and the Making of China* (London: Picador-Macmillan, 2011), 38, 63–67, 90–113, 297.

7. Darwin, *After Tamerlane*, 123–24; Mote, *Imperial China*, 961.

8. Rossabi, *China*, 196.

9. Trevor Royale, *Crimea: The Great Crimean War, 1854–1856* (Hampshire, UK: Palgrave Macmillan, 2000), 165–75, 501.

10. Rossabi, *China*, 196.

11. Mukminova and Mukhtarov, "Khanate of Bukhara," 35–38; Annanepesov and Bababekov, "Khanates of Khiva," 63–66.

12. Beckwith, *Empires*, 260, 262; Darwin, *After Tamerlane*, 212.

13. Seymour Becker, *Russia's Protectorates in Central Asia: Bukhara and Khiva, 1865–1924* (London: RoutledgeCurzon, 2004), Kindle edition, sections 237–55, 547–54, 640–705.

14. Ibid., 1169–77; Darwin, *After Tamerlane*, 293.

15. Rossabi, *China*, 721, 742–49.

16. James A. Millward, *Eurasian Crossroads: A History of Xinjiang* (New York: Columbia University Press, 2007), 118, 123.

17. Ibid., 121–22.

18. Lorge, *Asian Military*, 167–68; Millward, *Eurasian Crossroads*, 126.

19. Millward, *Eurasian Crossroads*, 130; Lorge, *Asian Military*, 168–69.

20. Fairbank, *Cambridge History*, 408.

21. Becker, *Russia's Protectorates*, 1439–45, 2088–95, 2509–78, 2764–65.

22. Beckwith, *Empires*, 251.

23. Rossabi, *China*, 189.

24. Beckwith, *Empires*, 250–51.

25. Fairbank, *Cambridge History*, 357; Rossabi, *China*, 194, 200.

26. S. C. M. Paine, *The Sino-Japanese War of 1894–1895: Perceptions, Power, and Primacy* (Cambridge: Cambridge University Press, 2003), 321.

27. Darwin, *After Tamerlane*, 351.

28. Sergei Witte is probably best known as a reformer on the domestic front of imperial Russia, as well as the chief negotiator for the Russians during discussions that led to the Treaty of Portsmouth. He was also active in establishing the funds and logistics for the construction of the Trans-Siberian Railroad and creating Russian Far

East policy in general. One might call him the last great statesman of the Formless Empire in imperial Russia.

29. Rossabi, *China*, 201.

30. Darwin, *After Tamerlane*, 352; Rossabi, *China*, 202.

31. Rossabi, *China*, 205.

32. Paine, *Sino-Japanese War*, 65, 321–22.

33. Rossabi, *China*, 206–7.

34. Ibid., 203.

35. Darwin, *After Tamerlane*, 354; Rossabi, *China*, 211–12, 238.

36. Fairbank, *Cambridge History*, 403.

37. Philip Jowett and Stephen Walsh, *Chinese Warlord Armies 1911–30* (Oxford: Osprey, 2010), 18.

38. Becker, *Russia's Protectorates*, 4520–27.

39. W. Bruce Lincoln, *Red Victory: A History of the Russian Civil War 1918–1921* (New York: Da Capo, 1989), 226–35, 244.

40. Richard H. Ullman, *Anglo-Soviet Relations, 1917–1921*, vol. 1, *Intervention and the War* (Princeton, NJ: Princeton University Press, 1961), 86, 95.

41. Paul E. Dunscomb, *Japan's Siberian Intervention, 1918–1922* (Plymouth, UK: Lexington Books, 2011), 34–35, 39, 85.

42. James Palmer, *The Bloody White Baron: The Extraordinary Story of the Russian Nobleman Who Became the Last Khan of Mongolia* (New York: Perseus, 2009), 75–77, 89.

43. Ibid., 95–104; Ullman, *Anglo-Soviet Relations*, 138–41; Lincoln, *Red Victory*, 258.

44. Ullman, *Anglo-Soviet Relations*, 272–75; Jamie Bisher, *White Terror: Cossack Warlords of the Trans-Siberian* (New York: Routledge, 2005), Kindle edition, location 2306.

45. Dunscomb, *Japan's Siberian Intervention*, 135, 148.

46. Ibid., 155, 202.

47. Ibid., 193.

48. Palmer, *Bloody White Baron*, 122–24.

49. Ibid., 95, 107.

50. Ibid., 196.

51. Peter Hopkirk, *Setting the East Ablaze: Lenin's Dream of Empire in East Asia* (London: John Murray, 1984), Kindle edition, sections 2161–78.

52. Ibid., 2178–86, 2318–27, 2351–60.

53. Ibid., 2377–85; Bisher, *White Terror*, 5706.

54. Hopkirk, *Setting the East*, 2394–428.

55. Palmer, *Bloody White Baron*, 234–45.

56. Becker, *Russia's Protectorates*, 4692–99, 5001–8, 5073–135.

57. Hopkirk, *Setting the East*, 980–1528.

58. Ibid., 781–90, 2463–89, 2557–724.

59. Becker, *Russia's Protectorates*, 5633–794.

60. Sonja D. Schmid, "Nuclear Colonization? Soviet Technopolitics in the Second World War," in *Entangled Geographies: Empire & Technopolitics in the Global Cold War*, ed. Gabrielle Hecht (Cambridge, MA: MIT Press, 2011), 128.

61. Hopkirk, *Setting the East*, 3161–69, 3462–70.

62. Rossabi, *China*, 229; Millward, *Eurasian Crossroads*, 196–97.

63. Millward, *Eurasian Crossroads*, 185; Hopkirk, *Setting the East*, 3555–63; Rossabi, *China*, 230.

64. Hopkirk, *Setting the East*, 3646–55.

65. Taiheiyo Senso, *Japan Erupts: The London Naval Conference and the Manchurian Incident 1928–1932* (New York: Columbia University Press, 1984), 6–8.

66. Ramon Myers and Mark Peattie, *The Japanese Colonial Empire, 1895–1945* (Princeton, NJ: Princeton University Press, 1984), 230–31.

67. Shinichi Yamamuro, *Manchuria under Japanese Domination* (Philadelphia: University of Pennsylvania Press, 2005), 98–99.

68. Louise Young, *Japan's Total Empire: Manchuria and the Culture of Wartime Imperialism* (Berkeley: University of California Press, 1998), 40, 42–46.

69. Prasenjit Duara, *Sovereignty and Authenticity: Manchukuo and the East Asian Modern* (Lanham, MD: Rowman and Littlefield, 2003), 186–88.

70. Yamamuro, *Manchuria*, 98–99.

71. This year, 1937, was the same one in which the now-infamous biological-weapons and human-experimentation laboratory Unit 731 began operations just south of Mukden, but as it was top secret, this was probably not known to the vast majority of even the Japanese spy network.

72. Duara, *Sovereignty*, 63–64; Young, *Japan's Total Empire*, 49.

73. Palmer, *Bloody White Baron*, 239.

74. Stuart D. Goldman, *Nomonhan, 1939: The Red Army's Victory That Shaped World War II* (Annapolis, MD: Naval Institute Press, 2012), Kindle edition, sections 501–9, 1405–1557, 1588–1792, 2114–20.

75. Ibid., 2381–2705; Edward Drea, *Nomonhan: Japanese-Soviet Tactical Combat, 1939*, Leavenworth Papers no. 2 (Ft. Leavenworth, KS: Combat Studies Institute of the US Army, 1981), 32–47, http://usacac.army.mil/CAC2/cgsc/carl/download/csipubs/LP2_NomonhanJapanese-SovietTacticalCombat_1939.pdf.

76. Goldman, *Nomonhan*, 3123–3211.

77. Drea, *Nomonhan*, 71–77; Goldman, *Nomonhan*, 3304–3533, 4200–4208.

78. Darwin, *After Tamerlane*, 421; Goldman, *Nomonhan*, 4050–59, 4141–48, 4178–85.

79. Drea, *Nomonhan*, 86.

80. A parallel could be made here to the traditional steppe army of a large light cavalry with a core of heavy cavalry.

81. Young, *Japan's Total Empire*, 406–9.

82. Rossabi, *China*, 267.

Chapter Six: Rebirth Through Smothering

1. John J. Stephen, *The Russian Far East: A History* (Stanford, CA: Stanford University Press, 1994), 164–65, 247, 262.

2. James Forsyth, *A History of the Peoples of Siberia: Russia's North Asian Colony, 1581–1990* (Cambridge: Cambridge University Press, 1992), 396.

3. Ibid., 363–65.

4. Svat Soucek, *A History of Inner Asia* (New York: Cambridge University Press, 2000), 230–36.

5. Darwin, *After Tamerlane*, 473.

6. Uradyn E. Bulag, *The Mongols at China's Edge: History and Politics of National Unity* (Lanham, MD: Rowman & Littlefield, 2002), 169.

7. Tsering Shakya, *The Dragon in the Land of Snows: A History of Modern Tibet Since 1947* (New York: Columbia University Press, 1999), 43, 139, 206–7.

8. James A. Millward and Nabijan Tursan, "Political History and Strategies of Control, 1884–1978," in *Xinjiang: China's Muslim Borderland*, comp. and ed. Stephen Frederick Starr (New York: M. E. Sharpe, Central Asia-Caucuses Institute, 2003), 87–88.

9. Millward, *Eurasian Crossroads*, 240–1, 253–55.

10. Rossabi, *China*, 267.

11. David J. Dallin, *Soviet Foreign Policy after Stalin* (London: Methuen, 1960), 490; Lorenz M. Luthi, *The Sino-Soviet Split: Cold War in the Communist World* (Princeton, NJ: Princeton University Press, 2008), 46.

12. Luthi, *Sino-Soviet Split*, 115–16; Sergey Radchenko, *Two Suns in the Heavens: The Sino-Soviet Struggle for Supremacy, 1962–1967* (Stanford, CA: Stanford University Press, 2009), 87.

13. Luthi, *Sino-Soviet Split*, 181.

14. Radchenko, *Two Suns*, 71, 172.

15. Luthi, *Sino-Soviet Split*, 214–16, 276–77, 299.

16. Alfred D. Low, *The Sino-Soviet Confrontation since Mao Zedong: Dispute, Détente, or Conflict?* (New York: Columbia University Press, 1987), 17.

17. Radchenko, *Two Suns*, 76.

18. Margaret MacMillan, *Seize the Hour: When Nixon Met Mao* (London: John Murray, 2006), 133.

19. Radchenko, *Two Suns*, 202; Luthi, *Sino-Soviet Split*, 299, 340.

20. Drew Middleton, *The Duel of the Giants: China and Russia in Asia* (New York: Charles Scribner's Sons, 1978), 141–46.

21. Ibid., 135–37; Radchenko, *Two Suns*, 204. According to Middleton, who was writing not long after the events he described, the general assumption among those who studied Soviet strategy was that the Soviet Union would launch a punishment expedition into Manchuria and possibly Xinjiang with the intention of stirring up the minorities and possibly looting the industry. Soviet "deep battle" strategy— essentially a massive, mechanized assault meant to break into the enemy's rear and

disrupt its logistics on a massive scale—was considered highly likely to break the less mechanized Chinese army. But the Chinese held the numerical advantage and could use guerrilla tactics in occupied territory, so any military action would be raid based and likely involve no permanent border changes except for the disputed territories. Middleton, *Duel*, 141.

22. Middleton, *Duel*, 135–37, 144.

23. Robert S. Litwak, *Détente and the Nixon Doctrine: American Foreign Policy and the Pursuit of Stability* (Cambridge: Cambridge University Press, 1984), 76–77.

24. Henry Kissinger, *Diplomacy* (New York: Simon & Schuster Paperbacks, 1994), 730.

25. Rossabi, *China*, 286.

26. Radchenko, *Two Suns*, 206–8.

27. Millward, *Eurasian Crossroads*, 277, 289.

28. Victor Spolnikov, "The Impact of Afghanistan's War on the Former Republics of Central Asia," in *Central Asia: Its Strategic Importance and Future Prospects*, ed. Hafeez Malik (New York: St. Martin's, 1994), 102; Melvin Goodman, "Perestroika: Its Impact on the Central Asian Republics and Their Future Relations with Moscow," in *Central Asia: Its Strategic Importance and Future Prospects*, ed. Hafeez Malik (New York: St. Martin's, 1994), 77.

29. Roderic Braithwaite, *Afghantsy: The Russians in Afghanistan, 1979–89* (London: Profile Books, 2001), Kindle edition, sections 753–837, 1002, 1746, 2272.

30. Ibid., 1994.

31. Spolnikov, "Impact of Afghanistan's War," 14–15.

32. Braithwaite, *Afghantsy*, 5062–5437.

33. Abdujabbar A. Abduvakhitov, "The Jadid Movement and Its Impact on Contemporary Central Asia," in *Central Asia: Its Strategic Importance and Future Prospects*, ed. Hafeez Malik (New York: St. Martin's, 1994), 68–70.

34. Beckwith, *Empires*, 304–5; Darwin, *After Tamerlane*, 478.

35. Soucek, *History of Inner Asia*, 237.

36. Hooman Peimani, *Regional Security and the Future of Central Asia: The Competition of Iran, Turkey, and Russia* (Westport, CT: Praeger, 1998), 2.

37. Ibid., 23.

38. Boris Rumer and Stanislaw Zhukov, eds., *Central Asia: The Challenges of Independence* (New York: M. E. Sharpe, 1998), 104, 130.

39. Dilip Hiro, *Inside Central Asia* (New York & London: Overlook Duckworth, Peter Mayer, 2009), 96, 148, 152.

40. Islam Karimov, *Uzbekistan on the Threshold of the Twenty-First Century* (Richmond, UK: Curzon, 1997), 103, 138, 191–92; Shireen T. Hunter, *Central Asia Since Independence*, Washington Papers no.168 (Washington, DC: Center for Strategic and International Studies, 1996), 98.

41. Hunter, *Central Asia*, 114–15; Lutz Kleveman, *The New Great Game: Blood and Oil in Central Asia* (New York: Grove, 2003), 74.

42. Hunter, *Central Asia*, 38–39.

43. Kleveman, *New Great Game*, 150.

44. Soucek, *History of Inner Asia*, 273; Boris Rumer and Stanislaw Zhukov, "Between Two Gravitational Poles: Russia and China," in Boris Rumer and Stanislaw Zhukov, eds., *Central Asia: The Challenges of Independence* (New York: M. E. Sharpe, 1998), 162; Dru C. Gladney, "The Chinese Program of Development and Control, 1978–2001," in *Xinjiang: China's Muslim Borderland*, ed. James A. Millward and Peter C. Perdue (New York: M. E. Sharpe, Central Asia-Caucuses Institute, 2003), 118.

45. Gladney, "Chinese Program," 109–11.

46. Yitzhak Shichor, "The Great Wall of Steel: Military and Strategy in Xinjiang," in *Xinjiang: China's Muslim Borderland*, comp. and ed. Stephen Frederick Starr (New York: M. E. Sharpe, Central Asia-Caucuses Institute, 2003), 120–23.

47. Soucek, *History of Inner Asia*, 302.

48. Tsedendamba Batbayar, "Geopolitics and Mongolia's Search for Post-Soviet Identity," *Eurasian Geography and Economics* 43, no. 4 (2002): 324.

49. Ibid., 327; Jennifer Anderson, *The Limits of Sino-Russian Strategic Partnership*, Adelphi Paper 315 (Oxford: Oxford University Press, 1997), 55.

50. Anderson, *Limits*, 57.

51. Ashley J. Tellis and Michael Wills, eds., *Domestic Politics and Grand Strategy in Asia* (Seattle: National Bureau of Asian Research, 2007), 47, 171.

52. Lena Jonson, *Tajikistan in the New Central Asia: Geopolitics, Great Power Rivalry and Radical Islam* (London: I. B. Tauris, 2006), 41–44, 45–50.

53. Muriel Atkin, "The Politics of Polarization in Tajikistan," in *Central Asia: Its Strategic Importance and Future Prospects*, ed. Hafeez Malik (New York: St. Martin's, 1994), 212–13.

54. Hunter, *Central Asia*, 94–95.

55. Oliver Roy, *The New Central Asia and the Creation of Nations* (London: I. B. Tauris, 2000), 190.

56. Hunter, *Central Asia*, 94.

57. Braithwaite, *Afghantsy*, 5465; Jonson, *Tajikistan*, 58.

58. Kleveman, *New Great Game*, 192.

59. Lena Jonson, *Vladimir Putin and Central Asia* (London: I. B. Tauris, 2004, 2006), 81, 86–87.

60. Jonson, *Vladimir Putin*, 112; Hiro, *Inside Central Asia*, 175, 184.

61. Ariel Cohen, "Yankees in the Heartland," in *Eurasia in the Balance: The US and the Regional Power Shift*, ed. Ariel Cohen (Burlington, VT: Ashgate, 2005), 69.

62. Hiro, *Inside Central Asia*, 301, 408–9.

63. Cohen, "Yankees," 87.

64. Jeffrey Mankoff, *Russian Foreign Policy: The Return of Great Power Politics* (Lanham, MD: Rowman & Littlefield, 2009), 194; Hiro, *Inside Central Asia*, 414.

65. Anderson, *Limits*, 79.

66. Kleveman, *New Great Game*, 192; Lowell Dittmer, "The Sino-Russian Strategic Relationship: Ghost of the 'Strategic Triangle'?," in *Challenges to Chinese Foreign Policy: Diplomacy, Globalization, and the Next World Power*, ed. Yufan Hao, C. X. George Wei, and Lowell Dittmer (Lexington: University Press of Kentucky, 2009), 98–101.
67. Mankoff, *Russian Foreign Policy*, 195, 222; Cohen, "Yankees," 158.

CONCLUSION

1. Darwin, *After Tamerlane*, 500–501.
2. Tellis and Wills, eds., *Domestic Politics*, 28, 138.
3. Karimov, *Uzbekistan*, 191.
4. Mankoff, *Russian Foreign Policy*, 225.
5. Sun Tzu, *Art of War*, 82.

BIBLIOGRAPHY

Abduvakhitov, Abdujabbar A. "The Jadid Movement and Its Impact on Contemporary Central Asia." In *Central Asia: Its Strategic Importance and Future Prospects*, edited by Hafeez Malik, 65–76. New York: St. Martin's, 1994.

Adle, Chahryar, and Irfan Habib., eds. *The History of Central Asia*. Vol. 5. Paris: United Nations Educational, Scientific and Cultural Organization, 2003.

Adshead, S. A. M. *Central Asia in World History*. Hampshire and London: Macmillan, 1993.

Ahmad, Zaid. *The Epistemology of Ibn Khaldun*. London: RoutledgeCurzon, 2003.

Alan, Muzaffar, and Sanjay Subrahmanyam, eds. *The Mughal State, 1526–1750*. Delhi: Oxford University Press, 1998.

Al-Din, Rashid. *The Successors of Genghis Khan*. Translated by J. A. Boyle. New York: Columbia University Press, 1971, first published 1317.

Anderson, Jennifer. *The Limits of Sino-Russian Strategic Partnership*. Adelphi Paper 315. Oxford: Oxford University Press, 1997.

Annanepesov, M., and H. N. Bababekov. "The Khanates of Khiva and Kokand." In *The History of Central Asia*. Vol. 5, edited by Chahryar Adle and Irfran Habib, 61–81. Paris: United Nations Educational, Scientific and Cultural Organization, 2003.

Arrighi, Giovanni, and Beverly J. Silver. *Chaos and Governance in the Modern World System*. Contradictions of Modernity, vol. 10. Minneapolis: University of Minnesota Press, 1999.

Asher, Catherine. "India: The Mughals 1526–1858." In *Great Empires of Asia*, edited by Jim Masselos, 175–88. London: Thames & Hudson, 2010.

Atkin, Muriel. "The Politics of Polarization in Tajikistan." In *Central Asia: Its Strategic Importance and Future Prospects*, edited by Hafeez Malik, 211–22. New York: St. Martin's, 1994.

Axworthy, Michael. *The Sword of Persia: Nader Shah, from Tribal Warrior to Conquering Tyrant*. New York: I. B. Tauris, 2006.

Baali, Fuad. *Society, State, and Urbanism: Ibn Khaldun's Sociological Thought*. New York: State University of New York Press, 1988.

Babur, Zahir ud-din Muhammad. *The Baburnama: Memoirs of Babur, Prince and Emperor*. Translated, edited, and annotated by Wheeler M. Thackston. Oxford: Oxford University Press, Smithsonian Institution, 1996. Originally completed 1530.

Ballantine, Karen, and Jake Sherman, eds. *The Political Economy of Armed Conflict: Beyond Greed & Governance*. Boulder, CO: Lynne Rienner, 2003.

Barfield, Thomas J. "Inner Asia and Cycles of Power in China's Imperial Dynastic History." In *Rulers from the Steppe: State Formation on the Eurasian Periphery*, edited by Gary Seaman and Daniel Marks, 22–43. Ethnographics Monograph Series, monograph no. 2. Los Angeles: Ethnographic Press, 1991.

Batbayar, Tsendendamba. "Geopolitics and Mongolia's Search for Post-Soviet Identity." Eurasian Geography and Economics 43, no. 4 (2002): 323–35.

Becker, Seymour. *Russia's Protectorates in Central Asia: Bukhara and Khiva, 1865–1924*. London: RoutledgeCurzon, 2004. Kindle edition.

Beckwith, Christopher I. *Empires of the Silk Road: A History of Central Eurasia from the Bronze Age to the Present*. Princeton, NJ: Princeton University Press, 2009.

Biran, Michael. *The Empire of the Qara Khitai in Eurasian History*. Cambridge Studies in Islamic Civilization. Cambridge: Cambridge University Press, 2005.

Bisher, Jamie. *White Terror: Cossack Warlords of the Trans-Siberian*. New York: Routledge, 2005. Kindle edition.

Blouet, Brian W., ed. *Global Geostrategy: Mackinder and the Defense of the West*. New York: Taylor & Francis, 2005.

Bogatyrev, Sergei. "Ivan IV: 1533–1584." In *The Cambridge History of Russia*. Vol. 1, *From Early Rus' to 1689*, edited by Maureen Perrie, 240–63. Cambridge: Cambridge University Press, 2006.

Braithwaite, Roderic. *Afghantsy: The Russians in Afghanistan, 1979–89.* London: Profile Books, 2001. Kindle edition.

Brysac, Shareen Blair, and Karl Meyer. *Tournament of Shadows: The Great Game and the Race for Empire in Central Asia.* London: Abacus, 2001.

Bulag, Uradyn E. *The Mongols at China's Edge: History and Politics of National Unity.* Lanham, MD: Rowman & Littlefield, 2002.

Burbank, Jane, and Frederick Cooper. *Empires in World History: Power and the Politics of Difference.* Princeton, NJ: Princeton University Press, 2010.

Buzan, Barry, and Ole Weaver. *Regions and Powers: The Structure of International Security.* Cambridge: Cambridge University Press, 2003.

Christian, David. *A History of Russia, Central Asia, and Mongolia.* Vol. 1, *Inner Eurasia from Prehistory to the Mongol Empire.* Oxford: Blackwell, 1998.

———. "Inner Eurasia as a Unit of World History." *Journal of World History* 5, no. 2 (Fall 1994): 173–211. Jstor.org. http://www.jstor.org/stable/20078598.

Chua, Amy. *Day of Empire: How Hyperpowers Rise to Global Dominance—and Why They Fall.* New York: Doubleday, 2007.

Cohen, Ariel. "Yankees in the Heartland." In *Eurasia in the Balance: The US and the Regional Power Shift,* edited by Ariel Cohen, 69–100. Burlington, VT: Ashgate, 2005.

Cohen, Saul Bernard. *Geopolitics of the World System.* Lanham, MD: Rowman & Littlefield, 2003.

Cornell, Svante E., and Frederick Starr. *The Guns of August 2008: Russia's War in Georgia.* Washington, DC: Central Asia-Caucasus Institute & Silk Road Center, 2009.

Cramer, Christopher. *Civil War Is Not a Stupid Thing: Accounting for Violence in Developing Countries.* London: C. Hurst, 2006.

Dale, Stephen F. *The Muslim Empires of the Ottomans, Safavids, and Mughals.* Cambridge: Cambridge University Press, 2010.

Dallin, David J. *Soviet Foreign Policy after Stalin.* London: Methuen, 1960.

Dardess, John W. "From Mongol Empire to Yuan Dynasty: Changing Forms of Imperial Rule in Mongolia and Central Asia." *Monumenta Serica* 30 (1972–1973): 117–165. Jstor.org, http://www.jstor.org/stable/40725972.

Darwin, John. *After Tamerlane: The Global History of Empire.* London: Allen Lane, 2007.

De Hartog, Leo. *Russia and the Mongol Yoke: The History of the Russian Principalities and the Golden Horde, 1221–1502.* London: British Academic Press, 1996.

Dennerline, Jerry. "The Shun-Chih Reign." In *The Cambridge History of China*. Vol. 9, pt. 1, *The Ch'ing Dynasty to 1800*, edited by Denis Twitchett and John K. Fairbank, 73–119. Cambridge: Cambridge University Press, 2002.

Dittmer, Lowell. "The Sino-Russian Strategic Relationship: Ghost of the 'Strategic Triangle'?." In *Challenges to Chinese Foreign Policy: Diplomacy, Globalization, and the Next World Power*, edited by Yufan Hao, C. X. George Wei, and Lowell Dittmer, 87–114. Lexington: University Press of Kentucky, 2009.

Drea, Edward. *Nomonhan: Japanese-Soviet Tactical Combat, 1939*. Leavenworth Papers no. 2. Ft. Leavenworth, KS: Combat Studies Institute of the US Army, 1981. http://usacac.army.mil/CAC2/cgsc/carl/download/csipubs/LP2_NomonhanJapanese-SovietTacticalCombat_1939.pdf.

Duara, Prasenjit. *Sovereignty and Authenticity: Manchukuo and the East Asian Modern*. Lanham, MD: Rowman and Littlefield, 2003.

Dunscomb, Paul E. *Japan's Siberian Intervention, 1918–1922*. Plymouth, UK: Lexington Books, 2011.

Fairbank, John K., ed. *The Cambridge History of China*. Vol. 10, pt. 1. *Late Ch'ing, 1800–1911*, Cambridge: Cambridge University Press, 1978.

Findley, Carter Vaughn. *The Turks in World History*. Oxford: Oxford University Press, 2005.

Forsyth, James. *A History of the Peoples of Siberia: Russia's North Asian Colony, 1581–1990*. Cambridge: Cambridge University Press, 1992.

Frank, Andre Gunder, and Barry K. Gills, eds. *The World System: Five Hundred Years or Five Thousand?* London: Routledge, 1993.

Franke, Herbert, and Denis Twitchett, eds. *The Cambridge History of China*. Vol. 6, *Alien Regimes and Border States, 907–1368*. Cambridge: Cambridge University Press, 1994.

Frye, Richard N. "Central Asian Concepts of Rule on the Steppe and Sown." In *Ecology and Empire: Nomads in the Cultural Evolution of the Old World*, edited by Gary Seaman, 135–41. Los Angeles: University of Southern California, 1989.

Gahrton, Per. *Georgia: Pawn in the New Great Game*. New York: Pluto, 2010.

Giersch, C. Patterson. *Asian Borderlands: The Transformation of Qing China's Yunnan Frontier*. Cambridge, MA: Harvard University Press, 2006.

Gladney, Dru C. "The Chinese Program of Development and Control, 1978–2001." In *Xinjiang: China's Muslim Borderland*, compiled and edited by Stephen Frederick Starr, 101–119. New York: M. E. Sharpe, Central Asia-Caucuses Institute, 2003.

Golden, Peter B. "The Qipchaqs of Medieval Eurasia: An Example of Stateless Adaptation in the Steppes." In *Rulers from the Steppe: State Formation on the Eurasian Periphery*, edited by Gary Seaman and Daniel Marks, 132–157. Ethnographics Monograph Series, monograph no. 2. Los Angeles: Ethnographic Press, 1991.

Goldman, Stuart D. *Nomonhan, 1939: The Red Army's Victory That Shaped World War II*. Annapolis, MD: Naval Institute Press, 2012. Kindle edition.

Goodman, Melvin. "Perestroika: Its Impact on the Central Asian Republics and Their Future Relations with Moscow." In *Central Asia: Its Strategic Importance and Future Prospects*, edited by Hafeez Malik, 77–94. New York: St. Martin's, 1994.

Gray, Colin S. "In Defense of the Heartland: Sir Halford Mackinder and His Critics a Hundred Years On." In *Global Geostrategy: Mackinder and the Defense of the West*, edited by Brian W. Blouet, 17–35. New York: Taylor & Francis, 2005.

Gray, John. *Black Mass: Apocalyptic Religion and the Death of Utopia*. London: Penguin, 2007.

Grousset, Rene. *The Empire of the Steppes: A History of Central Asia*. New Brunswick, NJ: Rutgers University Press, 1970.

Halperin, Charles. *Russia and the Golden Horde: The Mongol Impact on Medieval Russian History*. Bloomington: Indiana University Press, 1987.

Hao, Yufan, C. X. George Wei, and Lowell Dittmer, eds. *Challenges to Chinese Foreign Policy: Diplomacy, Globalization, and the Next World Power*. Lexington: University Press of Kentucky, 2009.

Hecht, Gabrielle, ed. *Entangled Geographies: Empire and Technopolitics in the Global Cold War*. Cambridge, MA: MIT Press, 2011.

Herz, John H. *Nation-State and the Crisis of World Politics*. Philadelphia: David McKay, 1976.

Hiro, Dilip. *Inside Central Asia*. New York & London: Overlook Duckworth, Peter Mayer, 2009.

Hookham, Hilda. *Tamburlaine the Conqueror*. London: Camelot Press, 1962.

Hopkirk, Peter. *The Great Game: The Struggle for Empire in Central Asia*. Peterborough, UK: Kodansha International, 1992.

———. *Setting the East Ablaze: Lenin's Dream of Empire in East Asia*. London: John Murray, 1984. Kindle edition.

Hunczak, Taras, ed. *Russian Imperialism from Ivan the Great to the Revolution*. New Brunswick, NJ: Rutgers University Press, 1974.

Hunter, Shireen T. *Central Asia Since Independence*. Washington Papers no. 168. Washington, DC: Center for Strategic and International Studies, 1996.

Ibn Khaldun. *The Muqaddimah: An Introduction to History*. Translated by Franz Rosenthal. Princeton, NJ: Princeton University Press, 1958. First published 1377.

Ignatieff, Michael. *Empire Lite: Nation-Building in Bosnia, Kosovo and Afghanistan*. London: Vintage, 2003.

Ingebrisen, Christine, with Iver Neumann, Sieglinde Gstohl, and Jessica Beyer, eds. *Small States in International Relations*. Seattle: University of Washington Press, 2006.

Johnston, Alastair Iain. *Cultural Realism: Strategic Culture and Grand Strategy in Chinese History*. Princeton, NJ: Princeton University Press, 1995.

Jonson, Lena. *Tajikistan in the New Central Asia: Geopolitics, Great Power Rivalry and Radical Islam*. London: I. B. Tauris, 2006.

———. *Vladimir Putin and Central Asia*. London: I. B. Tauris, 2006.

Jowett, Philip, and Stephen Walsh. *Chinese Warlord Armies 1911–30*. Oxford: Osprey, 2010.

Kalyvas, Strathis. *The Logic of Violence in Civil War*. New York: Cambridge University Press, 2006.

Karimov, Islam. *Uzbekistan on the Threshold of the Twenty-First Century*. Richmond, UK: Curzon, 1997.

Kaufman, Stuart J., Richard Little, and William C. Wohlforth, eds. *The Balance of Power in World History*. New York: Palgrave Macmillan, 2007.

Keay, John. *China: A History*. London: HarperCollins, 2008.

Kennedy, Paul, ed. *Grand Strategies in War and Peace*. New Haven, CT: Yale University Press, 1991.

Khodarkovsky, Michael. "Non-Russian Subjects." In *The Cambridge History of Russia*. Vol. 1, *From Early Rus' to 1689*, edited by Maureen Perrie, 520–38. Cambridge: Cambridge University Press, 2006.

King, Charles. *The Black Sea: A History*. Oxford: Oxford University Press, 2004.

Kissinger, Henry. *Diplomacy*. New York: Simon & Schuster Paperbacks, 1994.

Kleveman, Lutz. *The New Great Game: Blood and Oil in Central Asia*. New York: Grove, 2003.

Kwanten, Luc. *Imperial Nomads: A History of Central Asia, 500–1500*. Leicester, UK: Leicester University Press, 1979.

Lamb, Harold. *Babur the Tiger*. London: Robert Hale, 1962.

Laruelle, Marlene. *Russian Eurasianism: An Ideology of Empire*. Translated by Mischa Gabowitsch. Washington, DC: Woodrow Wilson Center Press, 2008.

Legg, Stuart. *The Heartland*. New York: Farrar, Straus & Giroux, 1970.

Li, Gertraude Roth. "State Building before 1644." In *The Cambridge History of China*, vol. 9, pt. 1, *The Chi'ng Dynasty to 1800*, edited by Denis Twitchett and John K. Fairbank, 9–72. Cambridge: Cambridge University Press, 2002.

Liddel-Hart, Basil Henry. *Strategy*. London: Faber & Faber, 1954.

Lieven, Dominic. *Empire: The Russian Empire and Its Rivals, from the Sixteenth Century to the Present*. New York: Cambridge University Press, 2003.

Lincoln, W. Bruce. *The Conquest of a Continent: Siberia and the Russians*. Ithaca, NY: Cornell University Press, 1994.

———. *Red Victory: A History of the Russian Civil War, 1918–1921*. New York: Da Capo, 1989.

Litwak, Robert S. *Détente and the Nixon Doctrine: American Foreign Policy and the Pursuit of Stability*. Cambridge: Cambridge University Press, 1984.

Lobell, Steven E., Norrin M. Ripsman, and Jeffrey W. Taliaferro, eds. *Neoclassical Realism, The State and Foreign Policy*. Cambridge: Cambridge University Press, 2009.

Lorge, Peter A. *The Asian Military Revolution: From Gunpowder to the Bomb*. New York: Cambridge University Press, 2008.

Lovell, Julia. *The Opium War: Drugs, Dreams and the Making of China*. London: Picador–Macmillan, 2011.

Low, Alfred D. *The Sino-Soviet Confrontation since Mao Zedong: Dispute, Détente, or Conflict?* New York: Columbia University Press, 1987.

Luthi, Lorenz M. *The Sino-Soviet Split: Cold War in the Communist World*. Princeton, NJ: Princeton University Press, 2008.

Mackinder, Halford J. "The Geographical Pivot of History." *Geographical Journal* 23, no. 4 (1904): 421–37. Jstor.org. http://www.jstor.org/discover/10.2307/1775498?sid=21105999540243&uid=2&uid=3739864&uid=4&uid=70&uid=3739256&uid=2134.

MacMillan, Margaret. *Seize the Hour: When Nixon Met Mao*. London: John Murray, 2006.

Mair, Victor H. *The Art of War: Sun Zi's Military Methods*. New York: Columbia University Press, 2007.

Malik, Hafeez, ed. *Central Asia: Its Strategic Importance and Future Prospects*. New York: St. Martin's, 1994.

Mankoff, Jeffrey. *Russian Foreign Policy: The Return of Great Power Politics*. Lanham, MD: Rowman & Littlefield, 2009.

Mann, Michael. *Incoherent Empire*. London: Verso, 2003.

Manz, Beatrice Forbes. *Power, Politics, and Religion in Timurid Iran*. Cambridge: Cambridge University Press, 2007.

———. *The Rise and Rule of Tamerlane*. Cambridge: Cambridge University Press, 1989.

Marozzi, Justin. *Tamerlane: Sword of Islam, Conqueror of the World*. Cambridge, MA: Da Capo, 2006.

Martin, Desmond H. "The Mongol Army." *Journal of the Royal Asiatic Society of Great Britain and Ireland* 1 (Apr. 1943): 46–85. Jstor.org, http://www.jstor.org/stable/25221891.

Martin, Janet. *Medieval Russia, 980–1584*. Cambridge: Cambridge University Press, 1995.

Masselos, Jim, ed. *Great Empires of Asia*. London: Thames & Hudson, 2010.

McNeilly, Mark. *Sun Tzu and the Art of Modern Warfare*. Oxford: Oxford University Press, 2001.

Megoran, Nick. "Revisiting the 'Pivot': The Influence of Halford Mackinder on Analysis of Uzbekistan's International Relations." *Geographic Journal* 170, no. 4 (Dec. 2004), 347–58. Jstor.org. http://www.jstor.org/stable/3451464.

Meskill, John. "History of China." In *An Introduction to Chinese Civilization*, edited by John Meskill and J. Mason Gentzler, 119–53. New York: Columbia University Press, 1973.

Meyer, Karl. *The Dust of Empire: The Race for Supremacy in the Asian Heartland*. London: Abacus, 2004.

Middleton, Drew. *The Duel of the Giants: China and Russia in Asia*. New York: Charles Scribner's Sons, 1978.

Millward, James A. *Eurasian Crossroads: A History of Xinjiang*. New York: Columbia University Press, 2007.

Millward, James A., and Nabijan Tursan. "Political History and Strategies of Control, 1884–1978." In *Xinjiang: China's Muslim Borderland*, compiled and edited by Stephen Frederick Starr, 63–98. New York: M. E. Sharpe, Central Asia-Caucuses Institute, 2003.

Morgan, David. *Medieval Persia: 1047–1797*. Harlow, UK: Longman Group, 1988.

Mote, F. W. *Imperial China 900–1800*. Cambridge, MA: Harvard University Press, 1999.

Mukminova, R. G., and A. Mukhtarov. "The Khanate of Bukhara." In *The History of Central Asia*. Vol. 5, edited by Chahryar Adle and Irfran Habib, 26–58. Paris: United Nations Educational, Scientific and Cultural Organization, 2003.

Murphy, Rhoads. "An Ecological History of Central Asian Nomadism." In *Ecology and Empire: Nomads in the Cultural Evolution of the Old World*, edited by Gary Seaman, 81–102. Los Angeles: University of Southern California, 1989.

Myers, Ramon, and Mark Peattie. *The Japanese Colonial Empire, 1895–1945*. Princeton, NJ: Princeton University Press, 1984.

Nicolle, David, and Richard Hook. *The Mongol Warlords*. Dorset, UK: Firebird, 1990.

Okada, Hidehiro. "Dayan Khan as Yuan Emperor: The Political Legitimacy in 15th Century Mongolia." *Bulletin de l'Ecole Francais d'Extreme-Orient* 81 (1994): 51–58.

Ostrowski, Donald. "The Growth of Muscovy: 1462–1533." In *The Cambridge History of Russia*. Vol. 1, *From Early Rus' to 1689*, edited by Maureen Perrie, 213–39. Cambridge: Cambridge University Press, 2006.

Paine, S. C. M. *The Sino-Japanese War of 1894–1895: Perceptions, Power, and Primacy*. Cambridge: Cambridge University Press, 2003.

Palmer, James. *The Bloody White Baron: The Extraordinary Story of the Russian Nobleman Who Became the Last Khan of Mongolia*. New York: Perseus, 2009.

Parker, W. H. *Mackinder: Geography as an Aid to Statecraft*. Oxford: Clarendon, 1982.

Peimani, Hooman. *Regional Security and the Future of Central Asia: The Competition of Iran, Turkey, and Russia*. Westport, CT: Praeger, 1998.

Perdue, Peter C. *China Marches West: The Qing Conquest of Central Eurasia*. Cambridge, MA: Belknap Press of Harvard University Press, 2005.

Perrie, Maureen, ed. *The Cambridge History of Russia*. Vol. 1, *From Early Rus' to 1689*. Cambridge: Cambridge University Press, 2006.

Rachewitz, Igor de, tr. *The Secret History of the Mongols: A Mongolian Epic Chronicle of the Thirteenth Century*. Leiden, Netherlands: Koninklijike Brill NV, 2004.

Radchenko, Sergey. *Two Suns in the Heavens: The Sino-Soviet Struggle for Supremacy, 1962–1967*. Stanford, CA: Stanford University Press, 2009.

Richards, J. F. "The Formation of Imperial Authority under Akbar and Jahangir." In *The Mughal State, 1526–1750,* edited by Muzaffar Alan and Sanjay Subrahmanyam, 126–67. Delhi: Oxford University Press, 1998.

Richards, Jon F. *The Mughal Empire.* Cambridge: Cambridge University Press, 1995.

Rossabi, Marcus. *China and Inner Asia from 1368 to the Present Day.* London: Thames and Hudson, 1975.

Roy, Oliver. *The New Central Asia and the Creation of Nations.* London: I. B. Tauris, 2000.

Royale, Trevor. *Crimea: The Great Crimean War, 1854–1856.* Hampshire, UK: Palgrave Macmillan, 2000.

Rumer, Boris, ed. *Central Asia: A Gathering Storm?* New York: M. E. Sharpe, 2002.

Rumer, Boris, and Stanislaw Zhukov. "Between Two Gravitational Poles: Russia and China." In *Central Asia: The Challenges of Independence,* edited by Boris Rumer and Stanislaw Zhukov, 153–66. New York: M. E. Sharpe, 1998.

———, eds. *Central Asia: The Challenges of Independence.* New York: M. E. Sharpe, 1998.

Samolin, William. *East Turkestan in the Twelfth Century.* London: Mouton, 1964.

Schmid, Sonja D. "Nuclear Colonization? Soviet Technopolitics in the Second World War." In *Entangled Geographies: Empire & Technopolitics in the Global Cold War,* edited by Gabrielle Hecht, 125–54. Cambridge, MA: MIT Press, 2011.

Scott, James C. *Seeing Like a State: How Certain Schemes to Improve the Human Condition Have Failed.* New Haven, CT: Yale University Press, 1998.

Seaman, Gary, ed. *Ecology and Empire: Nomads in the Cultural Evolution of the Old World.* Los Angeles: University of Southern California Press, 1989.

Seaman, Gary, and Daniel Marks, eds. *Rulers from the Steppe: State Formation on the Eurasian Periphery.* Ethnographics Monograph Series, monograph no. 2. Los Angeles: Ethnographic Press, 1991.

Senso, Taiheiyo. *Japan Erupts: The London Naval Conference and the Manchurian Incident 1928–1932.* New York: Columbia University Press, 1984.

Shakya, Tsering. *The Dragon in the Land of Snows: A History of Modern Tibet Since 1947.* New York: Columbia University Press, 1999.

Shichor, Yitzhak. "The Great Wall of Steel: Military and Strategy in Xinjiang." In *Xinjiang: China's Muslim Borderland*, compiled and edited by Stephen Frederick Starr, 120–162. New York: M. E. Sharpe, Central Asia-Caucuses Institute, 2003.

Shirk, Susan L. *China: Fragile Superpower: How China's Internal Politics Could Derail its Peaceful Rise.* New York: Oxford University Press, 2007.

Shpakovsky, Viacheslav, and David Nicolle. *Kalka River 1223: Genghiz Khan's Mongols Invade Russia.* Oxford: Osprey, 2001.

Smith, Graham. "The Masks of Proteus: Russia, Geopolitical Shift and the New Eurasianism." *Transactions of the Institute of British Geographers*, New Series 24, no. 4 (1999): 481–94. Jstor.org. http://www.jstor.org/stable/623236.

Sneath, David. *The Headless State: Aristocratic Orders, Kinship Society, and Misrepresentations of Nomadic Inner Asia.* New York: Columbia University Press, 2007.

Soucek, Svat. *A History of Inner Asia.* New York: Cambridge University Press, 2000.

Spolnikov, Victor. "The Impact of Afghanistan's War on the Former Republics of Central Asia." In *Central Asia: Its Strategic Importance and Future Prospects*, edited by Hafeez Malik, 95–116. New York: St. Martin's, 1994.

Standen, Naomi. *Unbounded Loyalty: Frontier Crossing in Liao China.* Honolulu: University of Hawaii Press, 2007.

Starr, Stephen Frederick, comp. and ed. *Xinjiang: China's Muslim Borderland.* New York: M. E. Sharpe, Central Asia-Caucuses Institute, 2003.

Stephen, John J. *The Russian Far East: A History.* Stanford, CA: Stanford University Press, 1994.

Sterling-Folker, Jennifer, ed. *Making Sense of International Relations Theory.* Boulder, CO: Lynne Rienner, 2006.

Sun Tzu. *The Art of War.* Translated by Thomas F. Cleary. Boston: Shambhala, 1988.

Taliaferro, Jeffrey W. "Neoclassical Realism: The Psychology of Great Power Intervention." In *Making Sense of International Relations Theory*, edited by Jennifer Sterling-Folker, 53–75. Boulder, CO: Lynne Rienner, 2006.

Tellis, Ashley J., and Michael Wills, eds. *Domestic Politics and Grand Strategy in Asia.* Seattle: National Bureau of Asian Research, 2007.

Tornnesson, Stein, and Hans Antlov. *Asian Forms of the Nation.* Studies in Asian Topics no.23. Richmond, UK: Curzon, 1996.

Tribathi, Prasad. "The Turko-Mongol Theory of Kingship" In *The Mughal State, 1526–1750*, edited by Muzaffar Alan and Sanjay Subrahmanyam, 108–124. Delhi: Oxford University Press, 1998.

Tsygankov, Andrei P. *Russian Foreign Policy: Change and Continuity in National Identity*. Plymouth, UK: Rowman & Littlefield, 2010.

Twitchett, Denis, and John K. Fairbank, eds. *The Cambridge History of China*. Vol. 9, pt. 1, *The Chi'ng Dynasty to 1800*. Cambridge: Cambridge University Press, 2002.

Tyler, Christian. *Wild West China: The Taming of Xinjiang*. London: John Murray, 2003.

Ullman, Richard H. *Anglo-Soviet Relations, 1917–1921*. Vol. 1, *Intervention and the War*. Princeton, NJ: Princeton University Press, 1961.

Van der Pijl, Kees. *Nomads, Empires, States. Modes of Foreign Relations and Political Economy*. Vol. 1. London: Pluto, 2007.

Vernadsky, George. *The Mongols in Russia*. New Haven, CT: Yale University Press, 1953. Reprint, London: University Microfilms International, 1979.

Von Hagen, Mark. "Empires, Borderlands, and Diasporas: Eurasia as Anti-Paradigm for the Post-Soviet Era." *American Historical Review* 109, no. 2 (Apr. 2004): 445–468. Jstor.org. http://www.jstor.org/stable/10.10861/530339.

Wallerstein, Immanuel. "Dependence in an Interdependent World: The Limited Possibilities of Transformation within the Capitalist World Economy." *African Studies Review* 17, no. 1 (Apr. 1974): 1–26. Jstor.org. http://www.jstor.org/stable/523574.

———. *Geopolitics and Geoculture: Essays on the Changing World System*. Cambridge: Cambridge University Press Syndicate, 1991.

Walton, C. Dale. *Geopolitics and the Great Powers in the Twenty-First Century: Multipolarity and Revolution in the Strategic Perspective*. New York: Routledge, 2007.

Weatherford, Jack. *Genghis Khan and the Making of the Modern World*. New York: Crown and Three River, 2004.

———. *The Secret History of the Mongol Queens: How the Daughters of Genghis Khan Rescued His Empire*. New York: Crown, 2010.

Yamamuro, Shinichi. *Manchuria under Japanese Domination*. Philadelphia: University of Pennsylvania Press, 2005.

Young, Louise. *Japan's Total Empire: Manchuria and the Culture of Wartime Imperialism*. Berkeley: University of California Press, 1998.

ACKNOWLEDGMENTS

I would like to thank my publisher, Bruce H. Franklin of Westholme Publishing, who showed great enthusiasm and encouragement from the start and answered my many and no doubt occasionally redundant questions. Before this study became a book, I was guided by Professor Andrew Williams of the University of Saint Andrews who was always willing to entertain ideas that were outside the bounds of a rigorously inscribed norm for studies. To him I owe a most thorough expression of thanks. I also owe thanks to Professor Christopher Beckwith, whom I have yet to meet but whose work did for the history of Central Asia what I seek to do for strategy and international diplomacy in the same field. By opening the door with a bold study over a large temporal scale, he showed that there is still room in the humanities for the grand, even in an era where the niche is dominant.

On a more personal level, I would like to thank the Room 13 crew, who were one with me in showing that the more bookish pursuits need not reject a sense of humor, fun, and in fact can be at the core of a strong group cohesion—or *assibiya*, as Ibn Khaldun would have called it.

INDEX